Acclaim for Edward Mendelson's

The Things That Matter

"Mendelson is an impassioned reader and he communicates that passion. . . . I don't think I'll read *Frankenstein* or *Wuthering Heights* or *Middlemarch* or *Mrs. Dalloway* in quite the same way again, thanks to his astute discussions."

—Eric Ormsby, *The New York Sun*

"Thought-provoking, imaginative, perfect to have a conversation about." —*The Washington Post Book World*

"The beauty of this book is the maturity of its thinking. Mendelson restores the novels to their original, moral context, but he does not upholster them in Victorian certainty. He shows the author struggling with their ideas. It's like watching Fabergé inspect diamonds." —Joan Acocella

"Takes the reader deep into the moral universe of his authors and pulls together thematic threads with extraordinary skill."

—*The New York Times*

"Rich, hugely readable." —*The Buffalo News*

"In this brilliant and humane book, Mendelson makes powerful progress toward repairing what academic criticism has done its best to put asunder—the connection between literature and life. This is a work of deep learning and deep feeling, a book whose consolations are worthy of the mighty genre it takes for its subject." —Thomas Mallon

"Thrilling. . . . [Mendelson's] readings will send you hungrily to these classics."

—Newsday

"Edward Mendelson's observations about literature are among the best I have read: deeply knowledgeable, appreciative and attentive, and expressed with the affinity of a scholar and critic who is himself an excellent writer. His book is a pleasure to read and to praise."

—Shirley Hazzard

"Elegant. . . . Enlightening. . . . Mendelson is an ideal companion. . . . [The book] reminds us that criticism of the sort that Mendelson practices is one of the things that matter."

—Los Angeles Times

"Heartfelt. . . . Illuminating." *—The New York Review of Books*

"Great works of fiction often not only tell a story but also reveal how we are to live our lives. This sympathetic, profound, and very readable work by one of the finest literary scholars of our time shows us how seven novels can help us with the stages through which we all must pass. Edward Mendelson's insights into the meaning of the novels he considers are acute. He reveals dimensions to these works that most of us will never have guessed at, showing, with grace and courtesy, both their deeper significance and the wisdom that they contain about life's challenges. Reading this book places one in the company of an urbane, erudite, and sure-footed guide."

—Alexander McCall Smith

Edward Mendelson

The Things That Matter

Edward Mendelson is a professor of English and comparative literature at Columbia University. He is the literary executor of W. H. Auden's estate and the editor of Auden's complete works. Among his previous books are *Early Auden*, *Later Auden*, and editions of novels by Anthony Trollope, George Meredith, Thomas Hardy, H. G. Wells, and Arnold Bennett. He lives in New York City with his wife and son.

Also by Edward Mendelson

Early Auden
Later Auden

The Things That Matter

The Things That Matter

What Seven Classic Novels
Have to Say About
the Stages of Life

Edward Mendelson

Anchor Books
A Division of Random House, Inc.
New York

FIRST ANCHOR BOOKS EDITION, NOVEMBER 2007

The Library of Congress has cataloged the Pantheon edition as follows:
Mendelson, Edward.
The things that matter : what seven classic novels have to say about the stages of life / Edward Mendelson.
p.   cm.
Includes bibliographical references and index.
1. Life cycle, Human, in literature.   2. English fiction—19th century—History and criticism.   3. English fiction—20th century—History and criticism.   I. Title.
PR868.l54M46 2006   823'.809354—dc22   2006043155

Anchor ISBN: 978-0-307-27522-6

Author photograph © Shannon Taggart
Book design by M. Kristen Bearse

www.anchorbooks.com

Printed in the United States of America
10   9   8   7   6

For, to, and about
James Mendelson

A thing there was that mattered; a thing, wreathed
about with chatter, defaced, obscured in her own life,
let drop every day in corruption, lies, chatter.
—VIRGINIA WOOLF, *Mrs. Dalloway*

She felt rather inclined just for a moment to stand still
after all that chatter, and pick out one particular thing;
the thing that mattered . . .
—VIRGINIA WOOLF, *To the Lighthouse*

CONTENTS

INTRODUCTION

This book is about life as it is interpreted by books. Each of the chapters has a double subject: on the one hand, an English novel written in the nineteenth or twentieth century, and on the other, one of the great experiences or stages that occur, or can occur, in more or less everyone's life. In writing about Mary Shelley's *Frankenstein* (1818) I have also tried to write about childbirth and its moral and emotional meanings. In writing about Emily Brontë's *Wuthering Heights* (1847) I have also written about the moral and emotional meanings of childhood. The remaining chapters follow a similar pattern: the chapter about Charlotte Brontë's *Jane Eyre* (1847) is also about the process of growth into adulthood, and the chapter about George Eliot's *Middlemarch* (1871–72) is also about marriage. In the three chapters devoted to novels by Virginia Woolf, the one on *Mrs. Dalloway* (1925) is about personal love; the one on *To the Lighthouse* (1927) is about parenthood; and the one on *Between the Acts* (1941) is about the stage when life surrenders to the next generation.

The book is arranged chronologically so that the sequence of chapters corresponds more or less to the sequence of experiences that occur in the course of life and also to the historical sequence in which the seven novels were written. Taken as a whole, it is designed to provide something on the order of a brief (extremely brief) history of the emotional and moral life of the past two centuries, an inner biography of the world of thought and feeling that came into being in the romantic era of the late eighteenth and early nineteenth centuries.

Anyone, I think, who reads a novel for pleasure or instruction takes an interest both in the closed fictional world of that novel and in the ways the book provides models or examples of the kinds of life that a reader might or might not choose to live. Most novels of the past two centuries that are still worth reading were written to respond to both these interests. They were not written to be read objectively or dispassionately, as if by some nonhuman intelligence, and they can be understood most fully if they are interpreted and understood from a personal point of view, not only from historical, thematic, or analytical perspectives. A reader who identifies with the characters in a novel is not reacting in a naïve way that ought to be outgrown or transcended, but is performing one of the central acts of literary understanding.

Scientists and mathematicians, in the course of their work, need not think about the course of their own lives, but that is exactly what literary critics ought to think about when they think about the shape of a novel or poem. This does not mean that they ought to impose their thoughts about their own lives on their readers. In most cases, the less that critics actually say about themselves, the better will be their criticism, but criticism is always more memorable, more convincing, more valid, when the critic's voice is—and sounds like—the personal voice of someone who has learned from unique personal experiences, rather than a dispassionate impersonal voice that sounds like the product of advanced professional training. In this book I have tried to contribute to literary studies in the professional sense by saying a few things that I think have not been said about these seven novels, but I have also tried to address that part of every reader—including every academic and professional reader—which takes a passionate interest in his or her own past and future. This book is written for all readers, of any age, who are still deciding how to live their lives.

The novels I discuss are the ones written in English that, as far as I know, treat most deeply the great experiences of personal life, even if, in some instances, their authors seem to me profoundly mistaken in some of their views. All these novels were written by women, three of them by Virginia Woolf. There is a reason for this, but it has nothing to do with any fantasy that women have inherent depths of feeling that men do not, or that women have greater moral and emotional intelligence than men have, or that women have any other essential qualities denied to men. The reason that women writers in the nineteenth and twentieth centuries were more likely than men to write about the emotional depths of personal life is that they were more likely to be treated impersonally, to be stereotyped as predictable members of a category, rather than recognized as unique human beings. A woman writer therefore had a greater motivation to defend the values of personal life against the generalizing effect of stereotypes, and to defend those values by paying close attention to them in her writing, by insisting that those values matter to everyone and that everyone experiences them uniquely.

An approach that treats these novels as defenses of the unique personality seems to make better sense of their larger shape and fine details than any treatment of them as examples of the category of women's writing. These novels do not speak for women as a group, nor for English or British women, nor for women writers, nor for any other group or category. Nor were these novels addressed to any group or category; they were written for the individual person whom Charlotte Brontë addressed as "Reader." Their authors differ among themselves on every important intellectual, emotional, and moral issue, and some of the most radical differences are to be found between the two who were sisters, Charlotte and Emily Brontë.

A unique individual is not someone who has a single undivided view of the world and speaks with one voice on every subject. In fact, the most certain sign that someone has anesthetized individuality in service of some ideology or party line is that he has a consistent, unequivocal answer to every question. Individuality is a continuous process of arguing against your own beliefs—an argument that is sometimes a friendly intellectual debate, sometimes a passionate emotional battle. The novels that I write about in this book all emerged from their authors' arguments with themselves. Everyone knows that fictional characters in novels debate different points of view with each other. What is less obvious is that, behind the scenes, unheard by the characters, the author's inner voices are also arguing with each other over which story to tell and how to tell it. This is not a sign of weak-mindedness or inconsistency, but of intellectual flexibility and strength. The authors refuse to be satisfied by simple or straightforward explanations of complex things, and they repeatedly correct the flaws of one explanation by exploring a different one. Some chapters of *Frankenstein* are narrated by the part of Mary Shelley that believes that people choose their own destinies; other chapters are narrated by the part that believes that people's lives are determined by events outside them. Different parts of Emily Brontë, Charlotte Brontë, and George Eliot argue among themselves in *Wuthering Heights*, *Jane Eyre*, and *Middlemarch*. Novelists also tend to argue against their own earlier selves whenever they write another novel. In *To the Lighthouse* Virginia Woolf disputes much of what she had written in *Mrs. Dalloway*, and disputes both books in the course of her arguments with herself in *Between the Acts*.

Virginia Woolf gets more attention than anyone else in this book because, I believe, she thought more deeply than any other English novelist about the moral and emotional aspects of personal life. The standard map of modern literature, taught in schools and taken for granted everywhere, places Yeats, Eliot, and Joyce on the highest slopes, with other writers arrayed in lesser and outlying positions. This account is based on the intellectual prejudice, shared by its three heroes, that archetypes are more real than individuals, that myths are more true than observations, that a vision of grand patterns matters more than any attempt to integrate the local particulars of individual lives. Hidden within this account is a deeper prejudice, which is that the shape and complexity of a work is the test of its greatness, that a work of art need not be emotionally moving except to the degree that its structure and patterns inspire inarticulate awe. Museums and concert halls and anthologies are filled with the unfortunate consequences of this assumption, but that does not make it any less mistaken. When you remember that all the great art of the past seems to have been created to be moving as well as to be ingenious, and that the same measure of greatness can still be applied to modern literature, the map of modern literature begins to look different from the version taught in schools. Virginia Woolf, who understood human life in terms of its changes through time, rather than in terms of permanent archetypal states, takes the central place in modern fiction, as W. H. Auden takes the central place in modern poetry, and Samuel Beckett—far more of a defender of individuality, far more of a moralist, than almost anyone other than his biographers recognizes—takes the central place in modern drama.

One of the themes of this book is its argument that the most intellectually and morally coherent way of thinking about human beings is to think of them as autonomous persons (the plural noun "persons," not the collective noun "people") instead of as members of any category, class, or group. A second theme, inseparable from the first, is that persons exist only in relations with other persons, that the idea of an absolutely isolated and independent person is intellectually and morally incoherent, that all ideas of personality and society that emphasize stoicism and self-reliance are at best only partially valid, while ideas that emphasize mutual need and mutual aid have the potential to be true.

Novels are more compact and better organized than life, and no one reads *Jane Eyre* or *Middlemarch* as a practical guide to action. Happy endings are always false and contrived. "The end of a novel," Anthony Trollope wrote at the end of *Barchester Towers*, "like the end of a children's dinner-party, must be made up of sweetmeats and sugar-plums." Miss Prism in Oscar Wilde's *The Importance of Being Earnest* states an indisputable truth when she summarizes the plot of her three-volume novel: "The good ended happily, and the bad unhappily. That is what Fiction means." In real life the good are not rewarded with wealthy and attractive spouses, nor are they rescued at the last moment from loneliness or oppression. In real life the race is to the swift and the battle to the strong. But in one small but crucial region of real life, the fiction proves to be true. In the inner life, in the psychological realm, to the degree that you can manage to belong to Miss Prism's category of "the good," you become more calm and more brave, less anxious and less envious, more capable of enduring injustice or disaster. And it is in this inner life that individuality takes shape, not in the outer world of appearances.*

Even the most psychologically detailed novels—Virginia Woolf's,

---

* The complex relations between inner individuality and outward expressions of it such as eccentric clothing and hair deserve a book to themselves. Someone who is deeply individual in her moral and intellectual life may choose to dress like everyone else because she doesn't care enough about how she looks to bother looking different; no one is more of an individual than Jane Eyre despite her gray, anonymous dress. Eccentricity of dress may be a sign of social courage or indifference—or merely a conventional way of posing as a rebel because rebellion confers a kind of glamour.

for example—cannot represent the inner life directly. At best a novel can report its characters' thoughts about their inner lives, or it can suggest through their outer actions what happens in their inner lives. All novels transpose in different ways the invisible unrepresentable events of psychological life into the visible representable events of narrative and plot, and the result is always slightly distorted and diagrammatic, like a flat map of the curved and textured earth. But sympathetic readers can make shrewd guesses about the inner reality that the novel both expresses and conceals.

One example of this kind of distortion is the way in which novels have a drastically smaller population than real life. In life, when a love affair falls apart, the two lovers find other people with whom to try again. In novels, which are typically populated by a few dozen characters at most, other people are in short supply, and the lovers tend to return to each other for better or worse. Thomas Hardy's *The Well-Beloved* presents a variation on this theme in which a sculptor falls in love with one woman, then twenty years later with her daughter, then twenty more years later with her granddaughter. Improbabilities such as these point toward the simple psychological truth that people repeatedly make the same mistake in relationships, no matter how many different people they find to make the mistake with. This transposition of the inner life into the outer one is true of all fiction, but more obviously and insistently true of novels of the nineteenth and twentieth centuries than of earlier ones. When Moll Flanders's first husband disappears early in her story, every modern reader anticipates his return at the end, but Defoe saw no need to bring him back and never mentions him again.

In the many generalizations in this book about novels, about literature in general, and about other matters, I have tried to follow the example of the critics who seem to me the most illuminating and enduring, and whose work is built on informed intellectual commitments about which books are most worth studying and which aspects of those books deserve the most attention. Such commitments are not the same as theories, which are attempts to describe objective general truths that stand regardless of the theoretician's stake in them. Theories belong to science, which relies on repeatable results that can be tested by experiment or refuted by fact; but where the goal is the knowledge of individual human beings or their works, repeatable results are the least interesting ones. Anyone who writes intelligently and interestingly about history and literature—things which are lived and made by human beings, not merely observed by them like atoms or galaxies—writes from an individual perspective that every reader is free to judge, and the dialogue between reader and writer is inseparable from the process of understanding.

A book could be written about the ways in which critics use the pronouns *I, we, one,* and *you* to refer to themselves and their readers. I have tried to avoid the presumptuousness of *we* (in the generalizing sense of "our sort of people") and the evasiveness of *one* (except where the alternatives to *oneself* were too cumbersome to bother with). That leaves *I* and *you.* Parts of this book are written in the second person singular, but that doesn't mean I assume you will agree with everything I say about you, just as I would not assume such a thing if we were talking face to face. And I don't expect you to agree with everything I say about books, but I hope our disagreements, when they occur, can provide the comforts of both heat and light.

The Things That Matter

1

BIRTH: *Frankenstein*

Frankenstein is the story of childbirth as it would be if it had been invented by someone who wanted power more than love.

The book's subtitle identifies Victor Frankenstein as "The Modern Prometheus." The ancient Prometheus stole fire from the gods so that he could give human beings its warmth and comfort. The modern Prometheus steals from nature "the cause of generation and life"—the secret of biological reproduction by which a new life is brought into being—and uses that secret to create a new species. In human beings the power of "generation and life" works through the partly instinctual, partly voluntary union of a man and woman who have little control over the outcome, and who typically feel—as Victor remembers his parents feeling about him—a "deep consciousness of what they owed towards the being to which they had given life." Victor, in contrast, feels no obligation to the being to which he has given life through "the horrors of my secret toil," and he sustains himself through his gruesome, pleasureless work with the thought that his creature will owe him more gratitude than any human child ever owed to its father. Frankenstein performs the act of creation alone, by conscious choice rather than through instinct, so that he alone can have total control over its outcome.

Victor creates new life by applying an electric spark to a dead body, not by embracing a living one. In this act and in every other he rejects his own bodily life, the bodily lives of those who love him, and the whole realm of the flesh. While building his creature, he "tortured the living animal to animate the lifeless clay." Later, while building a mate for the creature, Victor is so horrified by the prospect of their having children of their own that, "trembling with passion," he "tore to pieces the thing on which I was engaged." Victor thinks of his own impending marriage with "horror and dismay," and some of his feelings are justified by his creature's threat to be "with you on your wedding-night." But the deeper cause of his dismay is something that the book never names explicitly, but which it insistently points to—Victor's deep, unacknowledged horror of the human body and its relations with another human body. One effect of what he calls his "murderous machinations" is the murder of his own bride on their wedding night.

Choosing Beauty

The body is the part of yourself which is most obviously created and shaped by nature. No one can ever fully control its appetites, instincts, and desires, especially the impulses that erupt without warning at the end of childhood, when the body becomes sexually mature. Everyone wants to achieve at least some control over them, but Victor Frankenstein wants the total control over the flesh that he can attain by making a body to his own specification. His ambition is not merely to gain control over his own body—although he drives it to exhaustion and withholds satisfactions from it—but to conquer nature itself, to seize for his own use that mysterious instinctive power that gave his body life. "I pursued nature to her hiding-places," he says of his researches, as if he were a hunter and nature his prey.

When a child is born, nature determines whether or not it will have physical beauty, but Victor chooses for himself the appearance that he gives his creature: "His limbs were in proportion, and I had selected his features as beautiful." (The modern couple who advertises for a blond, blue-eyed egg donor is driven by a similar wish to control a new life.) He gives the creature the spark of life; he refuses it the warmth of his feelings. When Victor's work is done and the creature opens its eyes, reaches out its hand, and tries to smile at its creator, Victor flees in dismay. Earlier, when the creature existed only as an inert, lifeless thing in his laboratory, Victor could enjoy fantasizing about the gratitude it would give him, but as soon as the object of his generosity takes on a life of its own, as soon as it breaks free of his fantasies about it, "the beauty of the dream vanished, and breathless horror and disgust filled my heart." From this point onward, he thinks of his creature as "my enemy"—but the only thing it has done to deserve Victor's horrified disgust is to reach out for his affection.

What the creature wants from his creator is "sympathies," a word that recurs throughout *Frankenstein*. "Sympathy" was the word used in Mary Shelley's time for all the feelings of mutual understanding and affection that join individuals to each other. Sympathies bring together friend and friend, parent and child, wife and husband. The creature demands that Victor build a mate "with whom I can live in the interchange of those sympathies necessary for my being," and Victor later reflects that "one of the first results of those sympathies for which the daemon thirsted would be children." The sympathies the creature wants from Victor are those of a parent for a child. Victor offers only hatred.

But Victor's relationship with his creature is deeper and more mysterious than any mere hatred. Both Frankenstein and the creature believe they have rejected each other, yet they also half understand that they are not merely complicit with each other, but that in some deep and obscure way they are indivisible. They are joined in a passionate wish to destroy anyone who might break through their shared isolation. The creature responds to Frankenstein's rejection by committing violent acts of revenge, yet he takes his revenge not on Victor himself, but on Victor's family and friends and the foster sister who hopes to marry him. Victor perceives that his creature is the means by which his own spirit kills those whom he believes he loves: "I considered the being whom I had cast among mankind, and endowed with the will and power to effect purposes of horror, . . . nearly in the light of my own vampire, my own spirit let loose from the grave, and forced to destroy all that was dear to me." What Victor fails to perceive is that his family and friends—all those who want affection from him—are not dear to him at all. When he withdrew into the solitude of his laboratory, he also withdrew from everyone who wanted his love, and the creature, as if fulfilling a wish too dark for Frankenstein to see in himself, proceeds to destroy them all.

The creature never becomes, as a child does, an autonomous being. In a mysterious but inescapable way he is a hidden aspect of Frankenstein himself that has suddenly taken visible form. Victor's friends, siblings, and parents all assume that he feels as close to them as they feel to him, but Victor's only real relationship is with a monstrous emanation of himself. By the end of the book, he and his creature have withdrawn from all human society and made their way toward the frozen isolation of the North Pole in pursuit of one another. When Frankenstein at last dies—despite the creature's secret efforts to keep him alive—the creature has nothing more to live for, and rushes away toward his own death. The fruits of the solitary act of ambition, not love, through which Victor gave life to his creature are a deepening solitude, murder, and self-destruction.

Everything Has a Beginning

Mary Shelley's story of how *Frankenstein* came to be written has some of the drama and depth of the novel itself. She wrote an introduction to a revised third edition in 1831—the original version appeared in 1818 and was reprinted in 1823—in which she recalled the journey to Switzerland that she and Percy Bysshe Shelley made in 1816, when she was not yet nineteen. Their neighbor near Geneva was Lord Byron, who was there with his friend John William Polidori. After the four read some ghost stories, Byron decreed that they each would write a ghost story of their own. The three men immediately began writing their stories, and almost as immediately abandoned them. In contrast, Mary Shelley tried for some days to think of a story but could not, until one evening she heard Shelley and Byron talk about the possibility of reanimating a corpse, or of giving life to a body made up of separately manufactured parts. In bed that night, she suddenly saw in her imagination the scene in which Victor brings the creature to life, and the next morning she began writing the episode itself, beginning, "It was a dreary night in November . . ."

Other evidence suggests that Mary Shelley was retroactively improving on real events when she made so sharp a distinction between her slow patient start on her story and the quick impatience of her husband and friends, but her account points toward the themes that she knew she had woven into her novel. As she describes the events, she alone, unlike the three men in the party, brooded for days while awaiting the arrival of her story—the only one of the stories that grew into something finished and complete. "'Have you thought of a story?' I was asked each morning, and each morning I was forced to reply with a mortifying negative." In the next sentence of her recollections, she generalizes: "Every thing must have a beginning . . . and that beginning must be linked to something that went before." In *Frankenstein* the disasters that result from the beginning of the creature's story are linked to the events that preceded it. The miseries of the creature's life are inseparable from the way in which he was brought into life, and inseparable from his creator's conscious and unconscious attitudes toward what Victor calls "generation and life."

Mary Shelley gave *Frankenstein* its unique power by portraying its grotesque horrors as the consequence of the most familiar and ordinary causes. The whole moral and emotional content of her book is an extended restatement of a single sentence by her mother, Mary Wollstonecraft, in the first feminist manifesto written in English, *A Vindication of the Rights of Woman* (1792): "A great pro- portion of the misery that wanders, in hideous forms, around the world, is allowed to rise from the negligence of parents." In ordi- nary life, these hideous forms are concealed behind everyday faces. In *Frankenstein* they appear as they are, in all their horror. The hideousness of Victor Frankenstein's negligence of his creature is visible on the face of the creature itself as it wanders in hideous form around the world, inflicting and experiencing misery.

In lesser fictions of horror than Mary Shelley's book, the star- tling monstrosity erupts into the world from a remote laboratory on a mountain peak. In *Frankenstein* the monstrosity emerges from an extreme version of the sort of emotional negligence that anyone might commit. The book invites its readers to recognize them- selves in its hero. Almost all film and stage versions of *Frankenstein* portray horrors more spectacular but less unsettling than the book's, because the adaptations portray Frankenstein as absolutely different from ourselves—either a deranged scientist with an unlimited equipment budget or the rich nobleman Baron von Frankenstein, never the Victor portrayed by Mary Shelley, the child of loving parents who grows up to be a dedicated but otherwise ordinary student living in rented rooms near the university, who improvises a laboratory of his own, as every chemistry student did, because universities did not yet provide one.* The filmed versions of *Frankenstein* omit everything in the book that insists that Victor is an extreme case of someone to whom intimacy and obligation are intolerable—as they sometimes are to everyone.

Parents: Maternal and Otherwise

No greater book than *Frankenstein* has been written by an author who was not yet twenty years old, and this novel, more than Mary Shelley's later ones, combines the inchoate fears of childhood with the sophisticated intelligence of an adult. The fears that pervade the book are those of abandonment and death. Mary Shelley's mother died a few days after giving birth to her. At the time Mary finished writing *Frankenstein*, in 1817, she had abandoned her father in the middle of the night to elope with her lover; she had given birth to a daughter (who died a few days later) and a son; and she was now pregnant for a third time.† The children's father was Percy Bysshe Shelley, who abandoned his year-old child by his wife Harriet Westbrook when he and Mary eloped; Harriet was five months pregnant with their second child at the time. While

---

* Victor as mad scientist is a twentieth-century invention. In the nineteenth century he was always referred to as a student, as in Charles Dickens's allusion in *Great Expectations* (1860-61) to "the imaginary student pursued by the misshapen creature he had impiously made."
† The living son, William, died two years later at the age of three. Mary's third child was a daughter, Clara, who lived only a year. Her fourth child, Percy Florence, born a year later, was her only child who survived her.

the book was being written, Mary's half sister Fanny Imlay ran away from home, disguised her identity, and killed herself; two months later, Harriet killed herself, and was found to have been pregnant with a third child (the unknown father was possibly Percy himself, who could have encountered Harriet after he and Mary returned to London); Percy and Mary married soon afterward. Mary Shelley's critics have pointed to one or another of these experiences as the key to *Frankenstein,* but all that seems certain is that the young Mary Shelley learned about many different ways in which parents and children can be divided from each other in both death and life, about many different kinds of physical and emotional estrangement.

Her book dramatizes the emotional horror of separation while analyzing it in moral terms. Victor Frankenstein explains away the murderous disasters by placing all the blame on destiny and fate—and Mary Shelley emphasized his evasion by making it even more prominent in the heavily revised third edition of the book of 1831 than it was in the first and second editions of 1818 and 1823. But she knew that Frankenstein's claim to be the victim of malign impersonal forces is a way of evading responsibility, just as his isolated act of creation is a way of escaping intimacy.* Mary Shelley's father, the radical political philosopher William Godwin, had emphasized the ways in which human beings are shaped by the impersonal forces of their environment. Mary Shelley admired her father enough to dedicate *Frankenstein* to him, but she was chilled by his fury over her elopement with Percy Bysshe Shelley and by

---

* Mary Shelley's journals show that she herself was tempted to imagine that sufferings were required by fate. Writing in 1839, she interpreted the suicide of Shelley's abandoned wife Harriet, many years earlier, as the event to which "I attribute so many of my own heavy sorrows, as the atonement claimed by fate for her death." When she portrayed Victor Frankenstein making excuses for himself in attributing his sorrows to fate, she was both portraying and resisting a temptation of her own.

the cruelty of his refusals to sympathize over the deaths of her children. Victor Frankenstein's isolating evasions are, among other things, her oblique criticism of her father's evasions.

All the characters in her book take one of two opposite approaches to human relations. Either, like Victor Frankenstein, they flee from all mutual relations; or, like almost everyone else, they seek out those whom they can love and help, and, whether they are men or women, they act and live *maternally*. When Victor Frankenstein suffers a nervous collapse on the morning after he gives life to his creature, Victor's friend Henry Clerval, having just arrived on the scene, tends him through his long illness. "He knew," Frankenstein recalls of Clerval, "that I could not have had a more kind and attentive nurse than himself." When Mary Shelley wrote this, the noun "nurse" still commonly meant "one who feeds or cares for a baby." Clerval gives to Victor precisely the maternal nurture that Victor refuses to give to his creature. Victor says of Clerval, "Nothing but the unbounded and unremitting attentions of my friend could have restored me to life"—unwittingly alluding to his own different kind of unremitting attentions ("After days and nights of incredible labor and fatigue, I succeeded in discovering the cause of generation and life; nay, more, I became myself capable of bestowing animation upon lifeless matter"), and emphasizing the difference between Clerval's maternal, personal attention and Victor's indifference to the miscellaneous body parts that he too, in a less warmhearted way, had "restored . . . to life."

Frankenstein begins his life story by telling about his parents' wish to share their "inexhaustible stores of affection." A friend of his father, named Beaufort, had fallen into poverty and left his native Geneva in shame; the older Frankenstein, after ten months in search of his friend, finds Beaufort hiding in passive self-pity, tended by his daughter Caroline, who is working to provide them with subsistence. When Beaufort dies a few months later, the older

Frankenstein places Caroline in the care of a relative, and two years later, moved by "gratitude and worship," marries her. Deeply attached to each other, the couple bestow unstinting love on their firstborn, Victor:

> I was their plaything and their idol, and something better—their child, the innocent and helpless creature bestowed on them by Heaven, whom to bring up to good, and whose future lot it was in their hands to direct to happiness or misery, according as they fulfilled their duties towards me. With this deep consciousness of what they owed towards the being to which they had given life, added to the active spirit of tenderness that animated both, it may be imagined that while during every hour of my infant life I received a lesson of patience, of charity, and of self-control, I was so guided by a silken cord that all seemed but one train of enjoyment to me.

Victor chooses his words with passionate precision, emphasizing the way in which his parents' feelings toward their child were a combination of things that are not always found together: pleasure, charity, and obligation.

After a few years, Frankenstein's parents encounter an orphan child—the daughter of an Italian patriot who had died or been imprisoned while fighting for his country's liberty—and, in another impulse of generosity and love, take her into their family to raise as their own. The parents give their adopted daughter all the devotion and love that they have given their firstborn son, but Victor never quite understands that a child who arrives in a family without being born into it can be loved with the same depth of feeling as a biological child. On the day Elizabeth arrives, Victor's mother tells him playfully, "I have a pretty present for my Victor." He interprets her words literally, "with childish seriousness," and thinks of Elizabeth as "mine to protect, love, and cherish," not quite in the way that his parents thought of him as their plaything, idol, and child, but as "a possession of my own." The idea of ownership, rather than of mutual obligation, shapes all his relationships afterward.

When Elizabeth, some years later, falls ill with scarlet fever, Victor's mother, ignoring all warnings to preserve herself against the disease, tends Elizabeth with watchful care, and at last "triumphed over the malignity of the distemper." Elizabeth is saved; but, as Victor says, "the consequences of this imprudence were fatal to her preserver," because his mother contracts the fever from Elizabeth and dies. But the mother, unlike Victor, does not think of her generosity as an imprudence, and her only regret is that she will not live to see Elizabeth and Victor married so that they can experience the same happiness that she has felt in her own marriage.

Some years later, when the creature tells Victor the story of all that happened after the moment when he was simultaneously created and abandoned, he emphasizes the loving generosity of another noble-minded family whose members, like Victor's parents, sacrifice themselves for the happiness that comes from sharing their lives with others. The creature has been living in a hovel, from which he observes the De Lacey family, who occupy the adjoining cottage but are unaware of the creature's existence. The De Laceys are a father, son, and daughter who have chosen to live in poverty and exile, but for entirely different motives from those that drove the older Frankenstein's friend Beaufort from Geneva. They have been banished from France because the son, Felix, had rescued a Turkish merchant from an unjust sentence of death. The merchant's daughter Safie had fallen in love with Felix and fled from her father in the hope of joining him. When Safie's servant fell ill during the difficult journey to the De Laceys', Safie "nursed her with the most devoted affection"—with a maternal charity indifferent to her superior status, like Victor's mother at the time of Elizabeth's illness.

The De Laceys and the elder Frankensteins display the impossible moral virtues typical of melodramatic heroes, but Mary Shelley never suggests that goodness is limited to heroes. She gives similar virtues to her comic and unheroic characters. Henry Clerval's merchant father disdains education, forbids Clerval to study at a university, and insists that he become a merchant like himself—but even in his coarse soul, love triumphs over selfishness. As Clerval reports when he at last arrives at the university, "his affection for me at length overcame his dislike of learning."

Victor Frankenstein, unlike all these affectionate and maternal figures, is indifferent to everyone around him. Indifference leads sooner or later to an impenetrable loneliness—not the kind of loneliness that results from such external circumstances as isolation, exile, or loss, but the kind of chronic loneliness that cannot be relieved by the presence of others. Mary Shelley understood, as Victor does not, that the only way he could escape from his chronic loneliness would be to renounce his indifference. But he cannot renounce it because he believes it has been imposed on him by fate.

Original Virtue

Novelists who think deeply about moral issues tend to speak in two contradictory voices in the same book. One, the writer's official voice, expresses views the writer wants to believe but half secretly doubts. The other, unofficial voice expresses views the writer wants to deny but half secretly believes. The official voice states or dramatizes attitudes that may be admirable but tend to be morally simplistic. Even when it implicitly rebukes some failing, it simultaneously offers reassurance that reform is possible and easy, that simply by choosing the right action you can produce the right result. The unofficial voice, by contrast, offers no easy answers and tends to be audible mostly in metaphors and subtle juxtapositions that allude to difficulties, ambiguities, and contradictions that the official voice ignores.

Writing in her official voice, Mary Shelley endorses her mother's moralizing views on the monstrous forms of misery that arise from parental negligence: parental negligence makes the creature miserable; parental rejection makes him murderous. He knows from Frankenstein's journal (found in the pocket of the garment that the creature took with him when he first wanders away) that his creator was horrified by him even while preparing him for life. At first, the creature's feelings are instinctively generous, reverent, sympathetic. Only the misery and pain of abandonment goads him to violent hatred—which only increases his misery and pain. As he explains in the morally and biologically precise words of his final speech, "My heart was fashioned to be susceptible of love and sympathy; and when wrenched by misery to vice and hatred, it did not endure the violence of the change, without torture such as you cannot even imagine." Mary Shelley, speaking through the creature, endorses the central teaching of the most advanced and enlightened educational and psychological thinking of her era: the teaching that misery and hatred are unnatural, that human beings are inherently virtuous and free. These were ideas she absorbed as a child from the conversation of her father and his friends and then studied in detail in the writings of John Locke and Jean-Jacques Rousseau, and she knew they were the same theories of human nature that her mother, Mary Wollstonecraft, had used as the basis of her feminist manifesto.

John Locke taught that the human mind at birth is a blank slate, a tabula rasa, on which impressions are made by experience, that we are born without a predisposition to think in any particular way, and that we learn to be who we are from the examples set by others. Jean-Jacques Rousseau, accepting the essentials of this doctrine, added that human beings learn anger and greed from the society around them, not from any inner disorder of their own. When men and women first gathered into their hut villages, Rousseau theorized, they were sociable and generous—as Frankenstein's creature is before he is battered by hatred and rejection.

These teachings were intellectually revolutionary. They rejected the doctrine of original sin, the belief that all human beings are inherently sinful because everyone inherits sinfulness from Adam, and one of their effects was to overturn all traditional ideas about child-rearing. Locke's and Rousseau's writings about education excited parents and teachers throughout Europe with the prospect of a wholly new kind of education. Education would no longer aim to train children into the narrow roles required by the social status into which they had been born (as in traditional theories of education that derived from ancient Greece), nor to turn children away from their inherent tendency to sin (as in many Christian theories of education). Instead, love and the loving example of virtue and gratitude in their parents and teachers would guide children to goodness and happiness.

In *Frankenstein* the creature's moral and emotional life is the result of Mary Shelley's thought experiment in Locke and Rousseau's theories, her attempt to imagine how a child would develop in the extreme case of being born into total solitude. When Frankenstein's creature first comes to consciousness, his mind is empty of knowledge and experience, and he can find neither meaning nor order in his sensations: "No distinct ideas occupied my mind; all was confused." His biological instincts are limited to wishes for warmth and food, fear at finding himself alone, and pleasure at the sight of the moon lighting the sky. When he sees human beings, all his impulses toward them are generous and good. He instinctively learns how to feel reverence and love by observing the De Laceys' example; and by observing that they have needs which he is able to supply, he instinctively wants to help them and learns how to give them aid. Venturing out secretly by night, he leaves firewood at their door and clears snow from their path, actions that the De Laceys can interpret only as the work of a benevolent spirit.

The loving dignity of the blind elder De Lacey and the gentleness and beauty of Felix and his sister Agatha excite the creature with pleasing sensations, while his own reflection in a pond terrifies him with its monstrosity. He is moved to pain and pleasure by the exiled family's mutual expressions of love; their self-denying generosity affects him, he says, "sensibly"—so strongly that he experiences it in his physical senses, not only in his thoughts. Having absorbed their language, he can learn "even more deeply" about their relations: "I heard of the difference of sexes; of the birth and growth of children; how the father doated on the smiles of the infant, and the lively sallies of the older child; how all the life and cares of the mother were wrapped up in the precious charge; how the mind of youth expanded and gained knowledge; of brother, sister, and all the various relationships which bind one human being to another in mutual bonds." From all these mutual relations he knows he is banished: "No father had watched my infant days, no mother had blessed me with smiles and caresses."

The creature supplements his moral education through three books that he finds by chance: Johann Wolfgang von Goethe's epistolary novel about a sensitive young man who kills himself for love, *The Sorrows of Young Werther;* a volume of Plutarch's *Lives of the Eminent Greeks and Romans;* and John Milton's *Paradise Lost.* From the first he learns to sympathize with emotions so intense that Werther prefers to die than endure them. From the second he learns to admire just and peaceable lawgivers and to feel "ardour

for virtue . . . and abhorrence for vice." From the third he learns
that Adam, like himself, began in loneliness, but that Adam's "state
was far different from mine in every other respect," that the "espe-
cial care" Adam received from his creator was the opposite of the
abandonment endured by the creature. He later learns (by reading
the journal that Victor left in a coat pocket) that Frankenstein was
appalled by his creature—unlike the creator God of *Paradise Lost*
who, "in pity, made man beautiful and alluring, after his own
image." The creature knows himself to be a different kind of image,
"a filthy type of yours, more horrid even from the very resemblance." And when he commands Frankenstein to create a mate of
his own species, he knows he is demanding a gift that Adam
received without asking for it.

When the creature is alone, observing others in secret, his only
angry emotions are envy of the De Laceys—a feeling that he
recognizes in Satan's envy of God and the angels—and fury at
Frankenstein's abandonment of him. But he also loves the De
Laceys, and he wishes that Frankenstein would fulfill the role of
the creature's "natural lord and king" so that the creature could be
docile and grateful to him. The creature tries to imagine the De
Laceys as his benefactors and protectors—as Frankenstein should
have been—and has no wish to make them suffer. Even when violently struck by the terrified Felix, who finds him begging for sympathy at the feet of the blind elder De Lacey, the creature still
refuses to resist the evil done to him, although he knows he is far
stronger than his human attacker. And he still feels no wish to make
others suffer because he suffers. Soon afterward, in an instinctive
act of sympathy, he rescues a little girl from drowning in a river,
"with extreme labour from the force of the current," and uses
"every means in my power" to revive her. But her peasant father
grabs her away, and when the creature follows them ("I hardly
knew why," he says, only half understanding his wish for human

company), the father fires a gunshot that shatters the creature's flesh and bone.

Only this last agony of pain teaches him to feel "hatred and vengeance" and to vow "a deep and deadly revenge." Yet even now he still refrains from acting on his hatred. A few months later, coming across a beautiful child in the fields near Geneva, he thinks that because the child is too young to perceive him as horrible, he can take him away and educate him to be his companion and friend. But the child—who is Frankenstein's younger brother William—names his father as his protector while struggling in the creature's grasp. On hearing the name of the elder Frankenstein, the creature says, "you belong then to my enemy . . . you shall be my first victim"; but he does not quite murder him in cold blood. Instead, as William continues to cry out epithets that bring "despair" to the creature's heart, he grasps William's throat "to silence him"—and kills him. He had no wish to kill, but the sight of his dead victim gives him a sense of "exultation and hellish triumph" (he is alluding to Satan's triumph in bringing death to Adam and Eve), and the thrill of this exultation finally convinces him to choose evil as his good. But Mary Shelley has done everything possible to emphasize that the creature learns violence, hatred, and evil only from the violence, hatred, and abandonment inflicted on him by others—by the De Laceys who flee from him, the peasant who fires a shot at him, and his creator who was horrified by him.

Happiness and Vehemence

Mary Shelley devised the creature's story to serve as a proof of the psychological and educational theories that lie behind it—but at the same time she sensed that theories of inherent human goodness were sentimental and false. Even while she endorses them in her official voice, she refutes them through the story of Victor Frankenstein.

Victor descends into misery and despair, not because anyone abandoned or abused him as his creature was abandoned and abused, but because he willfully insists on doing so. Victor's parents raise him in a way that Rousseau—who was also born and raised in Geneva—would have approved. His parents, he says, were "the agents and creators of all the many delights which we enjoyed," and no one "could have passed a happier childhood than myself." When he visits other families, he recalls, "I distinctly discerned how peculiarly fortunate my lot was, and gratitude assisted the development of filial love."

But in the very next words he speaks, he explodes the theory that a climate of love produces a loving child. "My temper was sometimes violent," he says, "and my passions vehement." His violent temper and vehement passions can't be blamed on anyone—not even on himself. They issue from his irreducible individuality, his insistence on being himself despite all the shaping influences of education and instinct.

In this, he is human like everyone else, not the exceptional man portrayed in the horror films. The creature entirely lacks the kind of individuating impulse that drives Victor, but he lacks this impulse because he has no relations with others and doesn't need to assert his individuality against them. Individuality never arises in total isolation, only through relations with others—even antagonistic ones. To the ancient question whether the mind is shaped by nature or by nurture, Mary Shelley's answer is: neither, because everyone's individuality is willed, shaped by their own choices, not determined by forces outside them.

Mary Shelley believed in no religious doctrines, certainly not in the doctrine of original sin. But like many of her contemporaries, she continued to believe in the moral and emotional meanings of doctrines whose theological meanings she rejected as archaic and naïve. Victor's vehemence and temper seem in part to be the product of what might be called inherent willfulness—the ordinary everyday human insistence on getting one's own way whether or not it does you any good. But Mary Shelley seems also to suggest that Victor's vehement temper is the inevitable and unintended effect of exactly the kind of loving education that Locke and Rousseau recommended. Mary Shelley observed in her father's household the ways in which men and women who proclaim and practice benevolence can exert subtle control over others without knowing they are doing anything of the kind, and her subversive sense of the mixed effects of parental love is one of the most unsettling features of *Frankenstein*.

The Bonds of Love

The perfect upbringing that Victor receives from his parents corresponds in broad outline to the education that Rousseau imagined in his literary hybrid, the novel-treatise *Emile, ou De l'éducation*. Emile's tutor (who narrates the story) guides his pupil through an exactingly planned education based on love and example, until finally Emile is ready to love and marry Sophie, the young woman who has been given an equally exact education in feminine submission and sweetness. (This infuriated Mary Wollstonecraft, who wanted Sophie to get the same education as Emile.) Emile and Sophie have been chosen for each other in the same way that Victor and Elizabeth are destined for each other by their parents, and Rousseau's book ends with the triumph of their marriage—more of a triumph for the tutor than for the newlyweds, as the tutor manages every detail of their life, including their sex life, in order to prolong their happiness. Everything ends differently in *Franken-*

stein. Victor's childhood issues in monstrosity, not marriage; Elizabeth is murdered by the creature on the night of her wedding to Victor; and the one indissoluble union in the book is that of the creature and his maker.*

One of the unspoken questions in *Emile,* as in *Frankenstein,* is whether anyone can be guided to freedom and happiness by a coercive education, no matter how gentle the teacher and no matter how generous the teacher's goals. Emile's tutor allows nothing from the outside world to corrupt Emile's education, and it is the tutor who brings Emile and Sophie together when both are mature enough for sex. Rousseau imagined that Emile would feel only gratitude for his tutor's benevolence and care, and no resentment of the tutor's total control over his pupil's life. Mary Shelley was a better psychologist than Rousseau in her sense of the effect of care combined with power. In Frankenstein's story, Victor's loving mother shapes his emotional life in a more extreme way than anything Emile's tutor can imagine, and Victor's erotic life is blighted by his mother's hand—a "dead hand," in the legal sense of the term, in that her power over her son continues after her death.

Everything his mother says and does to shape Victor's life is loving and generous, but its effect is deadly. The crucial event occurs when she is on her deathbed, after succumbing to the disease from which she rescued Elizabeth. She joins Victor's and Elizabeth's hands and tells the two of them, apparently for the first time: "My children, my firmest hopes of future happiness were placed on the

---

* Historians like to point out that Rousseau wrote a few chapters of a sequel, *Emile et Sophie,* in which he seems to take a skeptical view of the effects of Emile and Sophie's education. In the fragment, the happy couple moves to Paris, where Sophie turns unfaithful and the marriage breaks down under the influence of urban immorality. But Rousseau's optimism was indomitable, and the fragment was not the whole story. Rousseau told a friend that the book was to end in a general recovery of happiness, with the revelation that Sophie, having been drugged with aphrodisiacs, had been morally innocent all along.

prospect of your union. This expectation," she adds, "will now be the consolation of your father." In effect, she withdraws her love from Victor by dying, and her last command is that he accept Elizabeth as her substitute. As for the rest of the family, Victor's mother tells Elizabeth, "you must supply my place to the younger children." Elizabeth has unintentionally caused Victor's mother's death by giving her the illness from which Elizabeth herself recovers, but the dying woman forbids any feelings of guilt on Elizabeth's part, or resentment on anyone else's, by insisting that Elizabeth can make good the loss: Elizabeth will now take on the role of mother to the younger children, and will later take on the role of wife by marrying into the family. Mary Shelley lived with the knowledge that she had caused her mother's death by being born—an exchange of life for death much like that of Victor's mother and Elizabeth. And Mary Shelley knew that any attempt to treat such an exchange in the calm daylight of rational benevolence inevitably leaves its real sufferings hidden in darkness.

The Fatal Wedding Night

Things hidden in darkness reemerge in nightmares. In the hours after Victor makes his creature come to life, he dreams about love and death:

> I slept, indeed, but I was disturbed by the wildest dreams. I thought I saw Elizabeth, in the bloom of health . . . Delighted and surprised, I embraced her, but as I imprinted the first kiss on her lips, they became vivid with the hue of death; her features appeared to change, and I thought that I held the corpse of my dead mother in my arms . . . I started from my sleep with horror . . . I beheld the wretch—the miserable monster whom I had created.

Victor's mother promised him Elizabeth as a substitute for herself, but his dream gives him his mother's corpse as a substitute for Elizabeth—and he opens his eyes to find the inhuman life that he has created in place of the human child who might have arisen from a marriage, the life that he made from corpses in "the unhallowed damps of the grave."

Later in the story, the creature demands that Victor make for him a female of his own species, so that he can have the mutual relations that Victor has denied himself. Victor consents, but after voyaging to a remote Scottish island to begin his second act of creation, he refuses to finish it. Victor reasons to himself that the creature had promised to leave Europe for the deserts of the New World, yet the creature and its mate would have children, "and a race of demons would be propagated upon the earth." So he destroys the unfinished female body that he has been making, while the creature watches in despair from a window.

Victor refuses his creature any hope of emotional and sexual sympathies, and the creature responds by denying the same hopes to Victor. When Victor hesitated earlier to build a mate for the creature, the creature had warned him: "I will work at your destruction, nor finish till I desolate your heart, so that you shall curse the hour of your birth." Now, after Victor destroys his work-in-progress, the creature warns him again: "Remember, I shall be with you on your wedding-night." Victor interprets this as a threat to kill him on his wedding night, but that is not at all what the creature says, and Victor characteristically, and almost willfully, neglects to remember that his bride will also be with him on his wedding night.

The day after Victor destroys the creature's unfinished mate, the creature continues his work of desolating Victor's heart by murdering Henry Clerval, a crime for which Victor is incarcerated until his innocence can be proved. Weeks later, as Victor makes his way back to Geneva after being released from prison, the creature's departing threat about his wedding night begins to take a clear and specific form. Elizabeth writes to Victor to reaffirm her love for him and to ask whether at last they will marry. If he hesitates, she asks, is it because he thinks of her more as a sister than as a bride? Or because he wants intimacy from someone else? "Tell me, dearest Victor," she begs. "Answer me, I conjure you, by our mutual happiness, with simple truth—Do you not love another?" Victor can find no plausible excuse for refusing to marry her, but he cannot answer her question "with simple truth," because the truth is hopelessly complex: he does not love another, but he is entangled with his creature in their intimate isolation more inextricably than any lovers can be entangled with each other.

"Alas!" Victor exclaims, revealing his unconscious sexual terror, "to me the idea of an immediate union with my Elizabeth was one of horror and dismay." His horror of sexual relations with a loving, beautiful woman arises from the same motives that drove him to create a new life in the solitude of his laboratory. Victor's fear of sex—and of its consequences, especially childbirth—is something he never states explicitly, but it pervades his story, and it is one form of his pervasive hatred and fear of the uncontrollable, unpredictable human body—the same hatred and fear that drove him when he "tortured the living animal to animate the lifeless clay." What he fears about the body and sex is that he cannot control them.

The myth of Cupid's arrow—or of Aphrodite maddening her victims with desire—is a way of describing the power that impulsive, instinctive sex has over men and women. Anyone who fears the power of sex, anyone who dreads losing control to nature and instinct, will try to avoid any relationship in which nature and instinct can take command of both partners by arousing them with mutual desire, any relationship in which both partners gratefully accept a power that acts equally on both of them, and helps to bring them together when resentments and angers push them apart. Such a person, like Victor, will prefer relations where unpredictable instinct has no place, and the only such relations are unequal ones in which one partner controls the other, and neither is controlled by unpredictable nature.

Victor fears sex, nature, and his own body. Elizabeth has no fear of sex and no fear of equality. She wants a free mutual relation with Victor, and would rather renounce her love than compel Victor to fulfill any obligation he might feel toward her. "Our marriage would render me eternally miserable," she tells him in her letter, "unless it were the dictate of your own free choice." Victor assents to their marriage, but in a way that makes it unequal even before it begins. He has, he tells her, "one secret," a "tale of misery and terror" that he will not reveal until the day after their wedding. "Until then," he writes to her, "I conjure you, do not mention or allude to it," and he adds, "I know you will comply." His promise to reveal his secret on the day after the wedding (because a marriage is traditionally irrevocable once it has been consummated) is the kind of promise that sinister bridegrooms make in folktales. (Before Jane Eyre learns the identity of the madwoman locked away in his house, Mr. Rochester promises that he will tell her the secret a year and a day after they are married.) Victor demands a relationship in which one party gains power over the other by concealing the truth about himself, not merely by keeping a secret concealed, but by winning the other party's willing consent to its concealment.

On the evening of their wedding, when Elizabeth is terrified by the fear she sees in Victor's face, he tells her that she must be calm until the night is over—but adds, "this night is dreadful, very dreadful." As if this were not enough to discourage a new bride on her wedding night, Victor sends her to bed alone while he wanders through the inn awaiting the catastrophe. It occurs, signaled by a scream from the bedroom where Elizabeth is and Victor is not. He rushes in to find her strangled, "thrown across the bed, her head hanging down," in a grotesque parody of sensual ecstasy, while the creature looks in through the window, exactly as he had looked through the cottage window in Scotland when Victor destroyed the creature's unfinished mate. "The Modern Prometheus" is also the modern Bluebeard who is not content to bring about the murder of his bride but also brings about the murder of everyone else with whom he has been intimate.

Power and Love, Politics and Nature

Human relations divide into two kinds: those based on love and those based on power. Relations based on love are maintained by obligations that are freely chosen; relations based on power are maintained by some kind of force. Most personal relations combine the two kinds, but one kind or the other tends to predominate in any specific relation, and a relationship can begin as one kind and then transform itself into the other. All the relations in *Franken-stein*, except for Victor Frankenstein's relations to his family and friends, are based predominantly on love and the promises and obligations of love. A promise to love and cherish someone is a voluntary renunciation of freedom that is enforced only by conscience and asks for no power over the beloved. As Elizabeth writes to Victor, her marriage would make her miserable if he does not choose it freely.

Mary Shelley recognized with great emotional and moral clarity that when promises are broken and obligations are refused, power and force take their place. The creature asks Frankenstein to create a mate for him; Frankenstein promises to do so, then changes his mind halfway through his work. When the creature confronts him, they exchange these words:

> "Begone [says Frankenstein], I do break my promise; never will I create another like yourself, equal in deformity and wickedness."
>
> "Slave [says the creature], I before reasoned with you, but you have proved yourself unworthy of my condescension.* Remember that I have power; you believe yourself miserable, but I can make you so wretched that the light of day will be hateful to you. You are my creator, but I am your master—obey!"

After the voluntary relation ends, what remains is the stagnant, sterile relation of master and slave. The relation between Frankenstein and his creature dramatizes the paradox that both parties in power relations are trapped—and in a profound sense powerless—in their involuntary loveless relation. Though Frankenstein admits to the creature that "the period of your power is arrived," he can still refuse to create a mate, and the creature, on hearing Frankenstein's refusal, "gnashed his teeth in the impotence of anger." Intransigence and impotence suffer with each other in a relation that can never change as long as they both shall live. After their symmetrical destruction of each other's brides, Victor and his creature are left alone to repel and pursue each other in dual solitude.

In Mary Shelley's novel, as in daily life, intimate voluntary relations, such as marriage and parenthood, tend toward equality, and are happier and more satisfying the more equal they are. A newborn infant is physically helpless, but its parents willingly give it

---

* "Condescension" in this context means a gracious willingness to treat social inferiors as equals, not an offensive display of superiority. Mary Shelley probably knew that the word was used in theology to refer to Christ's willingness to become human flesh.

absolute service, rising exhausted in the night to answer its cries. The child's physical powerlessness is balanced by its parents' psychological servitude; the relationship is far more equal than it appears. As the child grows stronger and more autonomous, the parents grow less willing to serve it; everything in the lives of each generation changes, but the balance between them constantly readjusts itself. Love relations have a past and a future; they grow and change over time to maintain an equality that would otherwise be lost. But when both sides reject equality, the result is the disabling stasis of a master-slave relation, the kind of relation that binds Frankenstein and the creature in an emotional embrace that can be broken only by death.

The same contrasts between equality and power relations apply to the politics of *Frankenstein*, and part of the greatness of the book is its ability to apply the same kind of moral intelligence to political and public issues as to intimate and private ones. The story is set mostly in Switzerland because the Swiss Republic was to Mary Shelley and her contemporaries a rare instance of an almost just society, a republic, not a monarchy, where class distinctions were less extreme than anywhere else in Europe and where even the status of a servant, as Elizabeth says in a letter to Frankenstein, "does not include the idea of ignorance, and the sacrifice of the dignity of a human being." Citizens in such a society have both individual freedom and mutual responsibility, but Victor Frankenstein demands the first while rejecting the second. Instead of feeling responsible to his living neighbors, he imagines himself the benefactor of a species that does not yet exist. Even the "fortunate country," as Elizabeth calls it, is unequal to the challenge of Frankenstein's radical withdrawal into himself: a Swiss court condemns an innocent to death when the servant Justine Moritz is found guilty of a murder committed by the creature. Ordinary justice suffices for ordinary crimes, but the motives that Frankenstein introduces into the world are so extreme that they cause an otherwise just society to act in ways that are all too similar to those of the creature whose existence it cannot acknowledge or understand.

Victor discovers his ambition, learns the powers of modern science, and builds his creature at the University of Ingolstadt, in southern Germany. Mary Shelley could have sent Victor to any of a dozen universities in or near Switzerland, but she chose the one that was widely believed to have been the ultimate source of the political ferment that led to the French Revolution. A historical study of Jacobinism (that is, extreme radical egalitarianism) by the Abbé Augustin Barruel, which both Mary and Percy Shelley read shortly before she wrote *Frankenstein,* blamed the upheaval in France on the revolutionary secret society called the Illuminati— the "enlightened ones"—which the professor of law at Ingolstadt had founded in 1776. Critics have made heavy weather of the idea that the creature therefore represents the French Revolution. It is tempting to interpret the abrupt emergence of the creature, its passage from idealism to violence, and its systematic destruction of those who brought about its own creation, as an allegory of the way the French Revolution descended into the political terror in which so many of its leaders destroyed each other.

This is a simpler and more diagrammatic equation than anything Mary Shelley seems to have had in mind when writing the novel, but she was vexed throughout her life by the contradictions between, on the one hand, the benevolent political intentions of William Godwin and Percy Bysshe Shelley and the radical political visionaries whom she met through both of them, and, on the other hand, the real emotional wreckage they inflicted on others without even noticing that they had done any harm. Percy Bysshe Shelley, inspired partly by the teachings of Mary's parents, invited her to join him in a new kind of personal life, unrestrained by ancient prejudices and taboos. In practice this meant that Shelley felt free to fall in love with other women, free to abandon them when he tired of them, free to encourage Mary Shelley to go to bed with his friends, and free to feel wounded by—and self-righteously superior to—the cold anger with which she reacted to all this. She also reacted by emphasizing the contrast between Henry Clerval's maternal loyalty and Victor Frankenstein's vehement ambition.

Mary Shelley may have been the first person to occupy a social role that became far more common in the twentieth century: the radical's lover. The radical's lover is at first dazzled by the radical's commitment to the causes of freedom and justice that she herself hopes to serve, at a time when she has not yet found a practical way to serve them. So she joins and encourages the radical in actions and attitudes that she increasingly recognizes as selfish and hypocritical, but which she cannot reject because she still admires the great causes that the radical claims to serve, and because she has irrevocably joined her life to the radical himself. Mary Shelley found herself increasingly dismayed and humiliated by Percy Bysshe Shelley's treatment of her, but his death by drowning in 1822 left her with a lifelong sense of guilt over her anger at him, and for the rest of her life she committed herself to idealizing his memory in private and public. Her deeper feelings flashed out in her 1831 revisions to *Frankenstein*, which highlighted Victor's vehemence and evasions, and also intermittently in her journals, notably in this entry from 1838:

> Some have a passion for reforming the world; others do not cling to particular opinions. That my parents and Shelley were of the former class, makes me respect it. I respect such when joined to real disinterestedness, toleration and a clear understanding . . . I have never written a word in disfavour of liberalism . . . But since I had lost Shelley I have no wish to ally myself to the Radicals—they

are full of repulsion to me—violent without any sense of Justice—
selfish in the extreme—talking without knowledge—rude, envious and insolent—I wish to have nothing to do with them.

Critics have cited this outburst as evidence that Mary Shelley
turned conservative as she grew older and betrayed her radical
past. It seems more likely that her attitudes did not change, that the
anger and distaste she made explicit in her journal were already
implicit in *Frankenstein,* and that she was able to put her feelings
into words because, as she grew older, she was more willing to trust
her own judgment. She still idealized her parents and her husband,
but now that all three were safely dead, she could finally put on
paper all the feelings that she had earlier suppressed out of love for
them. (William Godwin had died two years earlier.)

The only revolution that anyone anticipates in *Frankenstein* is
one that might overthrow Victor himself—because Victor, having
begun as a young rebel, has turned himself into a new kind of auto-
crat caught up in an unprecedentedly fatal kind of government,
one in which he and his creature both rule and destroy each other.
"I often sat for hours motionless and speechless," Victor recalls,
"wishing for some mighty revolution that might bury me and my
destroyer in its ruins."

The ideas of private and public ethics that underlie Mary Shelley's novel are those of a tolerant, conscientious Protestantism—
the same almost secular Protestantism that Rousseau learned in
Geneva. The confession by the Frankenstein family's servant, Justine Moritz, of a murder she did not commit, made under the
influence of a Roman Catholic priest and her own Catholic upbringing, has the effect of emphasizing by contrast the Protestant virtues.
The creature judges Victor's actions according to the example of
God in *Paradise Lost* who loved and clothed the creatures whom he
made in his image. The novel makes a similar judgment but in dif-

ferent terms, because Mary Shelley's religion as expressed in the novel itself is not Christianity at all but the romantic religion of nature, in which nature has the role that Christianity assigns to God. Like her father and husband, and everyone else in their circle, she revered *Paradise Lost* for its grandeur and vision without believing its religious doctrines. Victor's sin of pride is his attempt to usurp the powers not of God but of nature. In Mary Shelley's version of the romantic religion of nature, nature is inherently sexual; its creatures are male and female and its most sacred rituals are the acts of reproduction and childbirth. Victor commits a double sacrilege against the religion of nature through his usurpation of the powers of generation and by his refusal of the sexual relation offered to him by Elizabeth.

In the rare moments when Victor acknowledges the powers of nature instead of trying to usurp them, when he roams the Alps in the "glorious presence-chamber of imperial Nature," he is soothed and restored: "These sublime and magnificent scenes afforded me the greatest consolation that I was capable of receiving." His sins against divine nature are forgiven when he accepts nature's grace, but he almost always refuses it.

Knowledge and Power, Women and Men

The titanic passions of Victor and his creature disrupt the order of both society and nature in ways that ordinary human beings cannot. But these titanic passions are simply more intense and violent forms of ordinary human emotions, not the alien emotions of inhuman monsters. The story of Victor and his creature is framed within a parallel story, told in the opening and closing pages of the book, in which another character is driven by the same kind of ambition that drives Victor, but on a smaller and less destructive scale. This parallel story is that of the young English sea captain Robert Walton, who tells it in a series of brief letters to his married sister back home— letters in which he reports encountering Victor on an ice floe, taking him on board his ship, and writing down his story.

Walton is a youthful explorer who hopes to find a passage to the North Pole. He knows that the Arctic Ocean is icy and desolate, but he has convinced himself that the pole itself, if he could only arrive there, will prove to be a "region of beauty and delight" where the sun, always visible, gives the sky perpetual splendor. Two motives have driven Walton to buy a ship and hire a crew to join him in seeking the "undiscovered solitudes" of the pole: "the inestimable benefit which I shall confer on all mankind to the last generation" and the chance to "tread a land never before imprinted by the foot of man." Both these "enticements," as Walton calls them, are means of avoiding relationships. Someone who confers a benefit on present and future generations has no mutual relations with any of them: he confers, they receive. And the explorer who finds a place never seen by anyone else can be certain that he will not have to put up with annoying intrusions on his solitude. Like Frankenstein, Walton claims to regret his isolation, but he insists on maintaining it. "I have no friend," he tells his sister. This is his "one want which I have never yet been able to satisfy," yet he has chosen a way of life that cannot satisfy that want. "I shall certainly find no friend on the wide ocean."

A few days after writing this, he finds a friend when he encounters Frankenstein floating on a fragment of ice and takes him aboard his ship. Walton's transcript of Victor's narration—touched up and improved by Victor himself from Walton's hastily written notes—makes up the bulk of the novel. Walton and Frankenstein are both so isolated that they are not so much friends as mirror images, each searching for deeper solitudes. Having found each other, they grieve more than they rejoice. Walton explains to Victor that he is indifferent to his own life, that death seems "a small price to pay for the acquirement of the knowledge which I sought for the dominion I should acquire over the elemental foes of our race."* When Frankenstein hears that Walton, too, wants scientific knowledge so that he can have power over nature, he suffers "a paroxysm of grief" and bursts out: "Unhappy man! Do you share my madness? Have you drunk also of the intoxicating draught?"

Frankenstein contrasts two kinds of knowledge: first, the scientific, objective kind of knowledge that has no mutual relation with the things known (the stars don't care about the stargazer) and that, in many instances, gives power to manipulate those things; and, second, the mutual, emotional kind in which two persons gain mutual understanding of each other, as in the intimate relations between lovers or between parents and children. Frankenstein excuses himself again and again for keeping secrets from his father, Clerval, and Elizabeth, and making mutual understanding impossible. But he is obsessive in his quest for the objective knowledge sought by modern scientists—or "natural philosophers" as they were called in Mary Shelley's time. Victor keeps his own secrets, but he feels a "fervent longing to penetrate the secrets of nature." "Penetrate" is a suggestive word, part of the vocabulary of aggression, uncovering, and rape that Victor uses when he says, "I pursued nature to her hiding-places." Even the gentle professor Waldman at Ingolstadt uses this kind of language in his lecture on chemistry that rouses Frankenstein to his new ambitions. Modern natural philosophers, the professor says, "penetrate into the recesses of nature, and show how she works in her hiding-places."

At the heart of *Frankenstein* is a contrast between the desire to nurture others and the desire to dominate them, and this implies a contrast between feminine qualities of sympathy and masculine

---

* He means the forces of nature against which human beings struggle.

qualities of force. But Mary Shelley was too sane to imagine that feminine qualities belong only to women and masculine qualities only to men. Henry Clerval, though a man, is the best possible nurse Victor can have in his illness. The only woman in the book who actually works as a nurse—the woman hired by the benevolent magistrate to tend to Victor while he is imprisoned in Ireland—is brutal and unfeeling. All the men in the book, with the sole exception of Victor Frankenstein, combine the qualities of both sexes. Clerval is manly and brave, and, like Victor, seeks "no inglorious career," but his ambitions are different from Victor's. "Clerval had never sympathized in my tastes for natural science; and his literary pursuits differed wholly from those which had occupied me." The youthful Frankenstein pursues "the physical secrets of the world," while the young Clerval "occupied himself, so to speak, with the moral relations of things." Those moral relations are explicitly feminine. In the Persian, Arabic, and Sanskrit poetry that Clerval delights in, "life appears to consist in a warm sun and a garden of roses, in the smiles and frowns of a fair enemy, and the fire that consumes your own heart. How different from the manly and heroical poetry of Greece and Rome!"

Nature soothes Victor when he is alone among the awe-inspiring peaks and glaciers of the Alps; there, and only there, can he imagine that "maternal nature bade me weep no more." Clerval most loves nature where it provides a home for men and women who live and work together. Sailing down the Rhine with Victor, Henry exclaims at the sight of castles and villages: "Oh, surely the spirit that inhabits and guards this place has a soul more in harmony with man than those who pile the glacier [that is, climb it by driving stakes or piles into the ice], or retire to the inaccessible peaks of the mountains of our country." It is a sign of Mary Shelley's large-mindedness that Henry Clerval and Victor Frankenstein are both partial portraits of Percy Bysshe Shelley, each embodying different aspects of his character. In effect, in her relations with Percy Bysshe Shelley, she eloped with Clerval and found herself married to Frankenstein.

Victor is impassioned by modern experimental science because it promises him more power than anything else can, because no other civilized activity so thoroughly favors force over sympathy. Mary Shelley's repudiation of Victor's science is part of a wider romantic revolt against the impersonal objectivity of modern science; William Blake gave a slogan to this revolt in his prayer to be saved from "single vision and Newton's sleep." Mary Shelley's critique of science is extraordinary, even for its extraordinary times, in its moral clarity and intellectual subtlety, and in its recognition that different kinds of scientific research have entirely different kinds of moral value. Her critique is not directed against experimental science itself, some of which excites her to admiration and praise, but against the kind of knowledge that Victor Frankenstein chooses to pursue.

As a boy Victor is attracted not to science but to a heady mixture of science, alchemy, and magic, which he finds in the works of three occult magicians from earlier centuries: Cornelius Agrippa, Paracelsus, and Albertus Magnus. These three inspire him to wish for the philosopher's stone which transforms lead into gold, for the elixir of life which banishes disease, and for the magic incantations that raise ghosts and devils. Mary Shelley never read these three writers—Percy Bysshe Shelley, however, had read them as a boy— but she understood that the wishes for occult magical powers that Victor learns from them are the same wishes that motivate him in everything else.

Magic is different from modern science in two crucial ways. First, magic promises results that are spectacularly vast in comparison with the amount of effort that goes into them, and, second, only exceptional individuals can wield magical powers. The words of a magical spell can be spoken as easily as any ordinary words, but when spoken by the right person, they cause earthquakes and thunders. Only a magician can produce such powerful results; the same words spoken by ordinary mortals cause nothing to happen. In contrast, modern science assumes that the character of the experimenter has no effect on the results and accepts the fundamental principle of the conservation of energy, which affirms that the amount of energy expended equals the amount of work performed—in other words, you can't get something for nothing. The biblical decree that you must sweat for bread and labor for childbirth is a moral analogue of this principle. Everything worth having must be worked for, and everyone has to work to get it. Part of the appeal of the alchemist's magic is that it claims to give you something for nothing, provided that you are special enough to deserve it. (A similar fantasy of getting something for nothing seems to be behind the idea of "magic" in the realm of human relations: the husband or wife who complains that "the magic has gone out of my marriage" is perhaps disappointed at no longer being given something for nothing.)

Victor temporarily abandons his youthful wishes when, at the age of fifteen, he first encounters the reality of modern science. "A man of great research in natural philosophy" happens to be visiting Victor's family when lightning blasts a nearby tree, and the man is excited into telling his theory of "electricity and galvanism." This astonishes Victor and "threw greatly in the shade Cornelius Agrippa" and the other "lords of my imagination." As a result, he is not stimulated into an interest in modern science, but instead he loses interest in science altogether: "by some fatality the overthrow of these men disinclined me to pursue my accustomed studies. It seemed to me as if nothing would or could ever be known." Victor loses interest in science because the visitor's theory, although it eclipses ancient alchemy, is nothing more than a theory; not only does it fail to offer the kind of power that alchemy had offered, but it makes power and certainty seem unattainable by any kind of science at all.

Victor's interest revives in the next chapter when he arrives at Ingolstadt and learns that modern science actually offers more power than the alchemists had promised. M. Waldman says in his introductory lecture on chemistry: "The ancient teachers of this science promised impossibilities and performed nothing. The modern masters promise very little; they know that metals cannot be transmuted, and that the elixir of life is a chimera. But these philosophers, whose hands seem only made to dabble in dirt, and their eyes to pore over the microscope or the crucible, have indeed performed miracles." And when M. Waldman proceeds to enumerate their "new and almost unlimited powers," their ability to "command the thunders of heaven" like a modern Zeus, Victor's violent temper and vehement passions are rekindled. By joining scientific knowledge with his ambitions for magical power, he can attain the kind of domination and power that neither ambition nor knowledge could achieve alone.

As a scientist Victor is passionate in his desire for knowledge but indifferent to the objects of his knowledge. He wants knowledge only for the sake of power. In this he follows the example of the literary figure from whom Mary Shelley derived the essentials of both Walton and Frankenstein: the figure of Ulysses in Dante's *Inferno*. Dante's Ulysses is the same person as Homer's Odysseus, but Homer's Odysseus wants to get home to his wife and son and father while Dante's Ulysses has the opposite wish. He says of himself, "Not fondness for a son nor duty to an aged father, nor the love I owed Penelope, which should have gladdened her, could conquer within me the passion I had to gain experience of the world and of the vices and the worth of men." Abandoning those who love him, he sails out on the open sea, where he exhorts his small crew: "to this so brief vigil of our senses that remains to us, choose not to deny experience, following the sun, of the world that has no people." Having detached himself from all relationships, Ulysses can think of life as a "vigil of our senses": he watches and listens without sympathizing or participating. Following the sun, moving westward toward the future, he seeks knowledge of a world without people in it, the same remote world that the modern scientist observes through a microscope or telescope, a realm too large or too small or too hot or too cold for human beings to live in. The world without people need not be physically distant from the observer. It can be physically adjacent and morally distant, as it is for Victor in his upstairs laboratory, or as it is for any scientist who perceives other human beings in terms of numbers and statistics and anonymous impersonal forces, not as unique persons with names and faces.*

In the *Inferno,* Ulysses defies human limitations: he takes his ship through the Pillars of Hercules that had been set up at the edge of the ocean "so that men should not pass beyond." On the open sea, he rouses his crew to the exertions that bring them to the storm that drowns them: "You were not born to live as brutes," he says, "but to follow virtue and knowledge." These goals are

---

*Victor explicitly chooses a utilitarian and statistical approach to questions of personal suffering and moral obligation. He justifies to Walton his destruction of the creature's mate in these terms: "My duties towards the beings of my own species had greater claims to my attention because they included a greater proportion of happiness or misery. Urged by this view, I refused, and I did right in refusing, to create a companion for the first creature." This sounds noble until you remember that Victor is certain that by refusing to create a mate, he will bring about the murder of his friends—the creature promised to do exactly that—while he has no good reason to assume that by creating a mate with whom the creature can have children, the result will be a "race of demons," rather than the contented lives promised by the creature. And the creature never breaks his promises.

more ambiguous than they sound. Dante's *"virtute"* has a double meaning: not only moral excellence but also masculine power. Ulysses is in Dante's hell because he is a false counselor, one who has seduced others to seek goals that only brought them harm. Frankenstein echoes Ulysses' false counsel when he exhorts Walton's sailors, who have lost heart for their dangerous voyage: "Oh! be men, or be more than men . . . return as heroes who have fought and conquered."

The Self and Its Double

In many areas of life, objectivity is a source of clarity, disinterestedness, and justice. But not in all. Applied outside its proper boundaries, objectivity can spawn irrational horrors. By pursuing a single-mindedly rational and objective view of the world, you can all too easily repress your understanding of yourself as a *subject,* someone who makes choices and experiences emotions. In adopting a detached, objective relation to others, Frankenstein adopts a detached relation to himself. Just as he is unable to treat others as individuals with rights and freedom of their own, he keeps insisting that he himself is a mere passive object in the hands of destiny or fate. He is so detached from his own inner life that he cannot perceive that he makes his own choices, and insists that his acts are the work of invisible mythical forces such as "Destiny . . . and her immutable laws," or "the words of fate" (meaning the words of M. Waldman's lecture), or a purpose "assigned to me by Heaven," or "the Angel of Destruction."

By thinking of himself as a passive object, he denies the reality of everything in himself that makes choices or has feelings. He rejects everything in himself that might wish for sympathy, marriage, and love. But that part of himself cannot be repressed. Try to push it down, and it rises up again in a distorted form. In Victor's case, it reemerges as his *double*, the figure who is simultaneously his agent who carries out his secret wishes for him and his enemy who is determined to destroy him. Victor is vividly aware that his creature is not only something manufactured by his hands but something that has issued from himself, from that part of himself that is dead, "my own spirit let loose from the grave."

The myth of the double, which arose late in the eighteenth century and persisted through the early twentieth, served as the means through which literature interpreted the inherent doubleness of the human mind—its hatred of what it loves, its rejection of what it desires. In novels from *Frankenstein* and *Jane Eyre* to Dostoyevsky's *The Double* and Robert Louis Stevenson's *The Strange Case of Dr. Jekyll and Mr. Hyde*, the double performs the irrational destructive acts that its ordinary human counterpart consciously deplores. As Dr. Jekyll says, "This familiar [meaning a spirit or demon under human control] that I called out of my own soul, and sent forth alone to do his good pleasure, was a being inherently malign and villainous; his every act and thought centered on self; drinking pleasure with bestial avidity from any degree of torture to another; relentless like a man of stone." What makes Mary Shelley's version of this myth so profound is that the double's violence is not purely antagonistic like Mr. Hyde's; it turns violent because its wish for sympathy has been refused. The violent double more or less dropped out of literature around the start of the twentieth century, when the Freudian unconscious or id replaced the double as a way of portraying a division in the mind that had otherwise seemed unportrayable. (Clarissa has a double in *Mrs. Dalloway*, but of a very different kind.)

The relation between a character and a double is always irrational and mysterious. In *Frankenstein* Mary Shelley emphasizes that everything that occurs in the story has a rational explanation—except for the uncanny events that join Victor and his creature in a tangle of murder and betrayal when Victor destroys the female creature he had begun to make. Nothing else in the book is presented as an event that would be impossible in the ordinary world: Victor uses no magical art or spiritual aid in his researches; the unexpected gifts of food and firewood that Victor and the De Laceys attribute to miraculous spirits are provided by the all-too-real creature. But rational explanation collapses in the aftermath of Victor's destruction of the creature's mate.

In order to put together the female creature in safe obscurity, Frankenstein has journeyed to Scotland. Henry Clerval, believing that Frankenstein is traveling for rest, goes with him as far as Perth, but Frankenstein persuades Clerval to stay behind while he proceeds alone to a remote island in the Orkneys where he sets up his laboratory. After he destroys the half-finished mate, Victor rows away from the island to dispose of the fragments in the ocean. Having done so, he is unable to steer his way back to shore, and drifts to the coast of Ireland. When he lands there the next morning he is placed under arrest, because the murdered body of Clerval had been found on the shore the preceding night, only two miles away from the point where Frankenstein's boat had drifted in the morning. The creature had killed Clerval, and left his body in Ireland, hours before Frankenstein had even rowed away from the Orkneys—and the creature had placed the body in almost precisely the same spot where the unpredictable ocean would bring Frankenstein on the following day, so that Frankenstein could be charged with the murder. How did the creature know exactly where to leave Clerval's body the day *before* Victor's boat drifts there? How did the creature even know that Victor would set sail? The book gives no answers, because the connection between Victor and his creature is too mysterious and profound to be explained.*

Murderous Machinations

Victor exclaims over Clerval's body, "Have my murderous machinations deprived you also, my dearest Henry, of life?" He has created a new life through "machinations"—contrivance, planning, mechanics—without giving it any of his own life, as he would have done had the new life been created through a sexual act. What is ultimately murderous about his machinations, even though they at first produce life, is that they arise from a desire for power and control, a desire that cannot tolerate the freedom of someone else's life, from an insistence on treating life objectively. By devising the shape and form of his creature in advance, and then abandoning it as soon as it takes on independent life, he has set in motion a doomed struggle for power between creature and creator, master and slave. Parents who conceive a new life in a sexual act cannot control the form or even the sex of their offspring, and it is their understanding of a child as a subject, not an object, as an independent life with a mutual relation to their own independent lives, that makes it possible for the child to grow into autonomy and freedom.

Both Victor and the creature interpret the creature's coming to life as in some profound way an act that ends a life. Victor speaks

---

* Something similar seems to occur when Victor, approaching Geneva after hearing that his brother William has been murdered, glimpses the creature and instantly concludes that it was the murderer. At this point he has not seen or heard of the creature since his brief glimpse of it on the night he gave it life, but he is so certain of its guilt that he even says he has "proof" that Justine is innocent of the crime. He is right about the creature's guilt—but by what mysterious connection does he know it?

of his murderous machinations, and the creature says of himself to Walton, "I, the miserable and the abandoned, am an abortion, to be spurned at, and kicked, and trampled on." The creature says this while standing over the body of Frankenstein, who has at last died from exhaustion on Walton's ship. The creature's choice of words, here and everywhere in the book, is extraordinarily subtle: he is an "abortion" not at the moment of his own death, but at the moment when he has been abandoned, when his creator dies.*

"Oh, Frankenstein! generous and self-devoted being!" the creature exclaims over Victor's dead body. (This sounds like a paradox, but the creature is using "generous" as a synonym for "generative," which derives from the same root; the primary and usual meaning of "generous" multiplies the ironies of Victor's role as the self-devoted generator of a new species.) Only when the creature jumps to an ice raft to be borne away from Frankenstein's body and Walton's ship does he finally arrive at the state of total isolation described in the book's last words: "lost in darkness and distance." A few pages before this, the story of Walton and his crew came to a different end when Walton, without saying that he has done so, renounces his goals of vague benevolence toward the human race and impersonal power over nature, and chooses instead to give his sympathy to real persons. At his crew's insistence, Walton has taken the course that Ulysses refused to take, and has turned his ship away from a lonely and imaginary paradise. "I cannot lead them unwillingly to danger," he earlier told the dying Franken-

---

* Much earlier, when Victor renounced natural science after hearing a visitor explain his theory of electricity, he says of his renunciation that he "set down natural history and all its progeny as a deformed and abortive creation." (Most readers will not need to be reminded that Mary Shelley was using the idea of abortion as a metaphor, not as part of a moral and political debate that began more than a century later.)

stein, "and I must return." He writes to his "dear sister" that the circumstances of his failure are "bitter," but that "while I am wafted towards England, and towards you, I will not despond." He has lost the splendors of the North Pole and regained a sister and her children.

Walton succeeds through failure; Frankenstein fails through success. Walton accepts a life of sympathy and choice; Frankenstein insists on a life of objectivity and fate. Walton comes to understand that his life is shaped by his own free subjective acts and those of others; Frankenstein thinks of himself as driven toward an objective, inevitable destiny. The life that Frankenstein creates in his laboratory responds predictably to stimuli, behaves exactly as great philosophers predicted he would behave, but he has no freedom. His creator, convinced that he was giving his creature a benefit for which he would be grateful, brought him to life in full strength and power, rather than letting his body grow and his acts and choices bring him into his own freedom. He gave his creature life but denied him a childhood.

2

CHILDHOOD: *Wuthering Heights*

Wuthering Heights is a story of passion, but not the passionate sexual desire that drives adult men and women. Catherine and Heathcliff think only about each other, yet they are almost indifferent to each other's sexual lives. Catherine tells Heathcliff she feels no jealousy when he marries someone else; Heathcliff tells Catherine he is not jealous of her husband. They mean what they say, and are far too impulsive to disguise their feelings. What they want from each other is not the transient and incomplete satisfaction that adults find in sex, but the total unity that Emily Brontë portrays as the enclosed province of their childhood, a unity more profound and comprehensive than anything that ordinary adults can experience.

All the conventional values of adult life are reversed in *Wuthering Heights*. Childhood, in this novel, is a state of titanic intensity, adulthood a state of trivial weakness. Heathcliff and Catherine can find no words to describe the childhood unity they once shared, and everyone else disdains or ignores that unity, but nothing else in the book has its depth, strength, and dignity. In contrast, all the sexual flutterings of adults are silly and superficial. Their exchanges of gifts and endearments display the crass materialism of a bazaar; the things they do with each other's bodies are comically undignified. Adults in *Wuthering Heights* are childish to the degree that they are sexually interested in each other. Adulthood is childish. Childhood is not.

The tragedy of *Wuthering Heights* is not that Heathcliff and Catherine cannot marry each other, but that they grow into adulthood, in which mere sex and mere marriage are the closest substitutes that anyone can find for the unity that adults have lost forever. Everyone else in the book is distorted almost from birth by adult values, by wishes for possessions and status, by desires for sexual satisfaction. In the special world of this novel, wishes like these can only worsen the separation of one person from another. Catherine and Heathcliff have no such wishes when they are children, and as children they are undivided from each other. They feel the same scorn toward children who argue over possessions— as the coddled Linton children in Thrushcross Grange argue over a pet dog—that they feel toward adults who kiss and cuddle in order to be connected to each other. But Catherine and Heathcliff's unity is possible only in childhood, not afterward. They are doomed like everyone else to the divisions and frustrations of adulthood, condemned to be imprisoned in bodies and clothes that proclaim their differences in sex and status. They are divided both by their separation into man and woman and by the social distinctions that bar the questionable upstart Heathcliff from Catherine the landed lady.

Romantic Childhood

The vision of undivided childhood that pervades *Wuthering Heights* occurred in only one historical era: the century of romanticism between early Wordsworth and early Freud.* The writers, artists,

---

* Freud did not entirely banish the vision of undivided childhood. It persists in sentimental fiction by J. D. Salinger and more recent writers.

thinkers, and ordinary readers who experienced that vision interpreted it as a revelation of eternal truth, but in historical terms it
was an eccentric oddity, and even in its own era those who experienced it knew themselves to be outsiders in relation to the culture
around them, and knew they were unable to share their vision with
anyone else; everything that Emily Brontë believed about childhood and adulthood seems to have baffled or frightened her sisters
Charlotte and Anne. (Charlotte repeatedly suggests this in her
letters to friends and in her biographical note to the posthumous
second edition of *Wuthering Heights.*) The cult of childhood had
no church. Its believers communed only with their memories. As
Charlotte Brontë wrote of Emily: "Stronger than a man, simpler
than a child, her nature stood alone."

In most of the visions recorded by ancient and medieval writers, supernatural persons or things—God, the Virgin Mary, the
demons who tempted St. Anthony in the form of beautiful women—
suddenly made themselves visible to the eye. In the visions recorded
by nineteenth-century and later writers, a scene that until a moment
ago had seemed perfectly normal suddenly seems endowed with
great glory, immense beauty, and infinite significance—although
everything in the scene has exactly the same shape and location
that it had before.* Unlike a faith, belief, or creed, which can persist as long as a lifetime and is more or less consciously chosen, a
vision is brief, transient, and involuntary. It seems to be given
rather than chosen. A vision may later become the basis for a consciously chosen belief, but no one can choose to make a vision happen, and no one can choose to make a vision persist after it begins
to fade.

---

* Around 1293 Dante recorded a vision of a similar kind in *La Vita Nuova (The
New Life)*, where he sees the nine-year-old Beatrice and she herself does not
change in appearance, but he hears voices proclaiming great changes in himself
and telling him, "Now your blessedness has been revealed."

Emily Brontë was one of the romantic visionaries who, like William Wordsworth, seem to have built a system of belief on their recollections in adulthood of visions of nature and unity that they experienced in childhood. Her poems are less explicit about her visions than Wordsworth's were about his, but they both seem to have had visions of the same general kind. She experienced an overwhelming sense of the power and majesty of nature, and an overwhelming sense of sympathy and connection with it. Unlike other romantic visionaries, Emily Brontë seems to have retained into adulthood at least some of the visionary intensity of her child-hood, and she seems to have been able to live in the world of ordinary reality while half sensing the presence of an invisible realm around her and half mourning her loss of it. She stands alone in the depth and peculiarity of the beliefs that she constructed on the basis of her vision, even where those beliefs seem to match familiar romantic ideas about heroic individuality and passionate rebellion. All the passions that she portrays in the fully grown Catherine and Heathcliff are subtly but decisively different from the passions of adult life. Heathcliff, for example, derives from a long line of demonic heroes driven by despairs and ambitions that typically include a desperate and uncontrollable sexuality—as in, for exam-ple, Don Juan or Dracula, or in the fiery males in the novels of Emily Brontë's sisters Charlotte and Anne. But Heathcliff differs from his fictional predecessors in seeming to have no sexual appetite at all. The other demonic heroes in the line of Don Juan conquer women by seduction or by force. Heathcliff wants desper-ately to be merged with Catherine, to achieve with her the same bodily unity that he already has with her soul, and Emily Brontë portrays his wish not as an impulse to possess her, but as an impulse to dissolve the surfaces that separate them and to abolish their separate identities—something that never happens in sex, no matter how many poetic metaphors of merger and dissolution have been used to describe it.

The desire to merge two selves into one is entirely different from any sexual desire for another self, even if in real human beings these desires sometimes get confused with each other. Heathcliff only once shows any interest in kissing and caressing Catherine, and this occurs when she is delirious and dying, when the physical act of touching serves as a limited compensation for the spiritual union that is about to be broken by her death. Catherine's love for Heathcliff is remarkably sexless, and when Heathcliff returns to Wuthering Heights after a three-year absence, she does not withdraw any affection from her husband Edgar Linton. In fact, when she hears the news of Heathcliff's arrival, she hugs Edgar so tightly that he objects to being squeezed. Her sexual relationship with her husband flows along different channels of her mind from those that carry her sense of oneness with Heathcliff, and her excitement over Heathcliff's return only increases her impulse to make physical contact with her husband.

If, for a moment, you look up from the book and imagine Heathcliff as a woman, some of the more puzzling emotional aspects of the story begin to make sense, not because the story of Heathcliff and Catherine is secretly about homosexual desire—it is not about any form of sexual desire—but because it is about their wish to escape the divided condition that sex and the body impose on anyone who hopes to transcend division altogether. Seen from the perspective of adult sexuality, a perspective that Emily Brontë regarded as limited and debased, the story seems to conceal a secret sexual meaning. But it has no such meaning. For Emily Brontë, sex was not a hidden secret but a public mask over incommunicable passions that are frustrated by sex, never satisfied by it.

Two Bodies, One Self

As children, Catherine and Heathcliff are untroubled by sexual differences, or by any other differences, because they are scarcely aware of them. Even their clothes, as the young Catherine reports in her diary, are undivided. When they hide in a dresser, they conceal themselves behind a curtain made by fastening their two pinafores together; each wears the same unsexed children's clothing—as most children did until a century or so ago—and they combine that clothing into one covering for the two of them. A few paragraphs later, they prepare to slip out together to the moor, both covered by a single garment—the dairywoman's cloak.

That is the last time they feel wholly undivided from each other. After venturing across the moor, they peer through the window of Thrushcross Grange, the rich house of the Linton family, where they see Edgar and Isabella Linton illustrating the wrong way to be brother and sister, screaming and weeping after an argument over a pitiably domesticated lapdog. The Lintons' bulldog catches Catherine by the ankle as she spies on the house; during the ensuing uproar she is brought indoors and remains there for five weeks recovering from the dog's attack; when she at last returns to Wuthering Heights she and Heathcliff have been isolated irrevocably by sex and class. She leaves as a child and returns as a woman.

Emily Brontë writes about the change as if it were only a transformation in status, not also a biological change—although she carefully specifies that Catherine is twelve years old when it occurs. Catherine alights from the Lintons' carriage dressed in clothing that identifies her both as an adult woman and as a member of a class whose women are not obliged to use their hands for any harder work than holding their expensive clothing away from the dirt. "Instead of a wild, hatless little savage jumping into the house, and rushing to squeeze us all breathless, there lighted from a hand- some black pony a very dignified person, with brown ringlets falling from the cover of a feathered beaver [hat], and a long cloth habit which she was obliged to hold up with both hands that she might sail in." Newly divided against herself, Catherine delights in her new privileges and possessions, even if they seem insipid after her deep connection with Heathcliff. Emily Brontë herself was less delighted with such things; in one of the *devoirs* she was assigned to write when she and Charlotte Brontë were studying and teaching in Brussels, she refers to the "degrading privileges" to which women are "condemned by the laws of society."

Catherine's return makes Heathcliff fully conscious for the first time of his status as a servant, and self-conscious for the first time about his swarthy physical appearance. He no longer shares in Catherine's thoughts. When he overhears her telling the house- keeper Nelly Dean, "It would degrade me to marry Heathcliff, now," he stalks out of the house, to return three years later as a dig- nified, prosperous, fully grown figure with conventionally mascu- line attributes that, to Nelly Dean, "suggested the idea of his having been in the army." Like Catherine, he has taken on a new status and a sharply defined sexual identity, but unlike Catherine, he has done so in an attempt to restore their closeness. Much of his tragedy lies in his misunderstanding of his broken connection with Catherine; he does not understand that the more he defines himself in terms of class and sex, the less he is able to recover the classless and sexless unity that once had joined them.

That undifferentiated unity persists, however, even under the masks of sex and class, although neither Heathcliff nor Catherine seems to know that the other still experiences it. When Heathcliff hears Catherine say it would degrade her to marry him, *now*, he leaves too abruptly to hear the rest of her sentence: "so he shall never know how I love him; and that, not because he's handsome, Nelly, but because he's more myself than I am. Whatever our souls are made of, his and mine are the same, and Linton's is as different as a moonbeam from lightning, or frost from fire." Catherine does not feel much regret over Heathcliff's unsuitability as a husband, because the kind of connection she shares with him has nothing to do with the pleasures and responsibilities of marriage.

Catherine is convinced that the surfaces of her body are not the outer limits of her person. "I cannot express it," she explains to an understandably puzzled Nelly Dean, "but surely you and every body have a notion that there is, or should be, an existence of yours beyond you. What were the use of my creation if I were entirely contained here?" She experiences her body as a kind of porous container, inadequate to hold all that she is. She is speaking what she takes to be a literal truth when she says, "I *am* Heathcliff," and when she insists that he is always present in her mind, not as some-one else whom she remembers, "not as a pleasure, any more than I am always a pleasure to myself—but as my own being." Her whole existence depends on his: "If all else perished, and *he* remained, I should still continue to be," she says. And Heathcliff never doubts that Catherine is his own essential self that has somehow split off into a separate body, and when she is dying he demands of her: "would *you* like to live with your soul in the grave?"

Poetic lovers have declared for centuries that their beloved is the embodiment of their own soul. "Sylvia is myself," says Valentine in Shakespeare's *The Two Gentlemen of Verona*. "She is my essence," he says, more or less as Heathcliff and Catherine say. But for Heathcliff and Catherine this is not merely a poetic metaphor but literally true. Convinced that they *are* each other, not merely *like* each other, they are baffled at finding themselves separated. And because they are convinced of their unity while knowing them-selves to be divided, they each feel that they are somehow not themselves: each one's real existence is in the other one. Heathcliff cannot imagine living without Catherine, who is his soul. Catherine says of Heathcliff, "He's more myself than I am." Their single spirit is divided against itself when they are divided into two separate bodies, and the only way they can escape their bodily prisons, and reunite with themselves and each other, is to let their imprisoning bodies die.

What Cannot Be Spoken

Wuthering Heights is narrated by the shallow and fashionable Lockwood, who has rented Thrushcross Grange in order to enjoy a year in the countryside, and the sturdily practical Nelly Dean, both of them equally ignorant of transcendence, vision, unity, and everything else that matters in the story. They don't try to conceal the sublimity and depth of Catherine and Heathcliff's passion; they simply do not know it exists. Likewise, the first reviewers, believing what Nelly and Lockwood told them, read the book as a study in sordidness, not grandeur. One way in which Emily Brontë differed from other romantic visionaries is that she had no wish to communicate her vision to others; as her sister Charlotte wrote, with careful understatement, "My sister Emily was not a person of demonstrative character." She seems to have devised *Wuthering Heights* in such a way as to conceal its meaning from anyone who did not already understand and share her visionary passions. She wrote explicitly and straightforwardly about these matters only in her poems, many of them addressed to the inner source of the visions they triumphantly describe, the "God within my breast," unknown to everyone else.

Emily Brontë wrote these poems in secret. When she and her sisters were younger, they had shared all their writings with each other, but in their twenties "this habit of communication and con-sultation [as Charlotte Brontë called it] had been discontinued." Charlotte gives no reason for this change, but it seems likely that Emily withdrew first from the habit of sharing and that the other two did the same in order to avoid treating her as a unique outsider from the family circle. Emily kept her poems hidden until Char-lotte chanced to find them, and she erupted in fury at Charlotte's intrusion on her inner world. Charlotte recalled tactfully that "it took hours to reconcile her to the discovery." Even intruders as close as her sisters could not be expected to understand the inner riches they had stumbled on. When Charlotte proposed the idea of publishing Emily's poems together with poems written by Char-lotte and their sister Anne, Emily accepted the idea but seems to have said nothing further to anyone about her poems.

It was characteristic of her to transform her anger and discom-fort into a new triumph. The agony she felt at having her poems read by others who could not share her vision seems to have given her the idea of writing a novel about a hero and heroine whose visionary experiences are misunderstood and misinterpreted by everyone around them. Instead of writing poems in her own voice about visions that she fully understood, she would write prose in the voice of people such as Nelly and Lockwood, who tell—but never understand—a story about people who experience vision. Heathcliff and Catherine yearn for infinities—for what Heathcliff calls "one universal idea"—while everyone else in the book sees Heathcliff and Catherine as arbitrary, egocentric, grasping, and perverse.

When the Brontë sisters began writing their novels, they resumed their earlier habit of sharing their writings over the dining room table while their father was asleep upstairs, but even while all three shared their work, Emily seems to have kept her work's meanings secret to herself. She disguised *Wuthering Heights* as a story of doomed sexual passion perhaps because, in a complex reaction against one aspect of herself, she seems, consciously and deliberately, to have regarded her potential readers with something close to contempt. The mere fact that they read books, instead of seeking passionate intensity, meant that they could not understand what this book tells them. "I hated a good book," the young Catherine writes in the margin of one. "What in the name of all that feels," she says later about her husband, "has he to do with *books*, when I am dying?" Catherine's daughter (also named Catherine) remarks that "Heathcliff never reads." This understates Heathcliff's positive aversion to books, which he demonstrates by taking the trouble to destroy a few of them.

Books in *Wuthering Heights* are irrelevant to all forms of passion. They function as an economic medium of exchange, as a kind of paper money or scrip. Like sex (as Emily Brontë understands it), books serve as a superficial substitute for a visionary union. The younger Catherine, who experiences none of her mother's visionary longings, uses books to buy obedience and affection. She bribes a servant with books; she gives books to her cousin Hareton in order to seduce him into friendship. As she teaches Hareton to read, the two of them teach each other sexual intimacy, and their characteristic pose in the later chapters of the novel has Hareton struggling to decipher a page while the younger Catherine drapes her hand distractingly over his shoulder.

Concealed from the Reader

Emily Brontë's will *not* to be known or understood was one of her more unsettling qualities. Most people have both an inner self that they want to keep private and a public self that they want others to sympathize with and understand. Emily Brontë seems to have had only a private self. Her disdain for the uncomprehending reader of *Wuthering Heights* is at the farthest possible extreme from the confident expectation of others' sympathy in Jane Eyre's "Reader, I married him." After Emily Brontë outgrew her childhood closeness to her sister Anne, she seems never to have wanted intimacy or love, and she enjoyed the inarticulate company of dogs far more than she enjoyed the voluble company of men and women.

The intensity and inflexibility of her personality terrified her sisters, who were the only people who ever got close enough to perceive it. Charlotte described one incident to her friend Elizabeth Gaskell, who reported in her *Life of Charlotte Brontë:* "Charlotte saw Emily's whitening face, and set mouth, but dared not speak to interfere; no one dared when Emily's eyes glowed in that manner out of the paleness of her face, and when her lips were so compressed into stone." In a letter to another friend, Charlotte wrote this description of Emily's character: "Disinterested and energetic she certainly is; and if she be not quite so tractable or open to conviction as I could wish, I must remember perfection is not the lot of humanity."

Emily Brontë had seen the effects of sexual passion in the wreck of her brother Branwell, reduced to incoherent misery by his obsessive desire for the mother of the boy for whom he had been hired as a tutor. *Wuthering Heights* combines Branwell's desire for a sexually inaccessible beloved with Emily Brontë's longing for the realm of vision, and the book was shaped by her conviction that the kind of romantic passion that Branwell suffered could not be eased or satisfied by sex, and that, for all its sufferers, the unity and permanence they seek can be found only through dissolution and death. As Emily Brontë perceived, both through her reading and through her brother's disasters, all the transgressive forbidden desires, from the barrier-crossing passion of Romeo and Juliet through the adulterous passion of Tristan and Isolde, have less to do with sex than with a wish to escape the limits of being merely human, a wish to transcend the defeats imposed by time, the distractions imposed by other people, and the demands made by one's own body. In a thousand novels, plays, and films, the death of the transgressive lovers—who are never far from a convenient cliff they can drive over—is not a punishment for their transgressions but a triumphal reward.

An early reviewer of *Wuthering Heights* objected that "the hardness, selfishness, and cruelty of Heathcliff are in our opinion inconsistent with the romantic love that he is stated to have felt for Catherine." This is not the idealizing voice of Victorian propriety; it is an accurate response to the book's method, in which Emily Brontë seems to have invited her readers to make a false interpretation of Heathcliff and Catherine's relationship while—perhaps in order to please herself with her own novelistic skill—she pointed surreptitiously toward its real meaning. Virginia Woolf was the first reader to point out that in *Wuthering Heights* "There is love, but it is not the love of men and women." She also wrote that the book as a whole was Emily Brontë's "struggle, half thwarted but of superb conviction, to say something through the mouths of her characters which is not merely 'I love' or 'I hate,' but 'we, the whole human race' and 'you, the eternal powers . . .' the sentence remains unfinished." Virginia Woolf's imaginative generosity led her to conclude that Emily Brontë had attributed the possibility of vision to the whole human race, but the book itself suggests otherwise.

Heathcliff and Catherine differ from everyone else simply by knowing that the eternal powers exist. Each is convinced that what joins them to the other is an eternal and unalterable power. "My love for Linton is like the foliage in the woods," Catherine tells the uncomprehending Nelly Dean. "Time will change it, I'm well aware, as winter changes the trees—my love for Heathcliff resembles the eternal rocks beneath—a source of little visible delight, but necessary." Through Catherine, Emily Brontë gives voice to the fantasy that love persists by itself, that the lover need not do anything or will anything in order to sustain it, that it is sustained by the same quasi-divine powers that sustain the earth and the sky.

In the real world, although not in the world of vision, any adult love that lasts longer than an initial sexual attraction requires some element of choice, some quality of will and decision, or it withers (in Catherine's phrase) "like the foliage in the woods." Real-life couples who expect to be sustained by the eternal powers (acting perhaps through some "magic" in their relationship) soon begin looking for other partners with whom to be sustained. Emily Brontë was under no illusion that a magical wish can be fulfilled in ordinary human life, but she blames her disappointment on life, not on her wish, and she honors the lovers in her novel for perceiving the visionary truth that they can join the eternal powers only by renouncing bodily life.

The Force That Through the Green Fuse Drives the Flower

Like other romantic visionaries, Emily Brontë imagined that children could experience wholeness and vision as part of their daily lives; among adults such things could be glimpsed only briefly and by an exceptional few. She learned the doctrines of romanticism by reading the poems of Wordsworth and Shelley, and to a lesser degree Lord Byron and Friedrich Schiller, but she quickly surpassed her teachers. In her sense of the eternal powers, and of the connection between vision and childhood, she was untempted by the compromises and half measures that afflicted everyone else.

Unlike Wordsworth, she cared nothing about the social benefits that could be gained by teaching a child to outgrow the willful illusions of childhood. Unlike Shelley, she did not gain her vision by sacrificing her sense of the reality of other persons. The young girl in Wordsworth's "We Are Seven" talks as if her dead brothers and sisters were still with her; but Heathcliff and Catherine have no such fantasies, and their childhood experience of unity does not conflict with the ordinary visible reality that everyone around them thinks is all there is. Wordsworth looked back to remembered moments of visionary intensity in "Ode: Intimations of Immortality from Recollections of Early Childhood" and *The Prelude;* but Heathcliff and Catherine never bother to look back because they do not lose their visionary intensity even when they acquire the adult knowledge that conflicts with vision. Shelley imagined in "Alastor" and "Epipsychidion" that the most inward part of the soul communes with the soul of the world, and imagined himself suffering and dying because he had failed to find an image of his inner soul in a real woman; but Heathcliff and Catherine are never disillusioned, and never doubt that their vision is fully embodied in each other. For Heathcliff and Catherine, their vision of each other corresponds exactly to who they really are, and does not need to be fed by idealizing vagueness and poetic myth.

In Emily Brontë's version of the romantic religion of nature, vision and nature are ultimately the same. For her as for most other believers in nature-religion, visions of the truth of things are more likely to occur in wild nature than in the corrupt city, and an alpine peak is a more visionary place than a lowland farm. But for Emily Brontë, unlike Wordsworth, for example, the vision offered by nature contains no lessons in morality, and nature is entirely uninterested in what Mary Shelley called "the moral relations of things." Nature's gentleness, to Emily Brontë, is not a sign or version of goodness, nor its cruelty a sign or version of evil; nature's immense volcanic powers are inherently opposed to humanity with its legalistic ethics. Emily Brontë's sense of nature as amoral has since become more widespread—especially in America, where nature has tended to seem more like an implacable enemy than a nurturing mother—but it was not an idea that anyone around her shared. Charlotte Brontë, for example, seems never to have thought of anything like it.*

Until the seventeenth century, the idea scarcely existed of a nonhuman "green nature" distinct from "human nature," and the romantic idea that human childhood was intimately related to green nature had not yet occurred to anyone. When the ancients thought about the possibility of human beings returning to nature, they thought in terms of rejecting the artificial social order and returning to the natural state in which humanity began. Such teachings (which became associated with the thinker Diogenes the Cynic) assumed that human nature was part of nature, not something different from it. When Shakespeare's Prospero in *The Tempest* condemns Caliban as "a born devil, on whose nature / Nurture can never stick," the word "nature" refers to Caliban's inherently wicked qualities—his "born nature"—not to something originally innocent that had been distorted by Caliban's wickedness. Early traces of the idea of a green nature that is nonhuman appear in the seventeenth century in the poems and prose of John Milton and John Dryden, but the idea still had the quality of something eccentric and experimental. John Locke, writing in the second half of the seventeenth century, still assumed that the laws of nature include the laws of morality; it is nature that imposes on individuals the obligation to act morally, even if nature cannot compel them to do so.

For Rousseau, a few decades later (more or less as in the views

---

* Walton in *Frankenstein*, who leaves Europe for the inhospitable Arctic, refers to nature as an enemy when he alludes to "the elemental foes of our race." Victor Frankenstein fluctuates between thinking of nature as enemy and comforter.

attributed to Diogenes the Cynic), only primitive man in the uncultivated forest lived freely and according to nature. But Rousseau added an idea that had never occurred to the ancients: the idea that even in the modern social world, a newborn child was born free, in a state of nature, but grew to be chained by social conventions. Childhood, understood as a separate stage of life with its own special qualities, was not invented in the eighteenth century, as historians once liked to insist, but a new idea of childhood was invented then, together with new ideas of nature. Before these ideas took hold, people tended to think of children as innocent about sex—in the sense that they had not experienced sexual desire—but fully aware that sex exists and that adults have feelings about it. (This is the way Shakespeare portrays children.) Later, during the nineteenth-century triumph of these new ideas, childhood for the first time seemed both innocent of sex and unconscious of it, with neither sexual desire nor sexual knowledge. One consequence was that childhood became perceived as an oddly impersonal state, without conflict or inwardness, capable of being shaped and molded, and ending disastrously with an adolescent fall into sexuality and uniqueness.

For Emily Brontë, divinity was present both in nature and in the spirit of a lonely visionary like herself, but it was an impersonal deity. It had no face, preached no doctrine, and endorsed no creed; and unlike the nature divinity imagined by Mary Shelley, it cared nothing about sex. When Emily Brontë thought about the question, she seems to have believed that the divinity of nature was sometimes gentle and sometimes cruel, but she tended to focus on nature's ultimate cruelty more than its occasional and incidental gentleness. In one of the *devoirs* she wrote in Brussels, she recalls seeing a caterpillar destroying a flower: "at that moment the universe appeared to me a vast machine constructed solely to produce evil." Nature, she concludes, "exists on a principle of destruction:

every being must be the tireless instrument of death to others, or itself ceases to live." Inconsistently enough, the sight of the butterfly, and the knowledge that it emerged from a caterpillar, prompts Emily Brontë in the same *devoir* to think of the butterfly not as a symbol of a different aspect of nature that produces good instead of evil, but as "a symbol of the world to come." Instead of revealing a positive truth about nature that coexists with the negative truth symbolized by the caterpillar, the butterfly offers a visionary glimpse of "an eternal empire of happiness and glory," entirely distinct from the cruelty of nature—but also deriving from it, as the glorious butterfly derives from the destructive caterpillar. Like many writers and thinkers of the past two centuries, Emily Brontë seems to have assumed that you come closest to the truth about nature or anything else when you see what is worst about it.

When Catherine's father leaves on the journey to Liverpool from which he will return with the infant Heathcliff, Catherine asks him to bring her a whip (to make her horse go faster when she rides). For Catherine as a child, the whip is a sign of her imperiousness, energy, and force among the world of living beings such as horses; it is not yet a sign of the kind of cruelty to other persons that she will practice as an adult, because she has not yet experienced the division of nature and spirit that makes her seek dominion and power as compensation for her loss of unity. Only with the onset of adolescence are nature and spirit divided in both Catherine and Heathcliff, and they now perceive nature as a realm where power expresses itself in cruelty. Having been unconscious of the division of the sexes in childhood, now, as adults, they experience that difference as a reason to be cruel, not merely to others, but also to each other. Heathcliff now perceives Catherine as a torturer: "You are welcome to torture me to death for your amusement," he tells her. "Only allow me to amuse myself a little in the same style," he continues, talking about his plans to elope with Edgar's infatuated sister Isabella, whom he will ignore after impregnating her on their wedding night. In Emily Brontë's version of the religion of nature, adult sexuality is the curse that banishes human beings from the innocent garden; in Mary Shelley's version, sexuality is one of the innocent delights of the garden that Victor Frankenstein forfeits by his disobedience. Catherine and Heathcliff's deep identity with nature contrasts with the civilized shallowness of Catherine's weaker-minded brother Hindley, who asks their father for a fiddle when Catherine asks for a whip. Hindley's futile violence in adulthood—the knife he wields against Heathcliff closes on his own wrist—is a drunken parody of the more dignified cruelty of nature and of those who embody nature.

Emily Brontë never condemns Heathcliff and Catherine for their cruelty, although the book's lesser characters repeatedly do. No one even bothers to remark on the lesser characters' lesser cruelties: Hareton Earnshaw hangs a litter of puppies, an event mentioned only in a subordinate clause; Linton Heathcliff tortures puppies; the younger Catherine, before being civilized and diminished by sexual love, takes pleasure in the grief of her enemies. For Emily Brontë, cruelty and endurance are the natural conditions of life, not at all inconsistent with the beauty of visionary nature. When her favorite dog, Keeper, who was terrifyingly fierce to everyone but his owner, began resting his muddy fur on the beds at Haworth Parsonage, she broke him of the habit by beating him with her bare fists until his face was swollen.* And she was as calm in receiving pain as she was in inflicting it: when bitten by a dog reputed to be rabid, she took the poker from the fire and cauterized her own wound.

---

* This story has been questioned on the ground that the Brontës' servant, when interviewed many years later, did not remember it; but there is no reason to assume she would ever have known it. The Brontës kept many secrets from each other and everyone else.

Emily Brontë believed as strongly as did the Marquis de Sade that cruelty is inherent in nature, that it was one of the aspects of nature that human beings shared. But, unlike de Sade, she had no impulse to philosophize about the subject or to convince anyone else to share her point of view. De Sade is no more dangerous than a professor expounding transgressive ideas to a graduate seminar (which is one reason why de Sade has recently been in academic vogue); Emily Brontë is a more profoundly terrifying figure because she leaves behind the whole world of argument and discussion. If we don't already understand the cruelty of nature, she sees no reason to tell us about it; nature is not something that can be taught, and it has no use or need for our understanding.

Distant Consolations

In the same realm of nature that Emily Brontë in some moods saw as a machine for producing cruelty and destruction, in different moods she also found the soothing consolations found by other romantic pantheists, from Wordsworth among the English lakes to Victor Frankenstein in the Swiss Alps. In one of her poems, Earth itself speaks to her with the voice of the spirit. Among all the wildly pining souls of mortals, Earth tells the poet, "none would ask a Heaven / More like this Earth than thine." The poet's passion and inspiration now are spent, but the loss of passion is no reason to refuse Earth's eternal comforts:

> Shall Earth no more inspire thee,
> Thou lonely dreamer now?
> Since passion may not fire thee
> Shall Nature cease to bow?

Earth alone—no other divinity—can soothe this lonely dreamer: "Since nought beside can bless thee / Return and dwell with me," are Earth's welcoming words. And in *Wuthering Heights* the same two visionaries who seek unity in another world are those with whom nature feels special sympathy, even if they themselves do not notice that nature takes an interest in them. Nature itself is torn violently apart when Catherine and Heathcliff are separated: on the night when Heathcliff leaves Wuthering Heights and is divided from Catherine (aged fifteen and fully aware of her womanhood), a tree at the corner of the house is split in two by a thunderstorm, and a huge bough falls on the chimney.

As children, Catherine and Heathcliff understand life after death in a naïve but visionary way. When Catherine's father dies, she and Heathcliff first "set up a heart-breaking cry," but later, as Nelly Dean discovers, "the little souls were comforting each other with better thoughts than I could have hit on; no parson in the world ever pictured Heaven so beautifully as they did, in their innocent talk . . ." In Emily Brontë's universe, when the visionary child outgrows a passionate unity with nature, she can still find in herself a vision of glory, and can still see glimpses of the world to come. The speakers of the dramatic poems about the island kingdom of Gondal that Emily Brontë and her sister Anne invented as children reassure themselves that they are watched by the dead in heaven. And as Emily Brontë famously wrote in one of her nondramatic poems:

> So hopeless is the world without
> The world within I doubly prize.

The god of her universe is an inner god, created, chosen, and worshipped by her own imagination. She addressed it triumphantly in another poem:

And am I wrong to worship, where
Faith cannot doubt, nor hope despair
Since my own soul can grant my prayer?
Speak, God of visions, plead for me,
And tell why I have chosen thee!

Emily Brontë's poems suggest that she imagined this god of visions to be both in her heart and in the world of nature, but she did not believe it to be in other human beings in the same way—and she was too clearheaded to ignore the difficulty of making these ideas about it hold together in any coherent way. She strained, as Virginia Woolf wrote, to "say something" about the human race and the eternal powers, and what she was struggling toward seems to have been a statement about an unattainable marriage of the two worlds of human vision and inhuman nature.*

Like Emily Brontë, Catherine Earnshaw in *Wuthering Heights* longs for two things: to be out in the nonhuman world of nature, and to escape from the prison of the body into the realm of vision. Catherine's desire for nature is so strong that in a dream in which she dies and goes to heaven, she weeps so pitifully to come back to earth that the angels fling her angrily down to the heath, where she wakes sobbing for joy. Later, on Catherine's deathbed, she hopes to die into the world of vision, "to escape into that glorious world," she says, "and to be always there, not seeing it dimly through tears, and yearning for it through the walls of an aching heart; but really with it, and in it." Emily Brontë yearned for a heaven "like this

---

* Emily Brontë seems to have thought of the imagination as something that dwells within her but takes its strength from the vast impersonal forces of nature outside her; the "God within my breast" existed only because an impersonal nature divinity existed both inside and outside her. This idea seems to derive ultimately from Protestant theology in which the human intellect can never understand God, and one's awareness of God is a divine gift that can be accepted or refused.

Earth" (as Earth told her in the poem), yet yearning is not enough. The note of sorrow in her English poems and French *devoirs* suggests she had little hope that any kind of heaven really existed, on earth or elsewhere. Catherine's two wishes, one for life in nature, the other for vision in death, contradict each other, and much of the sadness of *Wuthering Heights* lies in Emily Brontë's belief that you can have nature or you can have vision, but that you can't have both and perhaps you can't have either. The romantic dreamer longs for a home that she is doomed never to find.

What Narrative Knows and History Doesn't

Like all complex and sophisticated works of fiction, *Wuthering Heights* is made up of two stories that the book tells at the same time. One story is the *narrative*, the sequence of events as they are reported to the reader from one page to the next, starting on the first page with Lockwood's arrival at Wuthering Heights in 1801, continuing through his convalescence as he hears Nelly Dean tell about events that occurred in earlier decades, and ending on the last page with his brief return in 1802, when he learns of Heathcliff's death and the impending marriage of Hareton and the younger Catherine. The other story is the *history* that can be extracted or inferred from the narrative, the story of the events in the book in the order in which they supposedly occurred, not the sequence in which they are told; this history of *Wuthering Heights* begins around 1771, with the childhood of Heathcliff and Catherine (in the fourth chapter of the *narrative*), and ends in the final chapter in 1802 as Lockwood stands over Heathcliff and Catherine's graves.

Part of the pleasure of writing such a book—and part of the pleasure of reading it—seems to lie in organizing and perceiving the elaborate pas de deux that these two stories perform. The book's *history,* the straightforward sequence of facts and events, is a conventional early Victorian novel of education and marriage. As the book's history presents it, Heathcliff and Catherine kill themselves off because, like Dora in *David Copperfield* or Mr. Casaubon in *Middlemarch,* their egoism or violence or some other moral flaw fatally disqualifies them to be the hero and heroine of a marriage story. After their death, Hareton Earnshaw, the potential hero who had been scorned by almost everyone, raises himself out of ignorance through his love for the younger Catherine, who now sees his hidden worth, and each is rewarded by marriage to the other. The wealth that Heathcliff had accumulated illegally in the bitterness of revenge is cleansed by being passed on to the young couple, who can enjoy it in guiltless luxury. In the history of *Wuthering Heights,* the marriage between two young people blessed with beauty, wealth, and hope is the sugarplum that Emily Brontë expected her readers to pull from her book as if it were a Christmas pie.

In contrast, the book's *narrative,* the story transformed by the shaping powers of the artist who made it, ascends to the austere sublimity of vision. The narrative begins in the lonely isolation of the living Heathcliff and the dead Catherine and ends in the union of their spirits after Heathcliff's death. Nelly Dean tells Lockwood that the country people are convinced that Heathcliff's spirit walks the earth, and in the closing paragraphs, as Lockwood makes a visit to their graves, a terrified shepherd boy tells him that he has seen the ghosts of Heathcliff and Catherine together on the moors. Heathcliff and Catherine's bodies rest in the earth, but their spirits meet on the moors that are, for them, more satisfying than heaven.

The shape of this visionary narrative is so well hidden that three-quarters of a century passed before anyone noticed it. In 1926 Charles Percy Sanger, an English lawyer, wrote a pamphlet, *The Structure of Wuthering Heights* (published by Leonard and

Virginia Woolf's Hogarth Press), demonstrating that the book was not a work of rough-hewn genius, as Emily Brontë's sisters and all other early readers took it to be, but a masterpiece of almost mathematical symmetry and economy, with every detail secretly keyed to the calendar of the moon and seasons and to the eternal cycles of earth. (Sanger's work was later supplemented by other scholars who settled most of the minor problems in chronology that he had left unsolved.) In an especially well-hidden example, the older Catherine dies and the younger one is born on the twentieth of March. Nelly Dean casually mentions the date a few lines after she refers to the younger Catherine's birthday, and a few chapters after reporting that the mother died two hours after the daughter was born. In the two years when the book apparently was written, 1845 and 1846, March 20 was the date of the vernal equinox. Catherine so fully embodies nature that she dies and gives birth to her successor on the first day of spring. In another example, the younger Catherine is born as "a puny, seven months' child," six and a half months following Heathcliff's return to Wuthering Heights after a long absence. Heathcliff is not the father—if he were, he and Catherine would not feel quite so tragic about their separation—but his mere presence in the neighborhood is potent enough to induce Catherine's pregnancy—with the help, perhaps, of the same physical excitement that prompts Catherine to embrace her husband when she first hears about Heathcliff's return.

The instinctual powers in Heathcliff and Catherine are strong enough to transform almost everyone around them, but the kinds of transformations that they spark vary with the people they transform. Heathcliff's presence induces fertility in the wild Catherine who feels at home in nature, but Catherine's presence as a ghost in Lockwood's dream near the start of the book has an altogether different effect on his repressed, civilized psyche. Earlier, at a polite seaside resort, Lockwood had been too timid to return a young woman's smile. Now, among the furies and passions of Wuthering Heights, he is roused to angry violence when he sees the dead Catherine—another young woman—in a dream: "Terror made me cruel; . . . I pulled its wrist on to the broken pane, and rubbed it to and fro till the blood ran down and soaked the bed-clothes."

Lockwood's dream of Catherine has a deeper function in the hidden narrative, one that no one seems to have noticed, Lockwood least of all. His dream leads directly to the resolution of the story, and through it the world of Wuthering Heights finally dislodges the unchanging misery that was afflicting it when he arrived there.

This is how it happens. In the years since Catherine's death, Heathcliff has been using his ability to plot and plan—everything about him that is not passionate, everything that has nothing to do with his feelings toward Catherine—to take legal possession of both Thrushcross Grange and Wuthering Heights. To the puzzlement of everyone else, all he plans to do with the two houses is to demolish them and everything within them. His motives for this destruction seem to be a vague idea of taking revenge on dead enemies and their living heirs who value the two houses, and an inarticulate hope that by destroying every artificial thing that intrudes on the natural landscape, he can destroy the barriers that separate himself from Catherine and from nature. For the same reason, he arranges to have the side walls of his and Catherine's coffins knocked away after his death so that their bodies can dissolve and decay into each other, and the artificial barriers built by human beings can be replaced by the open moors of inhuman nature. Then, suddenly and without warning, between the time Lockwood first visits Wuthering Heights and returns a year later, Heathcliff loses all interest in destroying the two houses—"I have lost the faculty of enjoying their destruction, and I am too idle to destroy for nothing"—and he half consciously begins to destroy himself instead.

Critics have puzzled over the motives behind Heathcliff's abrupt change of purpose, but Emily Brontë hid the explanation in plain sight by placing it at the start of the book, hundreds of pages before the change occurs. Heathcliff himself associates his new purposes with his new sense that he can see the dead older Catherine in the living faces of her nephew Hareton and the younger Catherine. But he had never seen her in them in all the years they were growing up in his house, and he can now sense Catherine's presence only because Lockwood, the least visionary person in the book, has unintentionally given him the idea that she is waiting for him on the moors. In the book's chronological history, this happened a short time earlier; but in the shape of its narrative, it occurred far back in the opening chapters, when the panicked Lockwood told Heathcliff his dream and Heathcliff wrenched open the window and sobbed, "Come in! come in! Cathy, do come. Oh do—*once* more! Oh! my heart's darling, hear me *this* time—Catherine, at last!" In the chronological history, this occurs shortly after Heathcliff told Nelly Dean that he was tormented by his belief that Catherine's ghost walked the earth, torturing him by keeping herself tantalizingly nearby but invisible. Now, because Lockwood has *seen* Catherine, Heathcliff's belief in her presence becomes a certainty, and, convinced that she is nearby, he is also convinced that by dying he can rejoin her. He is no longer distracted by his despairing romantic passion to plot the destruction of the two houses. Only the fact that he remains alive keeps him from what he wants. He tells Nelly Dean, "I have a single wish, and my whole being and faculties are yearning to attain it."

Because he is a visionary like Catherine, Heathcliff sees into the invisible heart of things, but aside from his vengeful plotting, he has no idea of what to do with his vision or with his whole existence. As if he were as helpless and controllable as a child, he has his direction set for him by dull, unvisionary adults. A scholar once wrote an essay that excitedly unmasked Nelly Dean as "the villain in *Wuthering Heights*" on the basis of the clear evidence that Nelly, by telling or not telling others about crucial events, shapes much of the action that produces the book's many personal and erotic disasters. Nelly does in fact shape much of the action, but she has no secret plan and no malicious intent. She is merely an unimaginative and unpassionate adult like Lockwood, someone who combines ordinary decency with a moderate inclination to preserve her comforts and increase her savings, and she makes ordinary casual decisions that visionaries are too otherworldly to bother with. Emily Brontë was brought to despair by her knowledge that mere adulthood triumphs, that vision and childhood die.

Remembering to Breathe

Earlier in the book, Catherine had hastened her own death by refusing to eat. At the end Heathcliff kills himself by the same method. His refusal is not a choice on his part; he acts on an inner necessity that he does not understand. He cannot stop himself from wanting something more significant than food and drink. "I have to remind myself to breathe—almost to remind my heart to beat," he tells Nelly. "It is by compulsion, that I do the slightest act, not prompted by one thought, and by compulsion, that I notice anything alive, or dead, which is not associated with one universal idea."

A few pages later, when he finds himself unable to touch the heaping plate that Nelly puts before him, even though he has not eaten for days, he speaks with passive wonder at his own lack of

will: "I'm animated with hunger; and, seemingly, I must not eat."
He is so intent on his goal that he can no longer bother with his
flesh, and after four days without food he fades quietly into death.
His body, when Nelly finds it, has its hand draped across the win-
dowsill, the lattice scraping it in the same way that Lockwood, in
his dream, had pulled Catherine's wrist across the broken glass.

In the next and final chapter, the shepherd boy sees the spirits of
Heathcliff and Catherine reunited on the moor, but the rational,
conventional Lockwood, inspired to insipid eloquence by the moths,
flowers, and soft winds of the graveyard, dismisses the boy's fantasies, and wonders "how any one could ever imagine unquiet slum-
bers, for the sleepers in that quiet earth." He is mistaken: in Emily
Brontë's private religion, the seemingly quiet earth thunders with
divinity and power. Two or three years after writing this ending,
Emily Brontë died of tuberculosis, having refused for days to speak
or eat. The village carpenter said her coffin was the narrowest he
had ever built.

To refuse to eat is to refuse your own body. A century and a half
after Emily Brontë died, this refusal tends to be regarded as an epi-
demic illness caused and spread by external factors such as fashion
or culture. But Emily Brontë was under no pressure to starve herself, and cultural pressure tends to affect only those who already
have a motive for succumbing to it. The most powerful motive that
drives someone to deny the body is the realization that the body
cannot be controlled. The moment when the body begins to have
the most disturbingly uncontrollable impulses is the time when
childhood ends and adulthood begins, and this is the moment when
the impulse to struggle against the body is strongest. In *Wuthering
Heights*, this is also the time when Heathcliff and Catherine sense
that a unity experienced in childhood has been devastatingly lost.

In his passion for Catherine, Heathcliff goes beyond what the
Anglican marriage service calls "forsaking all others." He actively

hates all others, and rejects all the ways in which one person depends on anyone else for food, shelter, and clothing, or for care and comfort when weak, injured, or ill. His passion to exclude others finally requires a corresponding hatred for his own body; his and Catherine's conviction that each one's soul is continuous with the other's requires them to think of their bodies as barriers. When Heathcliff grasps the dying Catherine's arm and Nelly sees "four distinct impressions left blue in the colourless skin," he is not simply being imperious in his passion, but is trying to break through to her soul, in the same way that he looks forward to the merger of their disintegrating bodies after death.*

The Fetish and the Idea

The two great disorders of erotic love are, on the one hand, a hunger for multiple partners with a commitment to none, and, on the other, an obsession with a single partner to the exclusion of every other kind of relationship. The emblematic images of the first disorder include the sultan with his well-stocked harem and Don Juan with his one-night seductions and anonymous encounters. The emblematic images of the second disorder include Tristan and Isolde, Romeo and Juliet, and Heathcliff and Catherine. The first disorder is an attempt to escape the uncertainties of time and change by starting again every night from the beginning, never growing, never moving onward to another stage of life, never becoming an adult with a past and a future. The second disorder is an attempt to escape the uncertainties of time and change by abandoning the

---

* The emotional logic of Heathcliff and Catherine's lives is that of the mad tea party in Lewis Carroll's *Through the Looking-Glass*, where "the rule is, jam tomorrow and jam yesterday—but never jam today." In the love that Heathcliff and Catherine have for each other, "yesterday" was childhood, "tomorrow" is death.

uncontrollable body in favor of an unalterable union of spirits, souls, or visions. The first disorder is an attempt to refuse death, the second an attempt to be rescued by its transforming power.

When Heathcliff says that he notices nothing that is "not associated with one universal idea," he is making a deep statement about the emotional and moral meaning of disembodied, abstract ideas. Emily Brontë chose Heathcliff and Catherine's vocabulary with exceptional care, and she makes Heathcliff refer to the "idea" in Plato's sense of an "idea" as an invisible, immaterial heavenly form, a "universal" (as Plato's name for it is often translated). A universal idea, Diotima tells Socrates in the *Symposium*, is superior to any earthly person, place, or thing: the goal of the lover and philosopher is to ascend from transient earthly things to imperishable universal ideas. Heathcliff has ascended from the tangible world of objects and bodies to the invisible realm of the universal idea, and he can think of nothing beneath it.

A platonic "idea" is a kind of *fetish*, an inanimate object worshipped for its supposed magical powers—not a visible fetish, but an invisible, sublimated one. Morally and emotionally, the philosopher who glories in the idea of the Good or the Beautiful is like a fetishist ogling a shoe or a foot. Both choose an abstract or symbolic substitute for a human being; both love an object that has no needs of its own, a thing that asks for nothing and is owed nothing. This is not a disorder of erotic love so much as a total rejection of it. Heathcliff is serene in his final days because in death he will be able to have what he wants without actually having to do anything to attain it.

In wishing to regain a lost imaginary unity of childhood in the imaginary unity of death, Emily Brontë turned away from the realities of time, growth, and love in which division can never wholly be overcome and all feelings, even the most intense, are mixed feelings. She cared about only a narrow part of human experience, but she saw that part with greater clarity than anyone whose perspectives were wider. The power of *Wuthering Heights* derives from her understanding of the impulse, more or less hidden in everyone, to find a refuge against time and change, and her understanding of the price you pay for having that impulse even if you never yield to it. Frankenstein's creature is doomed to misery because he lacks a childhood to grow out of, but Heathcliff and Catherine are doomed by being born into a childhood so glorious in its bright vision that they prefer death to the uncertainties—and possibilities—of growth.

3

GROWTH: *Jane Eyre*

Charlotte and Emily Brontë had the same two parents, spent most of their lives in the same isolated Yorkshire parsonage, and received more or less identical educations. But the two sisters wrote and thought in almost exactly opposite ways about nature, society, morals, love, sex, and truth. Emily Brontë wanted privacy in which to experience sublimity and vision. Charlotte Brontë wanted company with whom to seek justice and love. Everything that *Wuthering Heights* says about childhood, growth, and adulthood is contradicted by *Jane Eyre*. In *Wuthering Heights* all the means by which human beings communicate with each other—including speech, writing, drawing, and all the varieties of physical touch—are not worth using, and the public world of politics and religion scarcely exists. In *Jane Eyre* life is unimaginable without speech, writing, drawing, and touch, and the private intimacies of sex and affection are inseparable from the public ethics of justice and freedom.

Despite its fantasies and improbabilities, *Jane Eyre* offers the most profound narrative in English fiction of the ways in which erotic and ethical life are intertwined. It can do so partly because it understands the erotic and ethical appeal of its own fantasies, and fully acknowledges their improbability. Charlotte Brontë sees clearly everything that Emily Brontë neglects to notice. *Wuthering Heights* is the more finely crafted book, but *Jane Eyre* is the greater one. Most readers are more or less repelled by one or another aspect of *Jane Eyre,* either by the violent punishment that the plot seems to inflict on Mr. Rochester, or by the narrator's refusal to sympathize with the mad, imprisoned Bertha Mason, or by what seems to be Jane Eyre's unshakable satisfaction with herself. But in each of these apparent novelistic faults Charlotte Brontë was telling her readers uncomfortable truths about themselves, while at the same time making it easy for her readers to ignore them if they insisted on preferring fantasy to truth.

Even the most sympathetic critics of the book notice at least one flaw that can't easily be explained away: *Jane Eyre* is a novel of education in which the heroine seems to need no education. (She repeatedly thinks she must learn to become less passionate and rebellious; she is mistaken, but she is rescued from the effects of her mistake by external events, not by education.) Jane faces the same kinds of problems that, in the real world, you can solve only after a long, difficult process of learning to solve them; many of her problems seem impossibly difficult, but the problem of learning seems, for her, almost impossibly easy. As she grows older, she faces increasingly complex choices; the right answer becomes ever harder to find, and the consequences of the wrong choice become ever more dangerous. But unlike anyone in the real world, Jane never learns from her mistakes—because she never makes any. She learns to control and direct her passions, but her passions cause her physical and practical discomfort, not the moral discomfort that comes with questioning her own past; and in learning to direct her passions, she learns a practical lesson, not a moral one. She suffers repeatedly, yet she always ends by making the right moral choice, apparently without ever having educated herself into doing so. Charlotte Brontë provides a detailed model of how to act, but, most oddly for a novel of education, she seems to provide no model at all of how to *learn* to act.

For the kind of parable that Charlotte Brontë was writing, one in which each reader chooses whether and how to apply the story to the reader's own life, this apparent flaw proves to be an essential part of the design. What Jane Eyre learns is not how to act, but how to believe. Unlike real human beings, she does not learn by regretting wrong actions—not having committed them, she could hardly learn from them—but she does learn by regretting the wrong beliefs that had tempted her to wrong actions. Starting with nothing but curiosity about the world and resentment at its mistreatment of her, she educates herself in the ways she must think about her choices, in the beliefs she must use as the basis of her actions when the right choice may not be obvious. In moments of crisis, her beliefs are all she can hold on to:

> "I will hold to the principles received by me when I was sane, and not mad—as I am now. Laws and principles are not for the times when there is no temptation: they are for such moments as this, when body and soul rise in mutiny against their rigour . . . They have a worth—so I have always believed; and if I cannot believe it now, it is because I am insane—quite insane: with my veins running fire, and my heart beating faster than I can count its throbs. Preconceived opinions, foregone determinations, are all I have at this hour to stand by: there I plant my foot."

Almost everyone she meets tries to tell her what and how to believe—and everyone tells her to believe in different things in a different way—but she must find her beliefs by herself. In *Jane Eyre* as in life, the right choices are rarely new or surprising, but everyone has to discover anew the ways in which to learn to make those choices; you have to learn for yourself the ways—which are different for everyone—in which you can decide whether something that is not immediately obvious is nonetheless true, and you have to learn for yourself the ways in which you decide how to act on the truths you have chosen. In this kind of education, teachers, guides, and mentors are no help, except to the degree that they show by precept or example that you must make your decisions without—or despite—their help.

In *Wuthering Heights* no one learns anything from suffering; in *Jane Eyre* nothing can be learned without it. Jane Eyre has the paradoxical good fortune of being forced to suffer in childhood—and her suffering lets her perceive childhood as a state of ignorance and injustice, not a paradise that adults should sigh for. The cruelties Jane suffers in childhood are mean, not magnificent, and they never tempt her to identify with the oppressor. The opening chapters portray the young Jane's first tormentor, her cousin John Reed, as a boy who is more or less what the grown-up Heathcliff would be if you were to meet him in real life, without the visionary gleam that Emily Brontë gave him. John Reed announces that "all the house belongs to me, or will do in a few years," throws a book at Jane and makes her bleed, and grasps her violently when she protests. As Jane reports a few pages later, he "twisted the necks of the pigeons, killed the little pea-chicks, set the dogs at the sheep, stripped the hothouse vines of their fruit, and broke the buds off the choicest plants in the conservatory." Inequality is the most common injustice of childhood, and Jane Eyre, considered an inferior by her relations, is mistreated despite all her efforts to please, while John Reed and his two repellent sisters are coddled.

Unity or Equality

Jane Eyre records a journey out of a childish world into an adult one and a journey out of inequality and into equality. These are the same journey under different names. The injustices Jane suffers at the start of the book are committed by adults acting childishly; the equality she achieves at the end is possible only for those who have learned to become individual and adult. What she gains is equality, not unity. No one in the book is deluded by a desire for unity, which is the goal that drives the heroic passions of *Wuthering Heights*. Unity is a goal with no ethical meaning, an appealing-sounding but impossible condition that in the real world of emotional and political life is sought mostly by sentimentalists or tyrants. Equality, in contrast, is a difficult but plausible goal, with profound emotional and ethical meaning in both the private world and the public one. Mistrustful readers suspect that *in*equality is the real goal of *Jane Eyre*, because they believe either that Jane triumphs over Rochester in the end or—different readers discover different inequalities— that Jane yields submissively to Rochester's rule. But the evidence of the novel indicates that Charlotte Brontë thought Jane and Rochester arrive at something close to a fully equal relationship.

Unlike unity—which excludes as an enemy anyone who refuses to join in—the equality shared by Jane and Rochester embraces others who remain outside. A long tradition in love stories requires that the unsuitable suitor must be banished and humiliated when the lovers find their triumphant happiness, but *Jane Eyre* gives its triumphant final lines to a letter from her unsuccessful suitor, the missionary St. John Rivers. He writes his letter from distant India, not quite a place of banishment because he chose to go there to fulfill his vocation, but where he had intended Jane to go with him. His vocation has the same goal of equality that drives Jane and Rochester; as Jane reports, Rivers in India "hews down like a giant the prejudices of creed and caste." But by offering Jane Eyre a loveless marriage in which she would assist him in his service to God, he refuses equality to Jane and to himself, though he is willing to die while working to make it possible for others. I will suggest later in this chapter that in dying for the sake of an equality that he cannot accept for himself, St. John Rivers, with all his

Calvinist severity and heroic self-denial, shares his struggle with
an ally who would have appalled him had he met her, the mad
amoral pyromaniac Bertha Rochester, *née* Mason.

Equal Yet Not Equal

To become an adult in the world of *Jane Eyre,* you must escape or
defeat the inequalities that everyone more or less accepts during
childhood. The book opens at Gateshead, where Jane suffers under
the oppression of her uncle's widow, Mrs. Reed, and the three
Reed children. After Jane's initial revolt against John Reed, a servant warns her never to think of herself "on an equality with the
Misses Reed and Master Reed, because Missis kindly allows you to
be brought up with them." Jane is then sent to Lowood School,
where she and all the other pupils suffer under the rule of Mr.
Brocklehurst, the treasurer and manager of Lowood, and the son
of its rich founder. Brocklehurst, justifying himself by having "a
Master to serve whose kingdom is not of this world," explains that
his mission "is to mortify in these girls the lusts of the flesh; to
teach them to clothe themselves with shame-facedness and sobri-
ety, not with braided hair and costly apparel," to remind them of
their lowly status as charity girls, not least by letting them take in
the spectacle of his own richly dressed daughters.

But by listening to her Lowood classmate Helen Burns, Jane
learns a different way of thinking about unworldly kingdoms.
Helen Burns feels none of Jane's anger at the humiliations inflicted
at school; her faith in her own conscience and in a loving God
makes her indifferent to the cruelty she suffers. She has a moral
and religious vision of eternity, and trusts to invisible spirits that
guard the living. Helen's vision culminates in a creed which, she
says, "no one ever taught me," a creed that "extends hope to all" of

an eternity that will be "a mighty home, not a terror and an abyss." Jane respects but refuses Helen's creed because, Jane insists, she cannot be satisfied with spiritual rewards in the face of earthly indifference and hatred. It is not enough to think well of oneself and be loved by one's own conscience, Jane says to Helen: "if others don't love me, I would rather die than live—I cannot bear to be solitary and hated."

Later, as an adult engaged to marry Mr. Rochester, Jane returns briefly to her childhood home at Gateshead, where she finds Mrs. Reed psychologically and physically wrecked by the suicide of Jane's early tormentor John Reed, yet still sustained by her conviction that Jane is her inferior. Recalled to her earlier feelings of revolt after years of absence, "I felt pain," Jane reports, "and then I felt ire, and then I felt a determination to subdue her—to be her mistress in spite both of her nature and her will." She does not act on her impulse to dominate where she had once been dominated, but she does not renounce it until some days later, when, "pondering the great mystery" of Mrs. Reed's impending death, she "thought of Helen Burns: recalled her dying words—her faith— her doctrine of the equality of disembodied souls . . ." and this thought allows her to forgive the dying Mrs. Reed.

The faith expressed in Helen's dying words was that "God is my father; God is my friend; I love him; I believe he loves me." And Jane Eyre adopts Helen's faith for herself later in the book. But the "doctrine" that Jane learns from Helen Burns is not quite the doctrine that Helen Burns had expounded. If you look back a few pages from Helen's dying words to read what she actually said about her doctrine of disembodied souls, she turns out not to have spoken about their "equality." Helen's private creed, she said, "extends hope to all; it makes Eternity a rest—a mighty home, not a terror and an abyss." Helen believed that "debasement and sin will fall from us with the cumbrous frame of flesh, and only the spark of spirit will remain"; that this spark will return to the heaven "whence it came"; and then (in the most curious part of Helen's theology) perhaps be "communicated" to one of the angels, perhaps then to one of the seraphim, the highest angels of all.

This aspect of her belief derives less from orthodox Christianity than from ancient doctrines, loosely called Neoplatonism, that focused on the eternal, abstract oneness of God rather than on the physical world of the incarnate Christ and a multitude of individual persons. In Helen Burns's theology, more or less as in Neoplatonism, the spark of spirit seems not to retain its personal individuality as it ascends through the angels, but becomes part of the angels to which it is "communicated." This doctrine of dissolution into something much like an ultimate oneness or unity is very different from the doctrine that Jane Eyre arrives at when thinking about Helen Burns. What Jane believes (and Charlotte Brontë elsewhere said that she believed) is the ancient doctrine of universalism, which affirms that all individual souls, no matter what they choose to do in life, are ultimately saved; and that hell, if it exists at all, is not a state of eternal damnation, but of purgatorial cleansing from which each individual soul will eventually—and equally—emerge into salvation. Jane's version of this doctrine, unlike Helen's, emphasizes equality because Jane is tormented by the inequalities inflicted on her, while Helen is indifferent to inequality. Jane's doctrine of equality is one that no one taught her, and one in which, helped by painful experience, she educated herself.

The full effect of the emotional Rubicon that Jane Eyre crosses when she adopts the doctrine of equality does not emerge until a few pages later. Jane takes the idea of equality back with her from Gateshead to Rochester's house at Thornfield, where, after only one intervening chapter (the shortest in the book other than the brief opening and closing chapters), she puts her new doctrine to use in the first crisis of her romantic life. Rochester manipulates her into declaring her love for him so that he can propose marriage to her. She declares her love in a speech that climaxes with the assertion of her new creed:

> "Do you think, because I am poor, obscure, plain, and little, I am soulless and heartless?—You think wrong!—I have as much soul as you,—and full as much heart! And if God had gifted me with some beauty, and much wealth, I should have made it as hard for you to leave me, as it is now for me to leave you. I am not talking to you through the medium of custom, conventionalities, nor even of mortal flesh—it is my spirit that addresses your spirit, just as if both had passed through the grave, and we stood at God's feet, equal—as we are!"

Rochester repeats "As we are!" adding "so, Jane!" as he kisses her. Jane contradicts him: "Yes, so, sir, and yet not so." Disembodied souls may be as equal as her doctrine declares them to be, but living persons are not. Helen Burns was indifferent to the contradiction, because she knew she was dying and had put all her hopes on the life after death. But Jane wants to live, and, as she insisted to Helen, she cannot bear to be solitary and hated. Her living task in the rest of the book is to find on earth a physical, sexual, and economic equality that can approximate the disembodied equality in Helen Burns's heaven.

Before she can arrive at earthly equality, she must work her way through many barriers, the strongest of which are within herself. While engaged to Rochester, she is treated by him as a doll to be dressed in jewels and rich robes. Jane responds to this treatment with ritualized sadomasochistic playacting. The system she devises to relieve the feeling of being "kept" (the word she uses to describe her life as the object of Rochester's extravagant generosity) is one in which she torments him as much as possible. Having "worked him up to considerable irritation," having "thwarted and afflicted him," she provokes him into giving her the same treatment in return: "For caresses too, I now got grimaces; for a pressure of the hand, a pinch on the arm; for a kiss on the cheek, a severe tweak of the ear." They both enjoy it. "He was kept, to be sure, rather cross and crusty: but on the whole I could see he was excellently entertained; and that a lamb-like submission and turtle-dove sensibility, while fostering his despotism more, would have pleased his judgment, satisfied his common-sense, and even suited his taste, less." As for the punishment she receives from Rochester, "It was all right: at present I decidedly preferred these fierce favours to anything more tender."

By insisting on this mutual ferocity, Jane transforms into an erotic game a power relation that would otherwise be intolerable. But she knows the game is a mask over something more serious. She resists Rochester's social and physical strength because she is tempted into a more dangerous spiritual submission to him, a submission far deeper than the mere fact that she "would rather have pleased than teased him." She would rather have pleased him because, she says, "My future husband was becoming to me my whole world; and more than the world: almost my hope of heaven . . . I could not, in those days, see God for his creature: of whom I had made an idol." At this point Jane is willing to accept an unequal marriage for the sake of love, but Charlotte Brontë insists on something better. These sentences immediately follow Jane's descriptions of her erotic power games with Rochester: Charlotte Brontë understood the all-consuming quality of the kinds of games that Jane and Rochester play and, more profoundly, the way in which the partners in such games tend to lose sight of each other's individuality and see each other as embodiments of dominant and submissive roles. In one of the deepest paradoxes of erotic life, the more she becomes obsessed with Rochester, the less he seems a person and the more he seems "my whole world," a powerful but impersonal "idol" rather than a living, vulnerable human being.

The Nature Goddess and Others

In the next moral crisis of Jane's romantic life—a few hours after her wedding to Rochester is interrupted by the discovery that he has a living wife whom he cannot divorce—he asks her to leave England with him and live together outside of marriage.* Jane is first tempted to yield by her feelings of pity, with its half-concealed sense of her own superiority: "Think of his misery; think of his danger," she tells herself. When Rochester tells her the story of his marriage, how he was duped into it by his family and Bertha's, Jane exclaims, "I pity you—I do earnestly pity you." Rochester knows that pity is a mask over superiority, and says so in a speech that gradually shifts into an attempt to manipulate her pity to the point where it will convince her to join him:

> "Pity, Jane, from some people is a noxious and insulting sort of tribute, which one is justified in hurling back in the teeth of those who offer it; but that is the sort of pity native to callous, selfish hearts; it is a hybrid, egotistical pain at hearing of woes, crossed with ignorant contempt for those who have endured them. But that is not your pity, Jane; it is not the feeling of which your whole

* Divorce was a practical impossibility for many reasons. In England until 1857 a special act of Parliament was required for each individual divorce. Rochester has enough money and connections to get such an act passed, but it would be futile to try to do so, because the only legal ground for divorce was adultery—and Bertha cannot be judged to have committed adultery in a legal sense because, being insane, she is not responsible for her actions.

face is full at this moment . . . Your pity, my darling, is the suffering mother of love: its anguish is the very natal pang of the divine
passion. I accept it, Jane; let the daughter have free advent—my
arms wait to receive her."

Jane can resist this temptation, but she is also tempted by pity
for herself, by her own sense of insignificance. Why should she care
whether or not she is married, she asks herself after Rochester
leaves her alone for the night. "Who in the world cares for *you*? or
who will be injured by what you do?" Jane reports her answer to
her own question in heroic terms:

> Still indomitable was the reply—"*I* care for myself. The more
> solitary, the more friendless, the more unsustained I am, the more
> I will respect myself. I will keep the law given by God, sanctioned
> by man. I will hold to the principles received by me when I was
> sane, and not mad—as I am now . . ."

This is some of the most excited language in the novel, and its
excitement seems to suggest the depth of Charlotte Brontë's feelings about the emotional perception that lies behind it—the perception that the kind of romantic relations that you choose for
yourself are directly affected by your sense of self-worth.* (To the
degree that Charlotte Brontë learned about these matters from her
own experience, she seems to have done so by reflecting on her

---

* Jane Eyre refuses the kind of relations that Rochester had with his mistresses
during his years of wandering in Europe, relations that oscillate between contempt
for oneself and for one's lover. One modern counterpart of such relations is the
"open" marriage in which each partner feels free to jump from bed to bed, a relation accepted mostly by those who are convinced they are too unworthy to enjoy
the intimacy, trust, and depth that go with sexual faithfulness. Another modern
counterpart occurs with those whose sense of self-worth is so inflated that they
cannot imagine anyone as their equal, and therefore can never have anything better
than transient, unsatisfying affairs, even if some of these are formally legalized as
marriages.

unrequited passion for Constantin Heger, her married school-master in Brussels, to whom, after she returned to England, she wrote worshipful, impassioned letters that eventually prompted him to break off the correspondence. Unlike Jane Eyre, she knew she was in love with someone whose wife was very much alive and present.)

The quest for equality at the heart of *Jane Eyre* can succeed against all social and economic odds because nature itself, with its grand instinctive powers, takes an interest in it—and the kind of interest it takes is very different from the interest nature took in the doomed quest for unity in *Wuthering Heights*. Charlotte Brontë inverts the standard romantic equation of childhood with nature that Emily Brontë accepted without question. In *Jane Eyre* nature is closer to adults than it is to children, because nature, like every-thing else in Charlotte Brontë's universe, is moral, and because human beings can learn only through years of painful education the morality that nature already knows. Jane's relation with nature is not a matter of oneness and continuity but of mutual help and need, a relation shared between separate and autonomous beings. Even in her loneliest moments, she experiences nature as her mother and her friend in the same way that Helen Burns experi-enced God as her father and her friend:

> Nature seemed to me benign and good; I thought she loved me, outcast as I was; and I, who from man could anticipate only mis-trust, rejection, insult, clung to her with filial fondness. To-night, at least, I would be her guest—as I was her child; my mother would lodge me without money and without price.

Near the end of the book, when Jane is about to let herself accept St. John Rivers's icy proposal of a loveless marriage, and to "rush down the torrent of his will into the gulf of his existence," she hears Rochester calling her name from a hundred miles away. This, she insists, was neither a fantasy nor a supernatural intervention but simply "the work of nature. She was roused and did—no miracle—but her best."

Nature did her best because Jane Eyre had long since earned her care and concern. Near the start of the book, when summoned downstairs at Gateshead, Jane does not respond to the summons until after she has pulled open a window to feed a hungry robin; then, at Lowood School, when a friend returns to the schoolhouse, Jane stays behind "to plant in my garden a handful of roots I had dug up in the forest, and which I feared would wither if I left them till morning." In this novel's moral universe, small acts of charity like these (and like Jane's gift of a few coins to a beggar on the morning after her engagement) are as significant as large ones, and nature rouses herself at the end of the book to help Jane as Jane had helped nature by preventing a handful of roots from withering. Impersonal nature cares for Jane's unique personality: in her next great romantic and erotic crisis, when she is ready to submerge her own existence into the gulf of St. John Rivers's existence, nature transmits a voice that reminds her of her autonomous personal self by crying out her personal name: "Jane! Jane! Jane!"

St. John Rivers denies the powers of nature by repressing his desire for the beautiful Rosamond Oliver, a desire so intense that the sound of her voice startles him like a thunderbolt even while he exerts superhuman control over himself by resisting the impulse to turn and look at her. His renunciation is all the more difficult because Rosamond unmistakably desires him in return, and her wealthy father leaves no doubt that he would be honored to have St. John as a son-in-law. Through heroic self-restraint, St. John conquers his desire for Rosamond and instead proposes marriage to Jane, whom he neither desires nor loves. He sees Jane as a useful instrument for his missionary work, not as a unique person to be loved for herself. Jane had earlier noticed Rivers crushing a tuft of not-yet-opened daisies under his foot while crushing his desire for Rosamond in his heart—not unlike the young John Reed who broke the buds off the flowers at Gateshead—and he can only bring himself to propose to Jane after crushing in himself the erotic power of nature.

The lightning-injured tree in *Wuthering Heights,* its limb torn away on the night when Heathcliff and Catherine are torn from each other, has a notably different counterpart in *Jane Eyre.* On the same night when Rochester has proposed marriage to Jane— having neglected to mention the wife he keeps locked in a third-story bedroom—lightning strikes the great horse chestnut tree in the orchard and splits half of it away. A few days later, Jane looks at the cleft in the tree and sees the moon appear suddenly: "her disk was blood-red and half overcast; she seemed to throw on me one bewildered, dreary glance, and buried herself again instantly in the deep drift of cloud." Jane runs away to the sound of the wind's "wild, melancholy wail."

In the world of this novel, the moon wants to warn Jane Eyre of her moral predicament and is bewildered and dreary because it has no way of doing so. The moon finally succeeds at the more danger-ous moment when Jane is struggling against Rochester's proposal that they live together without being married. Falling into a troubled sleep, Jane dreams that the moon appears in the cloudy night sky—

as never moon yet burst from cloud: a hand first penetrated the sable folds and waved them away; then, not a moon, but a white human form shone in the azure, inclining a glorious brow earthward. It gazed and gazed on me. It spoke to my spirit, immeasurably dis-tant was the tone, yet so near, it whispered in my heart—

"My daughter, flee temptation!"

"Mother, I will."

Jane Eyre has no parents, only, in the person of Mrs. Reed, the novelistic counterpart of the wicked stepmother in a fairy tale. A child who has no parents, or who has parents too horrible to acknowledge, can easily be tempted by the fantasy that its only parent is nature itself. (This is the fantasy that Oedipus indulges in Sophocles' tragedy, when he claims nature as his parent in order to avoid acknowledging that Laius and Jocasta were his parents, and that he had killed one and married the other.) In *Jane Eyre* this fantasy flowers into a densely textured myth. Jane acknowledges two deities: the father-god of the Christianity she learns from Helen Burns and the mother-goddess who reveals herself in the form of the watchful cautioning moon.

Jane Eyre manages the nearly impossible feat of reconciling romantic nature worship with the ethical world of monotheism. Jane's two deities share the same purposes and the same goals, and each of these deities, unlike the nature deities of *Frankenstein* and *Wuthering Heights,* is a *person,* in the sense that each can speak in the first person and be addressed in the second person, and in the sense that human beings can have a personal relation with each of them. When Jane rejects Rochester's idea of fleeing England together by telling herself that she will keep the law given by God, the moon waits only a few paragraphs before warning her against the temptation to break that law. A few chapters later, when Jane is rescued from starvation by St. John Rivers (who turns out to be her cousin), she is welcomed and comforted by St. John's sisters, Mary and Diana, whose names allude to the Christian God who gives justice and mercy and to the nature goddess who gives warning and comfort.

In Emily Brontë's poems and in *Wuthering Heights* the divinities have no faces. They embody either the external divinity of nature, in which personalities and bodies dissolve into impersonal forces, or its inner counterpart, the god within the poet's breast who gives visions of escape from the limits of human existence. Compared to Charlotte Brontë's anthropomorphic divinity with a human face and a stern code of morals, Emily Brontë's idea of divinity seems, perhaps, more coherent, more consistent with the philosophical traditions that imagine a god who thinks only about mathematics or about the clockwork mechanism of the universe, never about human transience and disorder. But Charlotte Brontë's belief in a God with a face has some intellectual advantages of its own. The impersonal nature divinity of *Wuthering Heights*, like the philosophers' rational deity, has no connection with the individual person who believes in it. Faceless nature and timeless mathematics take no interest in human beings. The humanlike quality that can seem so naïve in Charlotte Brontë's version of a personal divinity makes possible an intimate connection between the personality of the observer and everything that the observer sees, no matter how distant or vast. In Charlotte Brontë's universe, the human personality is not cast out of nature and left to press its face against a closed window in envious wonder at the glory inside. Instead, the human personality and the things that matter to it are understood as an integral part of the whole. And, instead of Emily Brontë's despairing rush to dissolution and death, Charlotte Brontë portrays an urgent impulse toward integrity, so that the human personality can choose to achieve in itself something of the meaning and importance it perceives in the universe. As in many debates over great universal questions, the apparently naïve position turns out to be more profound than the apparently sophisticated one.

Jane Eyre's deities choose to help her because she chooses to help them, and the relation between them is voluntary, not a matter of destiny or fate. It is she who actively decides to keep the law that she describes as "given by God, sanctioned by man." Nature and religion aid her, but never impel her; no supernatural power leads her onward. Jane Eyre lives in a universe driven by free acts.*

The Unequal Sexes

Each of Jane's protective deities, the paternal Christian God and the maternal nature goddess, defends without compromise the equality of the sexes. The "temptation" against which the moon goddess warns Jane is not merely the temptation to adultery, but the temptation to accept the same subservience that Rochester's earlier mistresses accepted. Rochester himself has no illusions about the kind of relations he had with them: "Hiring a mistress," he tells Jane, "is the next worse thing to buying a slave: both are often by nature, and always by position, inferior: and to live familiarly with inferiors is degrading. I now hate the recollection of the time I passed with Céline, Giacinta, and Clara." Jane draws from this "the certain inference that if I were so far to forget myself and all the teaching that had ever been instilled into me, as—under any pretext—with any justification—through any temptation—to become the successor of these poor girls, he would one day regard me with the same feeling which now in his mind desecrated their

---

* The heroine of *Villette*, Charlotte Brontë's last completed novel, lives in an entirely different universe. "Fate took me in her strong hand; mastered my will; directed my actions," says Lucy Snowe, who believes her life is subject to "a vague arbiter of my destiny," and "the Fates had written their decree." Jane Eyre's choices are rewarded by a nature that is both motivated and moral; Lucy Snowe is deprived of happiness by the unchosen, unmotivated, amoral tumult of a storm at sea that drowns the man she loves. Charlotte Brontë's notion that success and happiness were her own doing while failure and misery were the work of fate was not necessarily inconsistent; it was a version of her deeper conviction that individual persons and deities ultimately produce good, while evil is the product of forces in nature and society that remain incorrigibly impersonal.

memory." Charlotte Brontë understood that an unequal sexual relation between adults is necessarily an unloving one; she also seems to have sensed that sex itself is experienced differently—that is, produces different physical and emotional feelings—in unloving relations and in loving ones.*

Even before Jane Eyre learns that Rochester has a wife locked away in an upper room, she has already perceived him as a master of female slaves in at least a moral or emotional sense. During one of the uncomfortable power games they play during their engagement, this exchange occurs:

> He chuckled; he rubbed his hands. "Oh, it is rich to see and hear her!" he exclaimed. "Is she original? Is she piquant? I would not exchange this one little English girl for the grand Turk's whole seraglio; gazelle-eyes, houri forms and all!"
>
> The eastern allusion bit me again: "I'll not stand you an inch in the stead of a seraglio," I said, "so don't consider me an equivalent for one; if you have a fancy for anything in that line, away with you, sir, to the bazaars of Stamboul without delay; and lay out in extensive slave-purchases some of that spare cash you seem at a loss to spend satisfactorily here."
>
> "And what will you do, Janet, while I am bargaining for so many tons of flesh and such an assortment of black eyes?"
>
> "I'll be preparing myself to go out as a missionary to preach liberty to them that are enslaved—your harem inmates amongst the rest . . ."

Here she fantasizes herself as a missionary; a few chapters later, her cousin St. John Rivers tries to convince her to become one in real

* *Post coitum homo tristis*—"After sex the human being is sad"—is far truer about unloving relations than loving ones. If the union between two partners is limited to the sexual act, then loneliness inevitably follows it.

life—and one reason Rivers can almost tempt her into agreeing is that he offers her the chance to become in India exactly what she imagines herself here: a missionary who preaches liberty to them that are enslaved.

In the course of Jane Eyre's education, the temptation to sacrifice sexual equality for the sake of sexual love is relatively easy to resist, and when Rochester asks her to become his mistress, she hesitates only briefly before leaving him. But she finds it less easy to resist the temptation to sacrifice sexual equality for herself in order to serve, through St. John Rivers's missionary work, the cause of sexual equality for other women. In a novel of education and growth, she is tempted to renounce the benefits of growth in order that others may grow and be educated. This is a hidden form of a temptation to superiority—a temptation to elevate herself over those whom she hopes to serve through the glories of sacrifice and duty—and it is far more dangerous to her than any temptation to subservience.

St. John Rivers, when Jane first meets him, has been planning for some months to start work as a missionary and "leave Europe for the East." But he does not say—possibly he does not yet know—exactly where in the East his work will take him. When he admires a painting of Rosamond made by Jane, Jane asks him whether he would want to have a painting like it when he is "at Madagascar, or at the Cape, or in India." She is reminding him that he has been notably unspecific about his plans. Perceiving that he does not feel at home in the house he shares with his sisters, she thinks: "the Himalayan ridge, or Caffre bush [among the Kaffirs of southern Africa], even the plague-cursed Guinea Coast swamp, would suit him better." Only later does St. John reveal that his destination is India, and he does so indirectly, by asking Jane to study Hindustani instead of the German that she has been teaching herself in order to read German poetry and drama. He gives no reason for choosing

India rather than the many other places where English missionaries were active at the time, but the book makes clear that the specific work he hopes to perform will be work that confronts the same problems of sexual inequality that Jane and Rochester had confronted earlier.

Years before she wrote *Jane Eyre,* Charlotte Brontë had thought about the need for a mission like St. John's to India, and she had explored the question in the first of the surviving *devoirs* in French that she, like her sister Emily, had written in Brussels. *"Sacrifice d'une veuve Indienne"* is the title of her imaginary account of a suttee (or sati), the traditional ritual in which a Hindu widow immolates herself on her husband's funeral pyre. The ritual was nominally a voluntary act by the widow, but the social pressure on her to perform it was in practice irresistible.* Charlotte Brontë's essay opens with the simple statement that India "is a slave." "What good," she asks, "are its diamonds and gold, as long as it is subject to the despotism of an arrogant and cruel Hierarchy?" The capitalized word emphasizes that the essential injustice of the suttee lies in its murderous inequality. She immediately asks herself, in language that looks forward to Rivers's mission, "Do all the mines of Golconda have the worth of a single ray from that star of Bethlehem which, long ago, the Magi saw in the East?" As Charlotte Brontë noted in her *devoir,* the British colonial authorities had banned forced suttees, but the ban had had little effect because the widows insisted that they were sacrificing themselves by choice. Near the end of the *devoir,* Charlotte Brontë imagines herself

---

* Recent historical scholarship suggests that the practice of the suttee seems to have begun after the British introduced European ideas of property into India, and probably began as a means of preserving the dead husband's property for his own family and keeping it out of his widow's family. The historical irony that Europeans were indignant over a practice that resulted from their own presence did not of course leave the immolated widow any less dead.

thinking and hoping that the widow she describes might renounce her sacrifice—"but no, either pride or religion sustained her to the end," and the widow sits beside her husband's corpse as the flames consume the pyre.

The same ritual of the suttee is a quiet but insistent presence in *Jane Eyre.* It is visible in the background of Jane's relations with both Rivers and Rochester. At one point, for no particular reason, Rochester sings to Jane a song that ends with:

> "My love has sworn, with sealing kiss,
>   With me to live—to die;
> I have at last my nameless bliss:
>   As I love—loved am I!"

Jane erupts, only half playfully: "What did he mean by such a pagan idea? *I* had no intention of dying with him—he might depend on that . . . I had as good a right to die when my time came as he had: but I should bide that time, and *not be hurried away in a suttee.*" Later, when Diana Rivers tries to dissuade Jane from going out to work as a missionary with St. John, whether or not she does so as his wife, she says: "You are much too pretty, as well as too good, to be grilled alive in Calcutta." Contemporary readers of *Jane Eyre* would have taken for granted that Rivers's work in India, like that of many of the missionaries who went there, would be focused most of all on the suttee as well as on a related form of sexual inequality, the infanticide of newborn girls. And in demanding that Jane accompany him, Rivers argues explicitly that he will need her help with his work among Indian women.

Like the opening sentences of Charlotte Brontë's *devoir, Jane Eyre* links two kinds of "Hierarchy": the suttee in the East and slavery in the West. (A third variety is the harem in Rochester's fantasy of himself as sultan; the harem, the suttee, and Rochester's mistresses are the novel's illustrations of Muslim, Hindu, and Christian varieties of sexual hierarchy.) Bertha Mason, Rochester's wife, is the daughter of a rich West Indian planter with "vast" possessions; Charlotte Brontë had no need to describe him as a slave owner; every reader knew he could not have been anything else. When Jane imagines herself going out as a missionary and preaching liberty to those that are enslaved, her reader may remember a detail from the proposal scene in the previous chapter, when Rochester alluded to a "West Indian insect" he had once seen. A few chapters before that, Jane had been much surprised to learn that Rochester had spent time in the West Indies. When Rochester eventually tells the story of his marriage, he portrays Jamaica as a realm of madness and disorder: Bertha's mother was "shut up in a lunatic asylum"; her brother was "a complete dumb [unspeaking] idiot"; Bertha herself was "intemperate and unchaste." Now locked away in Thornfield, Bertha Mason is large, violent, and dark; her obvious resemblance to the conventional image of a rebellious slave has often been noted. Bertha's mother is specifically identified as a Creole, a word that referred to someone born in the West Indies but of European (sometimes of African) descent; the word did not refer to skin color or any other physical characteristic, and typically referred to a specific person, not to her ancestors or descendants.* (Rochester refers to Bertha's "mother, the Creole"; Bertha herself is not a Creole.)

The moral resemblance between the African slave trade and the Indian suttee was evident to Charlotte Brontë's contemporaries,

---

* The *Oxford English Dictionary* records that the popular novelist Captain Frederick Marryat wrote in a novel published in 1832 that one of his characters "was a creole, that is, born in the West Indies, of French parents." Bertha's mother's name is Antoinetta, a name that suggests Italian origin, although Charlotte Brontë more probably imagined her as Spanish—one more instance of the continental immorality embodied in Rochester's French, Italian, and German mistresses.

partly because both evils were famously opposed by the same gentle and indefatigable legislator William Wilberforce, the great hero of Charlotte Brontë's evangelical circle, in which newborn boys were commonly christened Wilberforce.* William Wilberforce had taken the leading role in two great legislative triumphs: the bill that ended the slave trade in the British Empire (primarily affecting the British West Indies), and the bill that opened India to English missionaries, whom the East India Company had hitherto excluded on the suspicion that they were troublemakers who would disrupt established lines of colonial authority.

Not everyone in the book who lives on British colonial territory is implicated in the sins of "Hierarchy." Jane's uncle, John Eyre, from whom she eventually inherits wealth (he learns of her existence after the exposure of Rochester's intention to marry her), is another islander, but entirely unlike the hierarchical islanders of the West Indies. John Eyre lives on Madeira, where slavery had been abolished in the eighteenth century; his wealth derives from the wine trade, which unlike the sugar trade was untainted by a history of slavery. The novel's chronology makes it likely that John Eyre achieved his wealth during the years from 1807 to 1814 when Madeira was briefly ruled by Britain before being restored to Portugal.

Critical opinion about *Jane Eyre* at the start of the twenty-first century tends to assume that St. John Rivers is effectively an agent of British imperialism, implicated through his authoritarian per-

---

* In its social and political goals, evangelical Christianity in early nineteenth-century England differed from many later religious movements that also called themselves evangelical. The evangelism favored by Charlotte Brontë and her circle was synonymous with social and political activism on behalf of liberation and equality. It was one of the great driving forces toward legislation that limited working hours in mills and factories in Britain and abolished slavery and the slave trade in the British Empire.

sonality in imperialism's oppressions. Like many other dogmas that provide simple answers, this will someday seem naïve. Bertha Mason's father in the West Indies is Charlotte Brontë's image of the British colonialist, while St. John Rivers in the East is her contrasting image of the British missionary: one an exploiter, the other a liberator. Mason leaves a heritage of madness, disorder, and death. Rivers, as Jane Eyre describes his work in India in the swelling final paragraphs of the novel, leaves a heritage of enlightenment and freedom. "Firm, faithful, and devoted, full of energy and zeal, and truth, he labours for his race"—a word which in this context means what it often meant in the past three centuries: the entire human race. "He clears their painful way to improvement; he hews down like a giant the prejudices of creed and caste that encumber it."

St. John Rivers has "the sternness of the warrior Greatheart," who in John Bunyan's *The Pilgrim's Progress* is the special protector of women and children, yet he has a common purpose with the one person in the book who seems to be at the greatest moral distance from his severity and commitment. Bertha Mason, in her madness and disorder, more a Delilah than a Greatheart, struggles in her own way against the same inequities that Rivers opposes. St. John Rivers could not guess at the parallel between himself and the madwoman, and Bertha Mason's full role in the novel has come to be understood only gradually. More than a century elapsed before anyone detected the psychological and moral connections between Bertha and Jane, and the deeper connections between Bertha and other characters in the book remain almost entirely unnoticed.

Mr. Rochester goes out of his way to obscure the connection between Jane and Bertha. "Look at the difference!" he exclaims when his two brides are in the same room after the interrupted wedding. "Compare these clear eyes with the red balls yonder—this face with that mask—this form with that bulk." Virginia Woolf, in *A Room of One's Own*, seems to have been the first to detect a hidden connection between Jane and Bertha, but she dismissed it as a fault in the book and not the crucial element of its design that it was later recognized to be. She quotes the passage in which Jane walks along the third-story corridor at Thornfield thinking about the inequality of the sexes:

> Women are supposed to be very calm generally: but women feel just as men feel; they need exercise for their faculties, and a field for their efforts as much as their brothers do; they suffer from too rigid a restraint, too absolute a stagnation, precisely as men would suffer; and it is narrow-minded in their more privileged fellow-creatures to say that they ought to confine themselves to making puddings and knitting stockings, to playing on the piano and embroidering bags. It is thoughtless to condemn them, or laugh at them, if they seek to do more or learn more than custom has pronounced necessary for their sex.
>
> When thus alone, I not unfrequently heard Grace Poole's laugh . . .

Grace Poole is the keeper of Bertha Mason, of whose existence Jane is still unaware, and at this point in the book, Jane believes Grace to be the source of the frightening laughter heard in the locked third story. Virginia Woolf comments, without irony:

> That is an awkward break . . . It is upsetting to come upon Grace Poole all of a sudden. The continuity is disturbed. One might say . . . that the woman who wrote these pages had more genius in her than Jane Austen; but if one reads them over, and marks that jerk in them, that indignation, one sees that she will never get her genius expressed whole and entire. Her books will be deformed and twisted. She will write in a rage where she should write calmly.

In 1928, when this was written, no one had seen that Charlotte Brontë was in fact calmly affirming a continuity in this passage—

was expressing her genius "whole and entire"—because no one had yet recognized that Bertha Mason is Jane Eyre's double. If Jane has nothing to do with Bertha, then Virginia Woolf would have been right to see a discontinuity. The first hint that Jane and Bertha might be closely connected seems to have been made by Adrienne Rich, who wrote in an essay in 1973 that despite Bertha's violence, "she does not, interestingly enough, attack Jane," and that "the terrible figure of Bertha has come between Jane and a marriage which was not yet ripe, which would have made her simply the dependent adjunct of Mr. Rochester instead of his equal."

Adrienne Rich was arguing that the women in the novel were united in protecting Jane Eyre from the patriarchy. A more intimate connection between Jane and Bertha was first noticed in print in 1979, when Sandra M. Gilbert and Susan Gubar, basing their argument in part on Adrienne Rich's essay, demonstrated in their book *The Madwoman in the Attic* that Bertha is Jane's dark double. Jane as a child and Bertha as an adult are both condemned by others as wicked, passionate, and immoral. Jane as a child and Bertha as an adult are locked away in a room from which they issue a terrifying scream. ("And what a scream!" exclaims the housekeeper when the young Jane cries out; "What a cry," thinks Jane on hearing Bertha.) On the night before Jane's intended wedding to Rochester, Bertha terrifies her by entering her room and putting on her wedding garments—and, at that moment, Jane gets her first glimpse of Bertha's face *in her own mirror.* Jane has tried in vain to convince Rochester that she wants to wear a square of plain blond cloth instead of the extravagantly costly bridal veil he has bought for her. Bertha now settles the argument by tearing the expensive veil in half and trampling the pieces on the floor, and the next morning Jane goes to the wedding in the "plain square of blond after all." Earlier, when Jane, after thinking about the inequality of men and women, had heard Grace Poole's laugh, she was hearing the madwoman's inarticulate protest against the same injustice that Jane herself had been analyzing in her passionate but articulate sentences.

During one of Bertha's escapes from her locked room (when Grace Poole has drunk too much to be vigilant), she chooses a form of revolt that cries out with symbolic meaning: she sets fire to Rochester's bed, the nearest thing she can find to the marriage bed she once shared with him. Jane Eyre, while rushing to his rescue, sees "a candle burning just outside" his room, "left on the matting in the gallery." Inside the room, "tongues of fire darted round the bed: the curtains were on fire. In the midst of blaze and vapour, Mr. Rochester lay stretched motionless, in deep sleep." The whole scene is an image of the Indian suttee: the husband lies motionless amidst the smoke and flames ignited by the wife. In some Western accounts of the suttee (although not in Charlotte Brontë's French *devoir*) the widow carries the candle that ignites the pyre. By setting fire to the bed of a living husband and walking away to safety, Bertha Mason violently refuses and avenges the suttee.

In an episode near the start of the book, in Mrs. Reed's house at Gateshead, Jane herself is the victim of a psychological variant on the suttee. After striking John Reed in self-defense she is locked away in "the red-room," feeling desperate "like any other rebel slave." The red-room is kept as a sacred memorial to Mrs. Reed's dead husband. "It was in this chamber he breathed his last; here he lay in state; hence his coffin was borne by the undertaker's men; and, since that day, a sense of dreary consecration had guarded it from frequent intrusion." The focus of the room is "a bed supported on massive pillars of mahogany, hung with curtains of deep-red damask," which "stood out like a tabernacle in the centre." Abandoned in the ritually charged place where the dead husband had been, convinced of the injustice of her fate, finally screaming out in terror at the sight of a lantern flame outside the window, Jane is made to suffer a minor childhood version of the same injustice that Bertha Mason endures and avenges at Thornfield—and that St. John Rivers, more effectively than Bertha Mason, works to extinguish in India.

While Jane is living with St. John Rivers and his sisters, Bertha Mason continues to work, in effect, on Jane's behalf, although we and Jane only learn about Bertha's acts long after they occur. One night when Rochester is brooding alone at Thornfield over Jane's departure, Bertha Mason sets fire to the house—taking care to ignite the bed Jane had used—in a final evocation of the suttee. As Rochester, at great risk to his own life, tries to save Bertha by climbing up on the burning roof where she is standing, she leaps to her death. (Is she fleeing from him, or from the funeral pyre she has ignited for herself?) Rochester, though badly injured, is free to marry—and, at around the same time, Jane Eyre's uncle dies and bequeaths her a fortune. Bertha dies, and Jane inherits wealth and a potential husband. Some confused sense of jealousy seems to have prompted Bertha to destroy Jane's bed, but she gave Jane many benefits in doing so.

Bertha's death is also a crucial stage in the growth of Jane Eyre's feelings. All the angers and resentments that afflicted Jane Eyre in childhood and adolescence die along with Bertha, as does the adolescent temptation to romance that was part of Jane's attraction to Rochester. Jane at last grows into adulthood, and, as she listens to St. John Rivers's proposal of marriage, she is subject for the first time to an adult temptation—the weary temptation to accept something second-best while trying to convince yourself that it isn't.

Reader, I Married My Equal

Early in the book, before Jane is sent off to Lowood School, Mrs. Reed receives a visit from Mr. Brocklehurst, who asks to see his ten-year-old prospective pupil. He reminds her that wicked people go to hell and asks her what she must do to avoid it. She answers, "I must keep in good health, and not die."

Her answer is a childish misstatement of something that, in this novel, is an adult truth. Jane Eyre's idea of equality and justice includes a sense that she has a moral right, even an obligation, to find happiness through her body. To keep in good health, to enjoy the world through the medium of the body, is one way of defeating the murderous powers of hell. When she falls into childish despair after being thrust into the red-room, she is briefly tempted by the thought of "starving myself to death" like Heathcliff and Catherine, but immediately checks herself on moral grounds: "That certainly was a crime: and was I fit to die?" Later she affirms to Rochester, as explicitly as novelistic conventions allowed in England at the time, that she has as much right to enjoy sexual love as anyone richer and more beautiful. Later still, she understands that a loveless marriage with St. John Rivers would be as much a desecration as an unmarried love with Mr. Rochester.

Charlotte Brontë presents the struggle over Jane Eyre's body and soul as a struggle among many different Christianities. Mr. Brocklehurst's hypocritical piety ("Consistency, madam, is the first of Christian duties") imposes plain dress and physical discomfort on the pupils of Lowood and threatens Jane with hellfire. Helen Burns's sublime hope promises universal salvation in heaven, and makes possible her noble indifference to her earthly sufferings. Mrs. Reed's daughter Eliza withdraws into a ritualistic high-church Anglicanism before leaving for Belgium to convert to Roman Catholicism and become abbess of a nunnery which she has endowed with her fortune. Rochester, who sometimes sounds like a self-taught Protestant theologian, murmurs to himself that in marrying Jane with a wife still living, "I know my Maker sanctions what I do. For the world's judgment—I wash my hands thereof. For man's opinion—I defy it." St. John Rivers, in a sermon that leaves Jane Eyre feeling "an inexpressible sadness," preaches a cold Calvinistic creed to which all bodily pleasure must be sacrificed and in which predestination, not choice, is the only means by which anyone can be saved. Jane Eyre refuses all these heterodoxies, even while honoring the Christianities of Helen Burns and—as long as she need not marry him—St. John Rivers. Her Protestant conviction is that she must obey the law, but also that she must permit no one other than her own conscience to tell her what the law is. For her, the law is given by God, sanctioned by man, and codified by herself. The sure sign that St. John Rivers is wrong about her is that he is certain he knows best what God wants from her— that she join him in India as a missionary.

Marriage, as Charlotte Brontë understands it, is simultaneously a sexual and legal relation and an act of sacred symbolism. Here, as in much else, she took to heart the language of the Book of Common Prayer, where the husband says to the wife after they exchange vows: "With this ring I thee wed, with my body I thee worship, and with all my worldly goods I thee endow." However the daily reality of marriage differs from this threefold statement of intent, the language of the prayer book points toward the ultimate meanings of that reality. The ring is the symbol of constancy; the sexual act is the means by which one partner worships the other;*

---

* When the Protestant Episcopal Church in the United States revised the prayer book in the 1780s after separating itself from the Church of England, it omitted

and the bestowal of worldly goods indicates that marriage requires a mutuality that is as much social and economic as it is spiritual and sexual. Jane Eyre regards herself as commanded to achieve this kind of marriage in the same way that she is commanded to love her neighbor as herself. These commandments may be impossible to fulfill, but to strive for anything less—for example, to pursue some childish fantasy of blended bodies or unified spirits—is to abandon herself to moral and psychological slavery.

One reason that the marriage vow matters to Jane Eyre, and to Charlotte Brontë, is that, like any vow, it commits the person who makes it to a responsibility he cannot abandon without declaring himself a liar. When Jane escapes from making a wrong marriage, first with Rochester at the middle of the book, again with Rivers at the end, she escapes from marriages that would have been built on lies. At Jane's unfinished wedding ceremony, when the minister makes the traditional demand, "if either of you know any impediment why ye may not lawfully be joined together in matrimony, ye do now confess it," Rochester's silence is a falsehood, and if he had the chance to say his vows, he would be speaking further falsehoods. St. John Rivers, as an Anglican minister, knows perfectly well that if he were to marry Jane Eyre he would be lying when called upon to proclaim his sexual love for her in the words, "with my body I thee worship." By refusing Rochester and Rivers, Jane Eyre rescues them both. She rescues Rochester from the lonely inequality of keeping a mistress whom he would eventually despise. She rescues Rivers from his temptation to tyrannize her in his private life while liberating others in his public life. And Charlotte Brontë was clearheaded enough to know that Rivers's manifest

---

the phrase "with my body I thee worship," probably for theological reasons rather than for prudish ones. Puritans in England had been trying without success to alter or remove the phrase from the English version.

impulse to liberate others is not invalidated by his parallel hidden impulse to tyrannize others into acting as he thinks best.

Jane can have an equal marriage to Rochester only after she gains a fortune from her uncle (and she is still wealthy after transferring three-fourths of her inheritance to her cousins) and after Rochester, through his reconciliation to his wounds, loses the pride that makes him see himself only as one who gives, never as one who receives. Both these changes are deliberately troubling. Jane knows that she would need no wealth to be equal with Rochester "at God's feet," but while she is alive she cares more about earthly inequality, and Charlotte Brontë was practical and realistic enough to know that this always has a financial aspect. Rochester's injuries bring a more troubling change in his relations with Jane, and perhaps every reader, to some degree, protests against the wounds that Charlotte Brontë inflicts on her hero. D. H. Lawrence found *Jane Eyre* "verging towards pornography" in its account of Rochester's wounds, and counted Charlotte Brontë among "pornographical people," those to whom "the sex flow and the excrement flow is the same." (This is a curious instance of projection, in that Lawrence's phrase exactly describes the sexuality of Rupert Birkin and Ursula Brangwen that he endorses in *Women in Love*.) In Lawrence's reading of *Jane Eyre*, "sex has become slightly obscene, to be wallowed in, but despised. Mr. Rochester's sex passion is not 'respectable' till Mr. Rochester is burned, blinded, disfigured, and reduced to helpless dependence. Then, thoroughly humbled and humiliated, it may be merely admitted."

This seems to get *Jane Eyre* backwards. The book is not only a psychological novel but also a variety of folktale marked by the extravagant violence of the folktale universe. In the strands of the story that derive from folktales, the point of Rochester's injuries is not to humiliate him for having sexual feelings, but to transform him into someone who can enjoy the sexual satisfactions that only an equal relationship can provide. His wounds break down the emotional wall he has built around himself; in a deep moral paradox, they are not a punishment but the first step toward a reward. Rochester is wounded because he climbs to the roof of Thornfield in an attempt to rescue Bertha from the fire she has set; his action is braver and more generous-hearted than anything else in the book. Her leap to her death frees him to marry again, while his wounds make it possible for Jane Eyre to join him in the equal marriage that was impossible earlier. As Jane is fortunate for having suffered early in the book, Rochester is fortunate in suffering near the end. Once he loses the vigor and power that, for Jane, had elevated him to the status of an idol, she can love him for himself and not for his domineering powers.

Despite the symbolically charged fact that his wounds deprive him of the use of a more or less cylindrical thing and two spherical things—his hand and his eyes—his sexual capacity is undiminished, and through his marriage to Jane he becomes a father for the first time. (His ward Adèle seems to be the child of one of his French mistress's other lovers.) And the effects of his wounds are partly reversed: "When his first-born was put into his arms, he could see that the boy had inherited his own eyes, as they once were—large, brilliant, and black." When Jane left Rochester earlier in the book she abandoned one of the great erotic temptations: the fantasy of being rescued by someone stronger and better than oneself. When she returns to him, she does so without the parallel fantasy of acting as his rescuer, because he has retained more than enough strength to manage by himself.

The unity of Catherine and Heathcliff is so complete that it excludes everyone else. The marriage of Jane and Rochester is so fertile that it embraces others. "My Edward and I, then, are happy: and the more so, because those we most love are happy likewise. Diana and Mary Rivers are both married . . . Diana's husband is a captain in the navy; a gallant officer and a good man. Mary's is a clergyman; a college friend of her brother's; and, from his attainments and principles, worthy of the connexion. Both Captain Fitzjames and Mr. Wharton love their wives, and are loved by them."

Jane and Rochester's marriage is sociable. Nature makes the marriage possible, but nature does not summon them to rush away over the moors. Just as Jane is rewarded by nature for the care she showed to plants and birds earlier in the book, she is rewarded for the care she takes over the home she shares with St. John Rivers and his sisters. When Jane becomes wealthy, the first thing she does is keep house, a process she describes in a speech that ends in a serious joke about rites and initiation and about the sacred significance of home:

> My first aim [she tells St. John Rivers] will be to *clean down* (do you comprehend the force of the expression?) to *clean down* Moor House from chamber to cellar; my next to rub it up with beeswax, oil, and an indefinite number of cloths, till it glitters again; my third, to arrange every chair, table, bed, carpet, with mathematical precision; afterwards I shall go near to ruin you in coals and peat to keep up good fires in every room; and lastly, the two days preceding that on which your sisters are expected [having left their work as governesses after Jane shares her inheritance], will be devoted by Hannah and me to such a beating of eggs, sorting of currants, grating of spices, compounding of Christmas cakes, chopping up of materials for mince-pies, and solemnizing of other culinary rites, as words can convey but an inadequate notion to the uninitiated like you.

Near the end of the book, when Jane and Rochester, together at last, walk out to the fields outside his house at Ferndean and he again proposes marriage—"we must become one flesh without any delay," he says—Jane closes the chapter with a simple phrase that, in its context, speaks with overwhelming emotional force: "We entered the wood, and wended homeward." That one last word says everything that needs to be said about her new life. Until this moment, she has had, at best, only a room in someone else's home, but her care for Moor House has earned her a home of her own. The act of returning to Rochester's house with him makes his house the place to which she goes home. We turn the page, and the next words we see after "homeward" are: "Reader, I married him."

Jane Eyre and Edward Rochester have each endured loneliness and solitude in order to arrive at this point, because in the world perceived by Charlotte Brontë all roads to the gardens of intimacy pass through deserts of solitude, and no one can attain intimacy who has not accepted loneliness. When Jane Eyre says, "I married him," she insists on remaining herself, insists on saying "I," not "we," because only autonomous and equal individuals achieve intimacy and marriage.

4

MARRIAGE: *Middlemarch*

Nine characters in *Middlemarch* complete the quest that starts in solitude and ends in marriage—one of them does it twice—and a tenth starts on the journey but never finishes it. *Middlemarch* portrays these characters and the psychological and physical landscape of their quests with the exact detail of a Dutch painting. Through her sober realism and urbane maturity, George Eliot insists that the story she tells is driven by the ordinary realities of daily life, with all its routines and disappointments and boredom and compromises, with all its humdrum disorder and its gray interminglings of darkness and light. Yet much of the central story of *Middlemarch*, the story of Dorothea Brooke's impulsive, disastrous marriage to the aged Mr. Casaubon and her impulsive, triumphant marriage to the young Will Ladislaw, is less realistic than the book insists it is. Beneath its sober rationality, *Middlemarch* revels in the wondrous strangeness of legend and myth. Dorothea's story seems quietly ordinary in most of its day-to-day details, but in its overall trajectory and shape, it is driven by the same mythical energies and the same wish-fulfillment fantasies that drive the stories of Heathcliff and Catherine and of Rochester and Jane, and its crucial moments are marked by stark contrasts of brilliant light and obscure darkness, and the symmetrical clarity of myths.

Middlemarch is, I believe, the greatest English novel, even though, when I think in terms of George Eliot's whole career instead of this single book, she does not seem to me as great a novelist as Charles Dickens or Virginia Woolf. Part of the book's greatness is the eloquence with which it gives voice to two aspects of its author: an intellect that makes stern judgments on the faults of its characters, and a sympathy that forgives them for their faults and shares in their wishes. In the greatest moments of the book, and in the shape of the story as a whole, those two aspects do not conflict, but join in an effort to see truth and feel love simultaneously.

Mary Ann Evans, who as an adult spelled her name Marian Evans and published her novels under the pen name George Eliot, was the first English novelist who presented herself as a philosophical seeker after truth—and was honored and accepted as one.* She had the kind of morally passionate intelligence that experienced theories and ideas not merely as propositions to be thought about, but also as expressions of intense feeling. For her, an idea deserved to be thought about only if it expressed or answered a great human need, and the most important ideas were those that brought to light half-understood needs by articulating them in a way that taught us to recognize them in our own lives. Like Mary Shelley in her sense of the connections between intellect and emotion in Victor Frankenstein, George Eliot understood that ideas and passions were not opposed to each other but were different expressions of the same things. For her, an emotion could be fully understood only if the corresponding idea was also understood, and an idea made full sense only if you also understood the emotions that corresponded to it.

She also understood that some ideas and some emotions were

---

* Virginia Woolf promulgated the legend that the scholarly London Library kept George Eliot's novels on the shelves when everyone else's novels were banished as frivolous, but the legend reflects a genuine nineteenth-century sense that George Eliot was different from writers of mere fiction.

better and wiser than others, and that an idea could not be justified simply because it expressed a deep need. To be taken seriously, an idea must also withstand the cold scrutiny of dispassionate intelligence. The sober realism of much of *Middlemarch*—its claim to refuse the emotional temptations of fantasies and myths—is George Eliot's way of affirming that the ideas about marriage and morals propounded by the book's worldly-wise narrator are verifiably true and not merely driven by a wish that they might be true, unlike the passionate wish-fulfillments that so excited Charlotte Brontë and almost everyone else who had written about marriage and love.

And yet those fantasies and myths are precisely what bring *Middlemarch* to its satisfying conclusion. Dorothea Brooke and Will Ladislaw are brought together at last by a bolt of lightning sent down to them by nature so that they can be illuminated to each other, so that they can see each other in the light of their mutual need. The nature that does this is the same mythical, wish-fulfilling, and concerned nature that also sent down lightning bolts to illuminate the love lives of Catherine Earnshaw and Jane Eyre. Part of the artistic and intellectual triumph of *Middlemarch* is the way in which George Eliot's rational philosophical intelligence, having rejected the world of myth throughout most of the preceding chapters, participates in this conclusion. Her intelligence is large and generous enough to acknowledge that myths point toward truths that rationality alone cannot discover.

Unlike *Jane Eyre*, which praises and glorifies the mythical divinities who preside over its moments of crisis, *Middlemarch* tries to conceal those divinities altogether or disguises them as ordinary mortal characters. In *Jane Eyre*, the mother-goddess and the father-god both want to give Jane the same thing: a sensuous marriage of equals that is as satisfying to the spirit as it is to the flesh. In *Middlemarch*, as in *Jane Eyre*, two divinities again pursue their goals, but now their goals differ from each other, and they offer entirely different kinds of moral and sensual satisfaction. These two divinities are an instinctive, life-giving nature, intent on giving Dorothea a marriage of equals, and an angry moral deity who sends down into Dorothea's world a comforting and avenging angel named Will Ladislaw, who rewards Dorothea and punishes those who oppose her. Each of these divinities is the subject of a separate mythical story woven into *Middlemarch*. The first of these narratives dramatizes in mythical terms the intellectual wisdom propounded throughout the book by its philosophically adept narrator. The second, erupting in a remarkable scene of psychological sadism, suggests that even the narrator's imperturbably calm voice contains the furies that rage within everyone.

From Knowledge to Marriage

Middlemarch has five marriage plots: the stories of Dorothea Brooke and Mr. Casaubon, Dorothea's sister Celia and Sir James Chettam, Rosamond Vincy and Tertius Lydgate, Mary Garth and Fred Vincy, and Dorothea Casaubon and Will Ladislaw. In all these plots, as in the plots of almost all novels about marriage, the head and the heart dispute with each other over which one gets to choose the spouse who will be married to both. Marian Evans herself, after a series of failed relations, at the age of thirty-five found a mate who satisfied both head and heart. She lived for a quarter century with G. H. Lewes, a polymath writer on science, literature, and history, whom she loved and admired, and the happiness she felt with him seems to have released the creative energies that went into her fiction.*

---

* Marian Evans and G. H. Lewes lived together as husband and wife, but could not marry because Lewes was legally unable to divorce his wife, who had long

In its opening sections, *Middlemarch* seems to argue that the intellect deserves to win its argument with the emotions. The young and passionately virtuous Dorothea makes a spectacularly wrong choice in marrying the old egocentric Mr. Casaubon, not because she yields too much or too little to her feelings, but because she lacks the knowledge that she needs to act wisely. Unlike everyone else in the book, she is able to recognize that she lacks knowledge, but she proceeds to make the intellectual error of seeking it where it can never be found.

Dorothea is misguided and headstrong and egoistic, but *Middlemarch*, at least in its opening chapters, insists that she is not to be blamed for her faults; the narrator places the blame on the indifferent universe and the unjust society that together frustrate a woman's desire for knowledge. *Middlemarch* changed, however, in the course of being written, and the narrator's views changed with it. At the end Dorothea makes the right choice, not because she has found knowledge, but because she is pointed toward the right choice by instinctive feelings and mythical forces that make her choices for her—or point her in the direction of choices that she would otherwise not know how to make. She is saved less by the knowledge she seeks than by "involuntary, palpitating life" at its unconscious work, forcing knowledge on her at the last possible moment, just before it would be too late for her to use it.

Except in that final triumph of instinct—and in some brief earlier moments when Dorothea's feelings are deep enough to find something close to wisdom—*Middlemarch* tends to treat knowledge as the only useful starting point for action and morality, and especially as the only starting point for choosing a husband or wife.

---

since left him. In letters, hotel registers, and everywhere else where her legal name was not required, Marian Evans called herself Marian Lewes and referred to Lewes as her husband.

Everyone in the book is faced with intractable problems of knowledge: how to know enough about themselves and others to choose the right husband or wife, how to know enough about their own work to avoid losing their way in blind alleys or unchartable swamps, how to protect objective knowledge from subjective wishes. Almost everyone confronts or avoids the problem of choosing a mate, and they all choose wrongly to the degree that, instead of making their own choice on the basis of knowledge, they allow their choices to be decided for them "according to custom, by good looks, vanity, and merely canine affection."

A century afterward, George Eliot's arguments in favor of knowledge seem like platitudes, but she was consciously making a difficult polemical point, somewhat like a latter-day Galileo who had discovered the underlying patterns of emotion and was defending observed truth against conventional authority and egocentric illusion. She felt the urgency of staking out a new basis for action in a world that could no longer hope to find guidance in religion. In the same way that Matthew Arnold would predict a few years later that "most of what now passes with us for religion and philosophy will be replaced by poetry," *Middlemarch* argues that religion and philosophy must be replaced by knowledge. The opening "Prelude" points the moral of Dorothea's story by citing St. Theresa of Avila as an example of the ardent generous life that was once inspired by religion but can now be inspired by knowledge alone. Theresa's "passionate, ideal nature demanded an epic life," as Dorothea's nature thirsts for ideal greatness. Theresa "found her epos"—found a way of life worthy of epic poetry—waiting for her in the vocation of a Roman Catholic nun and the task of creating a new monastic order. But a would-be Theresa in the secular modern world is "helped by no coherent social faith and order which could perform the function of knowledge for the ardently willing soul."

Those last few words compress into a phrase a whole way of

thinking, a whole ideology. For George Eliot—or for many aspects of her personality—knowledge is the will's true guide; the various sets of socially agreed-upon convictions that had guided the will in the past served as more or less adequate substitutes for knowledge, never anything better. A modern ardent soul like Dorothea can find no epos waiting for her because social faith and order have disintegrated around her, because the social inequities between men and women bar her from the knowledge that she needs. So her ardor alternates between "a vague ideal and the common yearning of womanhood"—between an idealistic wish to do good without knowing what good to do, and an instinctive desire for love and children—"so that the one was disapproved as extravagance, and the other condemned as a lapse."

Knowledge, in *Middlemarch,* is the spirit that gives life. When Dorothea on her honeymoon journey with Mr. Casaubon is baffled by her confused impressions of Rome (at a time when she is also baffled by the total lack of sexual satisfaction that she finds in her marriage), George Eliot launches into an exalted metaphor of knowledge in the act of "quickening" matter—that is, giving life and soul to dead things—and connecting disparate objects: the narrator speaks of "those who have looked at Rome with the quickening power of a knowledge which breathes a growing soul into all historic shapes, and traces out the suppressed transitions which unite all contrasts"—those to whom Rome can still be the spiritual center of the world. To anyone who looks at Rome without the quickening power of knowledge, it looks like a mere jumble of ruins. (In the metaphors of *Middlemarch,* knowledge confers the same "quickening" power that Victor Frankenstein seizes when he discovers "the cause of generation and life"; "quickening" is the stage at which a pregnant woman feels the child making signs of life.) Many chapters later, when Dorothea at last achieves her moral triumph by rousing herself to help Rosamond and Ladislaw, despite having been injured by what she mistakenly perceived as Ladis-law's flirtation with Rosamond, her sympathy asserts itself, not in moral terms as a demand from her conscience, but instead in intel-lectual terms "as acquired knowledge asserts itself and will not let us see as we saw in the day of our ignorance."

In *Middlemarch* knowledge gives life and meaning; knowledge unifies and connects; knowledge rebukes our faults and demands our virtues. But knowledge in the world of *Middlemarch* is in desperately short supply, not merely because injustice and indif-ference prevent almost everyone from finding it, but ultimately because of the nature of knowledge itself. George Eliot is divided against herself on the question of what knowledge is and where it comes from. In her essays and letters she adopts the philosophi-cally sophisticated view that all knowledge is chosen and shaped by the mind from the raw stuff of an indifferent universe; it is not simply waiting to be found by a shrewd observer; the human mind *makes* it as much as finds it. In her novels, she expounds the same view of an indifferent universe, but she also longs for a different kind of knowledge, one that a sympathetic universe will ultimately offer as a reward to those who passionately seek it. The knowledge that matters most in *Middlemarch* is this second kind of knowledge—a knowledge of morals and emotion that is not objective like scien-tific knowledge but is just as true, just as focused on reality. In the world portrayed by *Middlemarch,* this kind of knowledge already exists outside you, and must find its way into you so that it can be transformed from mere passive understanding into a motive for action in all aspects of life—including the choice of a marriage. George Eliot yearns for this kind of knowledge while she also suspects, intellectually, that the indifferent universe has no such knowledge to give.

Two chapters after writing about the kind of knowledge that could quicken the dead objects of Rome, George Eliot worried aloud over whether knowledge could ever do anything of the kind. In the course of Dorothea's final conversation with Will Ladislaw in Rome, she asks whether he might become a poet:

> "That depends [Will answers]. To be a poet is to have a soul so quick to discern, that no shade of quality escapes it, and so quick to feel, that discernment is but a hand playing with finely ordered variety on the chords [i.e., strings] of emotion—a soul in which knowledge passes instantaneously into feeling, and feeling flashes back as a new organ of knowledge. One may have that condition by fits only."

"But you leave out the poems," Dorothea replies. "I think they are wanted to complete the poet." Dorothea adds that she understands Will's metaphor of knowledge passing into feeling, "for that seems to me just what I experience," but she says everywhere else that she lacks the knowledge she needs in order to quicken her feelings. And she notices that Will, by leaving out the poems, leaves out anything that might be made out of those sounding chords of emotion and bright flashes of feeling—chords and flashes that occur, as he says, in "fits only," not in anything as extended and organized as a poem, not in anything that might sustain a marriage or a life.

In the world of *Jane Eyre*, nature and spirit gave guidance to anyone in perplexity who asked for guidance. In the world of *Middlemarch*—almost until the last minute—all must find their way alone. Will Ladislaw and Dorothea Brooke are the hero and heroine of a uniquely modern kind of quest. Unlike the ancient heroes who know from the start what they are looking for, who set out on their journey with a clear sense that they intend to return to Ithaca and Penelope or steal the Golden Fleece or find the Holy Grail, George Eliot's modern wanderers do not know what they are looking for, and they must search for the knowledge that could tell them what they ought to want. In George Eliot's next and final novel, *Daniel Deronda,* the hero attains that kind of knowledge when he learns that he is a Jew, and he goes off to Palestine to find his epos in service to a social faith—as if he were the St. Theresa of the "Prelude" to *Middlemarch* reborn in a different sex, century, and religion. But no epos, no epic purpose or grandeur, is possible for the questers in *Middlemarch,* and George Eliot ends Dorothea's love story with her discovery of a knowledge that is as much a knowledge of her own heart as of any epic purpose. The lightning bolt that throws Dorothea and Will together does not have the power to keep them together, and when he prepares to leave a few minutes later, Dorothea brings him back forever by saying, "Oh, I cannot bear it—my heart will break."

Modern Knowledge, Modern Choices

Everyone makes the most important choices in life on the basis of some unique individual combination of lucid knowledge and blind trust. Even before making whatever choice you may consciously believe you are making, however, you have already made even more decisive choices about how much you require the security of knowledge and how willing you are to accept the risks of trust. The *way* you make choices—something you may never consciously think about—has a powerful effect on the choices you finally make. George Eliot confronts the moral and emotional consequences of this issue more deeply than any other novelist, more deeply than anything her sober, rational narrator knows how to explain.

The inexperienced Dorothea Brooke in the early chapters of *Middlemarch* has a youthfully naïve way of saying that knowledge is all-important, but the mature and sophisticated narrator endorses Dorothea's view of the matter. "I am often unable to decide,"

Dorothea tells her good-natured, unintelligent neighbor Sir James Chettam. "But that is from ignorance. The right conclusion is there all the same, though I am unable to see it." She later expresses this thought in grander terms that exactly echo the narrator's words in the book's "Prelude": "since the time was gone by for guiding visions and spiritual directors, since prayer heightened yearning but not instruction, what lamp was there but knowledge?" Dorothea is of course mistaken when she reasons that "learned men kept the only oil, and who more learned than Mr. Casaubon?" And she is mistaken when she imagines the "provinces of masculine knowledge" as "a standing ground from which all truth could be seen more truly." But she is mistaken only in her faith in masculine knowledge and in her reliance on someone else's knowledge rather than her own. At the end of the book, when Dorothea marries Will Ladislaw, one proof that George Eliot offers of Dorothea's moral excellence is her continuing humility before the veiled shrine of knowledge: "Dorothea herself had no dreams of being praised above other women, feeling that there was always something better which she might have done, if she had only been better and known better."

George Eliot, uniquely among English novelists, earned her right to adopt a magisterial tone for the voice of her narrator. Her novels expound more knowledge than any other body of fiction in English, and more wisdom than most. But a sophisticated modern intelligence like hers is vulnerable to a special kind of naïveté that blocks it from seeing its own prejudices, and part of George Eliot— but only a part—accepted a modern prejudice by assuming that knowledge is the most effective starting point for action. In *Middlemarch* she never explicitly questions her belief that the right knowledge reveals the right choice, even though the mythical tone and content of the novel's ending shouts otherwise. And she never explicitly questions her assumption that the right choice is already there waiting for us to discover it, that an answer already exists as a response to the questions we must learn to ask. When she reports that Tertius Lydgate, the ambitious young medical doctor in *Middlemarch,* has set himself a scientific question in terms that prevent him from finding "the awaiting answer," she takes for granted that this is the way in which all knowledge that matters comes into being—it already exists, quietly waiting to be found by someone who asks the right question.

Middlemarch is one of the few novels of which it can be said that it confronts an intellectual crisis. That crisis is George Eliot's struggle to reconcile, on the one hand, her explicit conviction that action requires knowledge, and, on the other hand, her understated awareness that, at least in the decisions that matter most, you never have enough knowledge to be certain that you are making the right choice. Any choice that you can make on the basis of knowledge alone is too trivial to write a novel about. A significant choice, such as choosing whom to marry, or choosing to have a child, no matter how well informed that choice might be, requires an active commitment to *make* it be the right choice, despite the real chances of failure, despite the inevitable blunderings and errors that will follow. Moral knowledge is not objective in the way that scientific or historical facts are. Nor is it eternal or unchanging; it does not preexist in a Platonist heaven, waiting to be found. It always includes an irreducible mixture of voluntary, subjective choice along with objective knowledge. Dorothea *almost* recognizes this in her dismal honeymoon in Rome, when she responds to Mr. Casaubon's dry description of some frescoes "which most persons think it worth while to visit" by asking the question that matters more: "But do you care about them?" A few paragraphs later, however, she is "humiliated to find herself a mere victim of feeling, as if she could know nothing except through that medium." What she will discover later is that *only* through the medium of feeling can she know anything that matters to her life.

The question with which *Middlemarch* opens and closes is: How is Dorothea to choose her life when the world around provides no guidance, no model, no direction? From the point of view of George Eliot's sober narrator, the answer that Charlotte Brontë gave in the 1840s would have seemed a jumble of unexamined ideas about nature and religion, a naïve enthusiastic fumbling backward toward the kind of faith that taught St. Theresa how to reform a religious order. The events in Dorothea's story occur forty years before George Eliot wrote about them in 1871 and 1872, but George Eliot presents Dorothea's problem as a new one, one that never occurred in earlier times; and a new question seems to require a new answer. George Eliot, like some but not all writers of the past two centuries, consciously thinks of herself as *modern*. She perceives her era as one in which the past can no longer serve as a guide for the present, where the young must find the shape of their own lives instead of using the old as their models. Mary Shelley and the Brontë sisters were not modern in this sense. Mary Shelley quickly disabused herself of her husband's fantasy that a new age called for a new morality, and the Brontë sisters never imagined they had been born into a radically new age at all, or that they and their contemporaries must find new ways of life to replace ways that had served once but were now obsolete. To be modern is to believe in a radical break between the past and the present. You can be thoroughly up-to-date—as Mary Shelley and Charlotte Brontë were—without being modern.

Modernity is a useful name for the social and intellectual conditions of the West in the past few centuries, but it can also be understood, perhaps even more usefully, as a state of mind rather than an objective fact. It is a special way of thinking about the relation between one's own age and earlier ages which seem to have been drastically different. In this sense, Euripides, John Donne, and Thomas Hardy were modern; Sophocles, William Shakespeare, and Charles Dickens were not. Virginia Woolf was modern in some of her novels but not in others. A modern writer is one who believes, as John Donne half seriously, half jokingly wrote, that "new philosophy calls all in doubt," and that now, for the first time, everyone must create himself anew:

> For every man alone thinks he hath got
> To be a Phoenix, and that then can be
> None of that kind, of which he is, but he.

The phoenix is absolutely unique, without ancestors, but also without friends, a culture, or a mate.

Dorothea Brooke is a phoenix misplaced in the comfortable society of her uncle's country house near Middlemarch. She has no suitable mate and no parents or friends who can help her find one; and she wouldn't want anyone's help if it were offered. When she marries Mr. Casaubon, she expects him to serve as a conduit to ancient wisdom that can guide her in the present. But Mr. Casaubon is absolutely without wisdom. He is a repository of secondhand information, all of it useless, incoherent, and disconnected from any personal experience. He marries Dorothea in an act of egoistic blindness, like every other unsuitable old man in comedies from ancient Athens until now who tries to marry a blooming young woman. *Middlemarch* transforms this ancient sexual joke about the lechery of old men into a thesis about historical change— it is not merely a story of an old man trying to control the erotic life of a young woman, but of an older society trying to limit, frustrate, and control a newer one. George Eliot also adds the sardonic twist that Casaubon lacks even the sexual desire that motivates his predecessors in Greek and Roman comedy, and adds a bitter historical twist to the old story by pointing to the ways in which it is not only the old but also the dead who hold back the young and the living. In the section titled "The Dead Hand," Dorothea learns after Mr. Casaubon's death that he wrote a codicil to his will specifying that she must forfeit the wealth she inherits from him if she marries Will Ladislaw; and Mary Garth learns that the last of many wills written by the grasping, rich Peter Featherstone (uncle to both Mary Garth and Fred Vincy by different marriages) leaves his whole fortune to an unknown illegitimate son and nothing to the debt-ridden Fred, who had hoped for an inheritance that would make him rich enough to marry.

In later chapters of *Middlemarch,* Dorothea gradually learns to find knowledge for herself, having realized that none is forthcoming from Mr. Casaubon, and she does so in the receptive spirit of a scientist seeking to make sense of her data without preconceptions. Back in England after her honeymoon, at the time when Will Ladislaw returns from Rome to England and visits her, "She was no longer struggling against the perception of facts, but adjusting herself to their clearest perception." Near the end of the book, after a dark night of the soul when she perceives the facts of her own emotions, she gains enough self-knowledge to recognize and declare her love for Will Ladislaw just as he is about to leave her forever. And in her last words in the climactic scene where she and Will declare their love, she is still talking about knowledge, this time the domestic knowledge that the wife of a poor man will need: "I will learn what everything costs." Starting with vague fantasies of being enlightened by a superior husband, she ends with a resolution to learn for herself the practical knowledge required in the day-to-day life of a marriage of equals.

Dorothea Brooke and Will Ladislaw have a modern psychology and modern problems, but they live in the same world with characters who are just as young as they are while having nothing at all modern about them. Mary Garth and Fred Vincy seem to have been written for a different novel from *Middlemarch*, perhaps a rustic novel of the eighteenth century; in finding their way to marriage they face a different problem from that faced by Dorothea and Ladislaw, and they find a different solution. This happens because their personalities are constructed according to a coarser and older model than the sophisticated modern one that George Eliot used in creating her major characters. Dorothea and Ladislaw suffer under the curse of modernity; having been expelled from the secure gardens of the past, they must labor to discover whom they love and must labor to become whom they are going to be. Mary and Fred face no such effort. They need not find out who they are or whom they love because they have known these things from the start. As children they used an umbrella ring to engage themselves to marry.

The reason Mary persists in refusing Fred is that he will not commit himself to being the person he already is. When his hopes for inherited wealth are destroyed, he threatens to become a clergyman, but Mary knows as well as Fred does that a clergyman is exactly what he ought not to be, and she refuses to marry someone who insists on being untrue to himself. Mary has another suitor, the Reverend Camden Farebrother, a worthy man whom she and everyone else likes and admires, but she refuses him even when Fred is in disgrace. Farebrother is a clergyman who performs his work responsibly, but he does so without passion or vocation, and he is self-aware enough to know that he should never have been a clergyman at all. Although Mary never says so, she refuses him because he has failed the same test that she fears Fred too will fail—the test in which you decide, or fail to decide, to become the person you know you ought to be. Fred finally passes the test by rejecting a future as a clergyman and working instead for Mary's father, partly to pay the debt he owes him, partly in order to become someone he has always (as Mary has always known) had the potential to become. By almost every other measure, Farebrother is the better man, but Fred, for all his fecklessness, has more integrity.

Fred and Mary can be measured by their integrity, that is, by their truth to their essential selves. Although they are variously more true or less true to themselves at different times, their essential selves remain the same; and because they know who their essential selves are, they do not suffer the agonies of unknowing that afflict Dorothea. They can solve their difficulties by accepting what they already know. No such solution is possible for essentially dynamic, modern characters like Dorothea who must seek for knowledge on a distant horizon that recedes as they approach.

Too Early or Too Late

To be one of the modern characters in *Middlemarch* is to be the last to learn the things that matter most, and to experience knowledge as a punishment for one's ignorant egoism. As a rule, in this book, the knowledge required to make a happy marriage arrives only after someone has made an unhappy marriage. Dorothea's experience conforms to the rule, but she alone is fortunate enough to have a second chance in which to use her hard-won knowledge.

Nicholas Bulstrode, the hypocritical evangelical who wants spiritual and financial dominion over all of Middlemarch, walks confidently through the streets of the town without sensing that everyone around him knows the guilty secret that he is responsible for the death of the drunken blackmailer Raffles and that he had cheated Will Ladislaw's mother of the wealth that she would otherwise have inherited. Lydgate is the last to know that he is suspected of complicity because he has accepted money from Bulstrode. When he too falls under suspicion—and while he remains unaware of it—his wife Rosamond cannot imagine why everyone refuses her invitations to a dinner. Lydgate does not know about Rosamond's begging letter to his rich uncle, does not know that she has sent out invitations, does not know that everyone refuses them because he is suspected of abetting Bulstrode's crimes, and does not know that Rosamond has begun to fantasize a flirtation with Will Ladislaw. Even when she sobs in Lydgate's arms after Will Ladislaw angrily rejects her—her shock at Ladislaw's rebuff is another instance of knowledge arriving too late—Lydgate does not know why she weeps.

Marriage in *Middlemarch* is a condition in which one partner lives in ignorance of the other partner's most intense thoughts and crucial acts, and knowledge always comes too late to be of use. Dorothea learns the depth of Mr. Casaubon's hateful resentment toward Will Ladislaw only when she learns the contents of his last will and testament. Mr. Casaubon never learns that Will's presence in Mr. Brooke's house nearby was not suggested by Dorothea, as he imagines in his brooding jealousy, but was Mr. Brooke's idea from the start. Lydgate and Rosamond learn each other's thoughts only after they wreck each other's hopes. Even in the contented marriage of the old-style static characters Caleb and Susan Garth (Mary Garth's parents), the wife learns too late that her husband's generosity with his signature has forfeited her savings and her son's chance of an education.

All these marital obscurities and secrecies result from a condition that in the world of *Middlemarch* is as general and universal as a law of physics or chemistry: knowledge is both indispensable and hard to come by. This condition governs all life in the book, not only married life. Both Mr. Casaubon, the backward-looking scholar, and Lydgate, the forward-looking physician, are seekers after intellectual knowledge who fail to find it, just as they and everyone else fail to find emotional knowledge in and outside marriage. The stories of Mr. Casaubon and Lydgate are the book's most vivid dramatizations of the ways in which emotions and ideas are inextricable.

The Key to All Mythologies is the book that Mr. Casaubon has spent a lifetime preparing himself to write. This book, he hopes, will demonstrate that all the mythological systems of the world are "corruptions of a tradition originally revealed"—that is, a tradition made manifest by the divine revelation given to Israel by the biblical God. Mr. Casaubon is a minister of the Church of England, but his religion takes the form of scholarship, not of faith, hope, and charity, and the goal of his scholarship is to confirm the authority of the Christian church, not to teach any moral or ethical truths. He does nothing for the parishioners who are nominally in his care; a curate is paid to perform all his clerical duties for him, except to preach the morning sermon, which remains Mr. Casaubon's responsibility, although he never actually performs it in the novel. "Mr. Casaubon did not preach that morning," the narrator reports during the one scene where Mr. Casaubon appears in church. His character as a husband may be predicted from his character as a clergyman.

In his researches Mr. Casaubon starts with the assumption that the words and acts of God as recorded in the Bible are both literally true and also "types," that is, they embody stories and characters that are universally relevant and true, such as the serpent, the murdering brother, the flood, the wanderings in the desert, and so on. The peoples who were scattered into different languages and different regions by the catastrophe at Babel took with them their distorted misrememberings of the original revelation in the form of stories that became ever more distorted with each retelling. Mr. Casaubon believes that traces of the original revelation remain among the myths, allowing an assiduous scholar like himself to identify the "correspondences" between the original truth and the distorted form of the myth into which the truth degenerated. George Eliot paraphrases Mr. Casaubon's assumption about the value of his work: "Having once mastered the true position and taken a firm footing there, the vast field of mythical constructions became intelligible, nay, luminous with the reflected light of correspondences."* Mr. Casaubon unsurprisingly perceives Dorothea as a character type—the devoted wife and amanuensis—rather than as a person with needs and intentions of her own.

Casaubon's historical method would have seemed valid enough in 1774, when Jacob Bryant published *A New System, or An Analysis of Ancient Mythology: Wherein an Attempt is made to divest Tradition of Fable.* George Eliot wrote in one of her early essays about "the orthodox prepossessions of writers such as Bryant, who saw in the Greek legends simply misrepresentations of the authentic history given in the book of Genesis." In the eighteenth-century intellectual world, at least among those who had what George Eliot called "orthodox prepossessions," a historical theory that traced the ancestry of all the world's cultures back to the ancient Near East could still make sense. However, by the early 1830s, German historical studies had shown that these and other cultures had arisen independently all over the world, and the radical implication of those studies was that the biblical story was neither the central nor the original story of the human species, and that, because no culture could claim to be the primary culture, none had an ancient or inherent right to claim authority over any other. All cultures were potentially equal.

---

* In nineteenth-century fiction, a dangling participle at the start of a sentence reporting a character's thoughts would not have been a grammatical error; it was used to represent the way in which you can think about a subject without quite connecting it to yourself.

As a scholar and as a husband, Mr. Casaubon is not prepared for new ideas about equality or for a wider perspective on the world than the one he already knows. His scholarship is being thrown away (as Will Ladislaw explains to Dorothea) "for want of knowing what is done by the rest of the world. If Mr. Casaubon read German he would save himself a great deal of trouble." George Eliot immediately exposes Ladislaw's motives in one-upping Dorothea's husband behind his back—"Young Mr. Ladislaw was not at all deep himself in German writers, but very little achievement is required in order to pity another man's shortcomings"—yet Ladislaw is right in what he says even if he has not quite earned the right to say it. Mr. Casaubon, in scholarship as in marriage, is fatally, irrevocably too late. He has always been too late, not simply because he has been bypassed by history, but because he fearfully and egoistically refuses to emerge from the past. In a book in which only modernity offers hope, however limited that hope might be, Mr. Casaubon is the antimodern man.

The Germans, Ladislaw explains, "have taken the lead in historical inquiries." Marian Evans herself, before she adopted her pseudonym, had done more than anyone else in England to follow the Germans' lead. After she abandoned the enthusiastic evangelical Christianity of her adolescence, she took a passionate interest in the new historical thought that her circle of friends in Coventry had partly learned from Germany and partly devised by themselves, and began studying the Bible as a historical document instead of as a vehicle of revealed truth. Her first book, in 1846, was a translation that she was invited to make of David Friedrich Strauss's *The Life of Jesus, Critically Examined,* a groundbreaking German study of the Gospels that claimed to winnow historical fact from mythical accretions, and demonstrated that the Christian tradition, far from having been a revealed truth, as Mr. Casaubon believes, was itself a mythical one. Strauss's critical, historical approach to religion corresponded with Marian Evans's own, though she found his book unsympathetic and cold.

A few years later, in 1854, she translated another German work that rebelled against traditional religious dogma, Ludwig Feuerbach's *The Essence of Christianity*. She found the book warm and sympathetic, and rendered Feuerbach's meditations on the transcendent power of love in an ecstatic, triumphant style. Feuerbach interpreted the Christian God—like every other god—as having no existence separate from the human imagination that created it. The difference between a pagan god and the Christian God who so loved the world that he gave his only begotten son was that the Christian God was a projection by human beings of their realization that love was the means by which they could transcend their existence, the means by which they could achieve what they called divinity. Divinity begins in the love between individual human beings, and culminates in universal love for all of humanity. What Marian Evans most appreciated in Feuerbach seems to have been his sense of the divinity of human love; what made him an important influence among European revolutionaries was his rejection of orthodox theology.

George Eliot became the medium through which radical European thought, with David Friedrich Strauss and Ludwig Feuerbach at its forefront, was made accessible in English. In this role, she gave rise to a new intellectual type that was to become far more common during the next century and a half: the apostle who brings exciting theoretical teachings from France and Germany to a reluctantly empirical Britain. Her public role as the translator of Strauss and Feuerbach resembled the roles adopted a century later by the first English translators of Jean-Paul Sartre, Martin Heidegger, and Michel Foucault. Unlike her successors in this role, she had no wish to be up-to-date at all costs, and seems to have had no self-conscious sense of herself as moving in advance of intellectual fashion; the idea of an intellectual avant-garde had begun to emerge in Paris, though not yet in Coventry or London. But Marian Evans felt both an obligation and desire to immerse herself in the most turbulent new currents of historical and scientific thought.

From Euripides until now, self-consciously modern writers have focused on the ways in which human behavior is ruled by unconscious motives, biological necessities, and large impersonal forces with names like History, Culture, Technology, and Society. (Other writers whose perspective is less self-consciously modern, less burdened by a myth of a fall that occurred in recent history—rather than outside history altogether, as in the myth of the Garden of Eden—focus instead on the effects of conscious knowledge, voluntary choice, and personal acts.) In the early nineteenth century the most up-to-date and modern psychological science was phrenology, the pseudoscience that identifies your emotional and moral character by mapping the bumps on your skull, in much the same way that more recent pseudoscience traces your voluntary actions back to the unchosen, involuntary workings of selfish or altruistic genes. A university chair in phrenology was established at Glasgow in 1845, and Charlotte Brontë, like most of her contemporaries, took it for granted that phrenology was valid science; Jane Eyre is conscious of her "organ of veneration" when Helen Burns recites Virgil, and observes on Rochester's forehead "an abrupt deficiency where the suave sign of benevolence should have risen," and Rochester observes in Jane "a good deal of the organ of Adhesiveness." But for Charlotte Brontë, phrenology was merely a familiar feature of her intellectual landscape. Marian Evans took it far more seriously as a new instrument of knowledge that called for her active participation in it. At the time she was translating Strauss's *Life of Jesus*, she arranged to have a full phrenological analysis made of herself, based on a plaster cast of her cranium, and the preparations for the analysis included shaving her head.

She abandoned phrenology for more plausible kinds of science long before she wrote *Middlemarch*, but the story of Tertius Lydgate shows that while writing it she continued to think of scientific and moral knowledge as intertwined, though in more subtle ways than any phrenologist imagined. Lydgate, like Casaubon, wants to find the single origin of apparently unrelated phenomena. What, he asks himself, is the building block from which all the various organs of living things derive? He thinks about living tissues in the same way that he thinks about women, intent on finding the essential quality that defines all of them rather than focusing on their individual uniqueness. George Eliot describes his research in terms resonant with meaning: "What was the primitive tissue? In that way Lydgate put the question—not quite in the way required by the awaiting answer, but such missing of the right word befalls many seekers." Following the lead of the latest French research, Lydgate seeks to "demonstrate the homogeneous origin of all the tissues" and identify the single "primitive tissue" that grew into all others; but he is leading himself down a blind alley, because (so George Eliot seems to have believed) each organ is derived from its own special and distinct kinds of building blocks, not from a single source. This erroneous theory of the separate evolution of individual organs seemed plausible to George Eliot because German philology had already proven a parallel theory about the separate evolution of national mythologies—each of which derived from its own independent origins, not from a single source in the Bible. Having found the excitement of a liberating modernity in German historical theory, she was predisposed to find the same merit in parallel biological theories.*

---

* For many years, scholars assumed that George Eliot's point was that Lydgate wasted his time because cell biology had not yet been invented. But this attributes twentieth-century knowledge to a novelist who was writing before modern biologi-

Lydgate uses the most advanced scientific instrument, "the microscope, which research had begun to use again with new enthusiasm of reliance," but, as the novel presents him, he cannot find the answer because he is looking for the wrong thing. As Casaubon is too late, Lydgate is too early. His impetuous youthful love for a French actress—who proved to have been a murderess—and his abrupt courtship of Rosamond are both instances in his erotic life of the central error of his intellectual life. He cannot find the happiness he seeks because he is looking for something that can never be found, not a real woman but an embodiment of a generalized feminine ideal. The French actress and Rosamond both seem to embody that ideal, so he rushes too quickly to embrace them. The road to success can be traveled only in the bright light of noontime, not, as Lydgate does, in the illusory shadows of dawn, nor, as Mr. Casaubon does, in the hopeless shadows of dusk.

One unsettling feature of George Eliot's learned and alert portrayal of intellectual and scientific history—which no other English novelist could even have attempted—is that she was harmlessly misled by her own intellectual prejudices in almost the same way that the seekers whom she pities in *Middlemarch* are fatally misled by theirs. The intellectual organizing principles that she believed had been discarded and discredited in her era reemerged among the dominant and organizing principles of another. Mr. Casaubon is led down a blind alley by the false organizing principle of a single ultimate source for all mythologies, but a similar principle returned in twentieth-century structuralist theories that (rightly

---

cal principles had been firmly established. Gillian Beer, in *Darwin's Plots* (1983; second edition, 2000), points out that G. H. Lewes, rejecting Darwin's idea of a single origin of life, postulated instead a variety of "diversified points," each of which grew into a specific kind of organism. The same idea, as applied to the origins of bodily organs, seems to be the one that Lydgate does not know enough to look for.

or wrongly) perceive a single universal grammar behind all varieties of language and culture. Even at the time when George Eliot was writing, Lydgate's search for a primitive tissue would already have justified itself in the cell biology of Matthias Schleiden, who recognized the "elementary particles of organisms" as cells, and in the evolutionary theory of Charles Darwin that posited a single origin for all forms of life.

In her deepest feelings about her work and ideas George Eliot seems to have had more in common with Casaubon, whom she largely despised, than with Lydgate, whom she largely admired. Like Casaubon, but with far more intellectual integrity, she both doubted and believed her own convictions. Throughout *Middlemarch* she seems tempted to believe that moral progress will inevitably result from advances in historical and scientific knowledge—and she portrays her own temptation through Dorothea's parallel wish to believe that her own moral progress will inevitably result from her access to masculine knowledge. As Dorothea starts from the false assumption that rational or factual knowledge brings with it moral knowledge, so the narrative voice of *Middlemarch*—which is not the same as the voice of George Eliot herself—looks forward to a world that will acquire enough rational or factual knowledge to become moral. The narrator never quite says that Dorothea breaks free from her temptation, but the story shows that she does.

Obscure Signs and Opaque Persons

George Eliot believed that there are answers to major intellectual and emotional questions, but that those answers remain elusive because we insist on asking the questions in the wrong way. All the characters in *Middlemarch* see all the others through the flattering and distorting lenses of subjectivity. Lydgate imagines that Rosamond offers the decorative submissiveness he thinks suitable to a wife. Dorothea imagines that Mr. Casaubon fulfills her wish for a great soul whom she can emulate. "For surely all must admit that a man may be puffed and belauded, envied, ridiculed, counted upon as a tool and fallen in love with, or at least selected as a future husband, and yet remain virtually unknown—known merely as a cluster of signs for his neighbours' false suppositions." Dorothea herself, who wants more than anything else to learn to see things clearly, is perhaps the first fictional heroine who is literally myopic. "I am rather short-sighted," she says of herself in an early chapter. Everyone in the book is morally shortsighted, but Dorothea is rewarded in the end partly because she alone learns to be fully conscious of her shortsightedness.

Middlemarch never fully escapes from a subdued but insistent tone of sadness, the consequence of its sometimes implicit, sometimes explicit sense that everyone is to some degree what the narrator calls a mere cluster of signs—an incoherent set of attributes with no underlying unity or underlying substance. (A century after George Eliot's death, an almost identical sense of disconnected signs and disjointed meanings was commonly described as the defining principle of a radically new postmodern condition; as with so many other ideas that seemed new to the twentieth and twenty-first centuries, the nineteenth knew all about it.) But in George Eliot's world, even if we could find the knowledge that we would need to see beyond mere clusters of signs, we would find the knowledge unbearable. "If we had a keen vision and feeling of all ordinary human life, it would be like hearing the grass grow and the squirrel's heart beat, and we should die of that roar which lies on the other side of silence. As it is, the quickest of us walk about well wadded with stupidity."

"What is *your* religion?" Dorothea asks Will Ladislaw. "I mean—not what you know about religion, but the belief that helps you most?" Ladislaw answers: "To love what is good and beautiful when I see it." Will's answer has the undertone of a love speech (Dorothea's husband is still alive), but George Eliot chooses his words with philosophic care: Will is someone who must *see* what is good and beautiful before he is willing to love it. He does not ask to nurture something imperfect that has as much need for him as he has for it. His wish for something inherently worthy to be loved is another version of Dorothea's and George Eliot's belief that rational or factual knowledge is the lamp that guides moral action.

The trouble with this belief is not, as offended critics complained a hundred years ago, that it lacks religion (which is what Dorothea asked Will about), but that it lacks charity, mutuality, and forgiveness. In the world of *Middlemarch*, the universe must do the heavy labor of providing something good and beautiful so that mortals can love it. Love, as George Eliot understands it in most of the book, is not a relation of mutual need, a relation that can exist only in a world of time and change where those who share in the relationship are constantly changed by it, but a relation in which whatever is good and beautiful is *already* good and beautiful, so no one risks anything by loving it. Almost everywhere in the world of *Middlemarch*, love requires from you neither faith nor hope nor charity, because the object of your love has already manifested itself as worthy, and needs nothing that your love might offer, including forgiveness. Your love does not—as it does in real life— give its object goodness and beauty that you could not perceive if you did not love it, and does not transform it from an autonomous object into a subject with whom you can have a mutual relation.

The sadness in *Middlemarch* is deepened by the book's portrayal of a world in which the goal of knowledge—whether in mythology, science, or marriage—seems to be even less accessible at the end of your journey than it is at the start. A recurring motif in *Middlemarch* is nostalgia for a lost time when one could begin a great intellectual or moral enterprise and do so full of hope. The narrator says of the period when Lydgate begins his researches:

> Perhaps that was a more cheerful time for observers and theorizers than the present; we are apt to think it the finest era of the world when America was beginning to be discovered, when a bold sailor, even if he were wrecked, might alight on a new kingdom; and about 1829 the dark territories of Pathology were a fine America for a spirited young adventurer.

In the brief "Finale" to *Middlemarch*, Will Ladislaw's London career begins in the same mood, with the same presentiment of darker times to come: "Will became an ardent public man, working well in those times when reforms were begun with a young hopefulness of immediate good which has been much checked in our days . . ." The word "young" points to the world of young love as much as it does to the world of young politics.

In *Middlemarch* change is the same as loss, just as change is the same as loss in every frame of mind or system of thought that is based on the idea of a goodness and perfection that has no need for the human beings who love it when they see it. George Eliot continually weaves together the intellectual and emotional realms of her book; the disappointments inevitable in the intellectual realm are equally inevitable in the emotional one. Part of the greatness of *Middlemarch* is its simultaneous portrayal of the marriage of Dorothea and Will Ladislaw as both a happy ending and a sad one.

The Better and the Worse

George Eliot, like Charlotte Brontë, believed that happy marriages require equality between husband and wife, but the only equal marriages that she portrays—rather than merely reporting in a few brief sentences in an epilogue—are those of staid people such as Caleb and Susan Garth or Sir James and Celia who have no towering ambition or passion for anything outside their marriage. All the marriages in which either the husband or wife is passionate and intelligent are unequal and therefore unhappy. George Eliot understood exactly what a happy marriage requires in the real world, and her narrator spells it out while moralizing over Rosamond's idle fantasies that she could have been happy had she married Ladislaw instead of Lydgate: "No notion could have been falser than this, for Rosamond's discontent in her marriage was due to the conditions of marriage itself, to its demand for self-suppression and tolerance, and not to the nature of her husband." The conditions of marriage are portrayed throughout the novel, but are portrayed only as inducing the misery of defeat.*

The marriages of Dorothea to Mr. Casaubon and of Lydgate to Rosamond are both unequal, not so much in terms of power (which was the kind of inequality that interested Charlotte Brontë) as in terms of inherent moral stature. Dorothea and Lydgate are the moral superiors of Casaubon and Rosamond, and the emotional task that George Eliot sets for these superior figures is the task of learning charity toward those who are inferior to them. Dorothea, through her heroic charity, overcomes her resentment and anger at Mr. Casaubon, and chooses to consent to his demand that she commit herself to following his wishes after his death—even though he will not tell her what those wishes are. She is spared from carrying out her promise only because Mr. Casaubon

---

* Divorce was still legally almost impossible at the time of the novel's action, and only slightly less impossible at the time the novel was written. Dorothea and Lydgate are as trapped in their unhappy marriages as Mr. Rochester was in *Jane Eyre*.

dies moments before she comes to him to offer it. Lydgate learns to accept and shelter Rosamond after she fails in her social ambition and he realizes at last that she is driven by ambition, not love. Similarly, Harriet Bulstrode sits quietly and loyally by her husband's side after he has been exposed as morally the murderer of Raffles. When Dorothea visits Rosamond after the crisis at the end of the book, Rosamond feels "something like bashful timidity before a superior."

All three of these morally superior figures give sympathy, compassion, and comfort to a wife or husband from whom they have lost all hope of receiving any such feeling in return. Each offers pity without love—the kind of pity that Mr. Rochester furiously rejected in *Jane Eyre* as a gift from a superior to an inferior. Dorothea is prompted to yield to Mr. Casaubon because she is compelled, not by law, but only by "her husband's nature and her own compassion, only the ideal and not the real yoke of marriage"—that is, by an abstract idea of love, not by love for anyone in particular. As for Lydgate's commitment to Rosamond, the narrator explains:

> Lydgate had accepted his narrowed lot with sad resignation. He had chosen this fragile creature, and had taken the burthen of her life upon his arms. He must walk as he could, carrying that burthen pitifully.

And Harriet Bulstrode is terrifyingly superior in the eyes of her disgraced husband: "The duteous merciful consistency of his wife had delivered him from one dread, but it could not hinder her presence from being still a tribunal before which he shrank from confession and desired advocacy."

What is striking about all these resolutions is that they are morally one-sided. Each is based on the fantasy that only the other person needs forgiveness, not you. The superior parties effortlessly acknowledge their minor flaws—too minor to require forgiveness—and the inferior parties painfully acknowledge or endure their major ones. This is emotionally satisfying—all readers can identify to some degree with one or the other of the superior figures—but psychologically false. In real life, reconciliations like these are temporary and incomplete; after the novelist brings down the curtain at the end of the scene, the time soon arrives when the inferior party, with some real justification on his side, refuses to accept an inferior status, and the cycle of mutual misunderstanding and frustration resumes. (George Eliot alludes to this later time in her epilogue, where she reports that Rosamond regained enough complacency to think of her second marriage to a rich old physician as "a reward." After offering a comforting fantasy in one of her chapters, George Eliot invariably corrects it in a later one.)

Some persons are more beautiful, more intelligent, more loving, more charitable than others, but only those who have murdered their conscience can seriously believe they are members of a *category* of human being that is, permanently and by nature, inherently superior to persons in other categories, that they themselves never lapse into moral blindness or injustice, that their angers are always righteous. George Eliot achieves her moral authority by anatomizing psychological errors and complexities that afflict everyone—but she subverts her own authority by treating her heroes and heroines as members of a special category that is exempt from conditions that, in her novel, are otherwise universal. Her happily married couples can be exempt only because she does not pretend to portray these couples with any depth. In contrast, she purports to treat her not-yet-married heroes and heroines with the most exacting scrutiny, but she does not give Dorothea any psychological motive for marrying Mr. Casaubon other than the mere facts of Dorothea's inherent superiority over her other potential suitors, combined with her inadequate surroundings and education. (George

Eliot knew that she herself had tended to seek what she called "father-confessors," but having grown out of her temptation, she was content to lampoon it rather than explore her motives for having yielded to it.) Dorothea belongs to a different moral species from everyone around her, including her sister Celia: "Here and there a cygnet is reared uneasily among the ducklings in the brown pond, and never finds the living stream in fellowship with its own oary-footed kind."

Middlemarch is capacious enough to express a sense that human beings divide into inherently superior and inferior people and the entirely different sense that everyone is subject to the same temptations. The doctrine of inherently unequal moral classes is an ancient one; it has a long history of being invoked as a justification for slavery; and it has always been endorsed by cultures and religions that regard wealth and success as signs of God's special favor. It was articulated most memorably in Plato's division, in the *Republic,* of human beings into guardians, auxiliaries, and producers. Many centuries of ethical thought were required before an opposing doctrine took shape in biblical and classical thought, the doctrine that held that the best and the worst share common impulses and desires, that the very qualities that distinguish the best can have the paradoxical effect of tempting them to act like the worst. This latter way of thinking is expressed by Charlotte Brontë in Helen Burns's "doctrine of the equality of disembodied souls," and by Virginia Woolf in the moral complexities of *Mrs. Dalloway* and *Between the Acts.*

It is easier, but less illuminating, to write a novel of education based on the first and more self-flattering of these opposing doctrines (the doctrine of inherently unequal moral classes) than on the second and more unsettling one (the doctrine of the equality of souls). The first doctrine grants the hero an inherent superiority that justifies the attention paid to his development through writing a novel about it. Even Charlotte Brontë was unable to solve the problem of writing a novel of education in which the heroine is not inherently superior to everyone else; despite the novel's doctrine of equality, Jane Eyre is the only major character in her story who does no wrong. (Her plainness and poverty are flaws only in the eyes of those whose flaws are inward, not outward like hers.) George Eliot faced the same problem, and for all her sophistication and genius, found it equally difficult to solve. Parts of *Middlemarch* suggest with evenhanded clarity that Dorothea makes the same kinds of egoistic errors that everyone else makes, but other parts of the book seem to be written as a warning against miscegenation between superior and inferior beings.

The Avenging Angel

With all her superiority, Dorothea is incapable of finding her own way to marriage, but must be rescued from loneliness by the only person in the world of *Middlemarch* who is superior to herself. Will Ladislaw starts out with the same egoistic blindness that afflicts everyone else, but he soon teaches himself to shed his egoism and think only of Dorothea—while at the same time he attains the freedom, rightness, and power that the book repeatedly insists is impossible for human beings because of their egoism and blindness. Ladislaw is beloved both by the small urchins who follow him about and by the ancient but almost equally small Miss Noble, who is so devoted to him that she announces her willingness to use his shoes as a pillow. In the closing chapters, Will is transfigured into a miraculous liberator who is also a violent avenging force, who punishes the malefactors Bulstrode and Rosamond by rejecting an offer of money from the one and of affection from the other, and with the power to redeem Dorothea by gracing her with his love.

Alone among the chief actors in the book, Will Ladislaw is free to escape from—and return to—the otherwise closed world of Middlemarch. Like Heathcliff, he transforms himself offstage, and he rescues Dorothea at last by taking her from the constraint and stagnation of provincial Middlemarch to the prospects and energies of metropolitan London. Only one other character, a minor one, shares Will's freedom of movement: the ambiguous criminal figure of the blackmailer Raffles, who comes and goes unpredictably, and who is an instrument by which Bulstrode is punished, more or less as Will is an instrument by which both Bulstrode and Rosamond are punished. Raffles dies in well-deserved drunken misery while Ladislaw is rewarded with marriage to moderate wealth and great beauty, but both Will and Raffles are subject to a different set of novelistic rules and conventions from those that govern everyone else in the book. They seem to have strayed from the worlds of Balzac or Dickens where spectacular interventions occur in the normal order of things. And George Eliot brings them into her otherwise realistic story because her plot requires precisely that kind of intervention in order to be resolved.

Charlotte Brontë's heroines have a habit of referring to their lovers—who may also be their employer or teacher—as "my master," but those heroines simultaneously long for equality. The equality they finally achieve is one of moral stature as well as of mere power. Mr. Rochester's moral heroism in his attempt to rescue Bertha from the fire redeems all his earlier errors and makes him Jane's equal in virtue while his wound reduces him to her equal in strength. George Eliot, in contrast, never abandons her fantasy of Will Ladislaw's inherent moral superiority and superhuman power. Near the end of the book, when Dorothea discovers Ladislaw and Rosamond talking together in apparent intimacy, she walks out again coldly, convinced that Will has been speaking words of adulterous love—when in fact he has been telling Rosamond in passionate terms that he loves only Dorothea. Rosamond commits no moral fault in this scene, however many faults she had committed earlier, but Will is understandably furious at finding himself so drastically misjudged because of her presence. When Rosamond flatters herself that she can comfort Will's distress with a touch of her fingers, his reply is the first of this episode's many images of physical violence: "'Don't touch me!' he said, with an utterance like the cut of a lash." When she responds with sarcasm, telling him that he can easily go after Dorothea "and explain your preference," he finds a "vent for his rage" in the feelings and vocabulary of Heathcliff:

"Explain! Tell a man to explain how he dropped into hell! Explain my preference! I never had a *preference* for her, any more than I have a preference for breathing. No other woman exists by the side of her. I would rather touch her hand if it were dead, than I would touch any other woman's living."

And in the next paragraph, although Will says nothing, he is as indifferent and cruel as Heathcliff at his worst:

Rosamond, while these poisoned weapons were being hurled at her, was almost losing the sense of her identity, and seemed to be waking into some new terrible existence. She had no sense of chill resolute repulsion, of reticent self-justification such as she had known under Lydgate's most stormy displeasure; all her sensibility was turned into a bewildering novelty of pain; she felt a new terrified recoil under a lash never experienced before. What another nature felt in opposition to her own was being burnt and bitten into her consciousness. When Will had ceased to speak she had become an image of sickened misery: her lips were pale, and her eyes had a tearless dismay in them. If it had been Tertius who stood opposite to her, that look of misery would have been a pang to him, and he would have sunk by her side to comfort her, with that strong-armed comfort which she had often held very cheap.

Let it be forgiven to Will that he had no such movement of pity . . .

Startling as it seems to find quasi-pornographic sadism in a book with the dignity and authority of *Middlemarch*, that is exactly what this paragraph is. (D. H. Lawrence's mistaken reading of Rochester's wounding in *Jane Eyre* as a pornographic punishment for sexual desire would have been accurate had he written it instead about this passage in *Middlemarch*.) The punishing lash, the burning and biting, the sickened misery of the beautiful victim, the unrepentant tormentor are all standard features of a book like *Histoire d'O*—as is Rosamond's submissive return to the husband whom she had "mastered" until she herself is transformed by humiliation, with her "vagrant fancy . . . terribly scourged." Dorothea unintentionally participates in these exchanges of mastery and punishment when she speaks to Rosamond the following day and produces this response: "Rosamond, with an overmastering pang, as if a wound within her had been probed, burst into hysterical crying . . ."

In *Jane Eyre* the exchange of torments and captivities between Rochester and Jane is something very different: a serious game of role-playing in which two lovers give stylized expression to the dangerous temptations of inequality, not a means by which the lovers hope to resolve those temptations or find their way out of them. The game is not an end in itself, and they lose interest in it when they resolve, through other means than role-playing, the inequalities that gave rise to it. In *Middlemarch* Will's torment of Rosamond is itself the means by which a crisis is resolved, and it concludes an important line in the plot. George Eliot seems unaware of the sadness behind her fantasy of a vagrant fancy terribly scourged, or of the futility of any wish to resolve the tensions of a relationship merely by acting them out or turning them into a performance that need never end. The erotic role-playing of *Jane Eyre* is emotionally realistic in that the two lovers are able to reverse the roles of dominant and submissive, in that both are anxious about their unresolved relation with each other, and in that their anxiety can finally be resolved because each would prefer to abandon role-playing altogether. Jane and Rochester, who are never indifferent to each other, can become adults, wounded but transformed by change. Will and Rosamond have no such future.

In the world of *Middlemarch* no emotional resolution can occur because no one is willing to endure the difficulties of a relationship built on shared, mutual change. In the episode when Will torments Rosamond, the novel makes it explicit that there is nothing mutual about their relationship: he is indifferent to her while she is transfixed by the thought of him. When Dorothea and Will first tell each other about their love for the good and the beautiful, George Eliot describes them as "looking at each other like two fond children"—not like adults who are aware of the pains and possibilities of growth and change. More than forty chapters later, in the climactic episode when they finally confess their love for each other, they are childlike again, first when they stand "with their hands clasped, like two children, looking out on the storm," later when Dorothea tells Will she can live without much of her fortune, and speaks to him "in a sobbing childlike way." For Will and Dorothea, as for Heathcliff and Catherine, adulthood is a barrier to intimacy, not the means of achieving it.

Revealed by Lightning

Also like Heathcliff and Catherine, Will Ladislaw enjoys a special relation with nature. George Eliot's philosophical, rational narrator is so intent on denying the existence of any sympathetic nature of the kind that surrounds the lovers in *Wuthering Heights* that the book is never explicit about the connection between nature and Will Ladislaw. But George Eliot finds ways to slip it in among her metaphors whenever Ladislaw appears on the scene. Will embodies the energies of nature itself: "he looked like an incarnation of the spring whose spirit filled the air." His unconscious acts are the acts of unconscious nature; at one point, he shakes his head "somewhat after the manner of a spirited horse." Dorothea can participate in nature as he does only when she and Will are together; in one of their early meetings, "Each looked at the other as if they had been two flowers which had opened then and there." (A double standard seems to apply here: when Will resembles a flower he is admirable, but when Rosamond looks like a flower, as she does repeatedly, she is contemptible.) On his first appearance in the book, Ladislaw is gently mocked by the narrator for believing that genius "may confidently await those messages from the universe which summon it to its peculiar [that is, particular, individual] work, only placing itself in an attitude of receptivity to all divine chances." But it is precisely Ladislaw's receptivity—in terms of human beings, not the whole universe—that is later a sign of his moral excellence, and the means by which he achieves love and success. As Dorothea perceives, "he was a creature who entered into everyone's feelings, and could take the pressure of their thought instead of urging his own with iron resistance."

Will Ladislaw is an exception to the general condition in *Middlemarch* that leaves everyone else blocked from nature. The lightning that strikes when Jane Eyre accepts the already-married Mr. Rochester refrains from striking when Dorothea accepts Mr. Casaubon, and when Dorothea encounters Will at Mr. Casaubon's house after her return from her honeymoon journey to Rome, the weather is merely rainy. But at the last possible moment when nature might be able to do any good, it makes the same spectacular intervention that it made again and again in the imagination of the Brontë sisters. As Will and Dorothea are about to part from each other, unable to speak their love, "there came a vivid flash of lightning which lit each of them up for the other"—and Will seizes Dorothea's hand "with a spasmodic movement." "Spasmodic," in this medically expert novel, signifies an involuntary movement, the work of nature and instinct, with no element of conscious choice.* The nature-divinities of Mary Shelley and the Brontë sisters had not entirely absconded.

In the real world, of course, everyone is inured to the knowledge that nature, despite all your wishes about it, is indifferent. Even the fanatics who attribute an earthquake or flood to God's anger against people they dislike do not suppose that nature itself is angry. Everyone can see that sea, land, and sky alike ignore human suffering and human happiness. Everyone knows that myths and stories in which nature takes an interest in human lives are comforting fantasies. But those fantasies are not entirely false. When you look at the sea, the land, and the sky and see nothing but nature's indifference, it may be because you are looking in the wrong place. The sea, the land, and the sky are indeed indifferent,

---

* George Eliot is not the only self-consciously modern writer who, at the end of a novel, slips in the idea of *interested* nature after devoting hundreds of pages to the task of denying that nature takes an interest in anything. E. M. Forster, having portrayed the vast indifference of nature in almost every chapter of *A Passage to India*, changed his mind somewhat when writing the final paragraph. Fielding asks Aziz why they cannot be friends: "It's what I want. It's what you want." The narrator continues: "But the horses didn't want it . . . the earth didn't want it . . . the temples, the tank, the jail, the palace, the birds, the carrion, the Guest house . . . didn't want it . . . they said in their hundred voices, 'No, not yet,' and the sky said, 'No, not there.' " This begins as an emphatic statement of nature's disinterestedness, and ends in metaphors and images that show nature actively opposing a friendship here and now while wanting it to happen at another time in some other place.

but they exist on a drastically different scale from the world in which human beings live their lives. Human beings live on the much smaller scale of their own bodies, a scale measured in inches, not miles, and on that scale, nature takes the deepest possible interest in their thoughts and emotions. It punishes anger and fear with headaches and indigestion; it rewards love and trust with a steady heartbeat and deep sleep. The lightning bolt in *Middlemarch* recalls Will and Dorothea to their bodily selves; it reminds them of the vulnerability and hunger, the need for warmth and contact that is always present in sexual love—and it also reminds them of the "merely canine affection" that the narrator had dismissed at the start of the book. The mythical sympathetic nature of *Jane Eyre*, and of the final chapters of *Middlemarch*, is finally closer to the truth than the narrator's rational, disillusioned denial of it. George Eliot was at her most generous to Ladislaw and Dorothea when she restored them to a full relation with nature, and it is a sign of her greatness that she was most wise when she was most generous.

From Marriage to Adulthood

Dorothea becomes childlike as the lover of Will Ladislaw, but she had earlier become an adult as the wife of Mr. Casaubon. Her words to Rosamond, when she senses that Rosamond is being tempted into adulterous love for Will Ladislaw, veer toward mere moralizing, but she has earned the right to her words:

> "Marriage is so unlike everything else [Dorothea says]. There is something even awful [that is, awesome] in the nearness it brings. Even if we loved some one else better than—those we were married to, it would be no use"—poor Dorothea, in her palpitating anxiety, could only seize her language brokenly—"I mean, mar-

riage drinks up all our power of giving or getting any blessedness in that sort of love. I know it may be very dear—but it murders our marriage—and then the marriage stays with us like a murder—and everything else is gone. And then our husband—if he loved and trusted us, and we have not helped him, but made a curse in his life . . ."*

The depths of this simple-sounding speech, and the process by which Dorothea makes herself able to say it, is one of George Eliot's imaginative triumphs. After the pain of seeing Will Ladislaw and Rosamond together in what looks like intimacy, Dorothea suffers a night of agony when she mourns over her lost love and her lost belief that Ladislaw was worthy of her love. Then, with the coming of dawn, in one of the most splendid scenes in nineteenth-century fiction, Dorothea forces herself to turn away from her own pain to the sufferings of Lydgate, Rosamond, and Ladislaw himself. Pulling back the curtains, she looks through the window:

> On the road there was a man with a bundle on his back and a woman carrying her baby; in the field she could see figures moving—perhaps the shepherd with his dog. Far off in the bending sky was the pearly light; and she felt the largeness of the world and the manifold wakings of men to labour and endurance. She was a part of that involuntary, palpitating life, and could neither look out on it from her luxurious shelter as a mere spectator, nor hide her eyes in selfish complaining.

* Seen from the perspective of another century with other mores, Dorothea's metaphor of adultery as murder illuminates the one modern instance in which adultery is entirely justified: when a marriage is already ruined but the two partners cannot manage to bring it to an end, one partner's adultery can serve as a mercy killing that puts the marriage out of its misery and sets both partners free.

Her tentative perception of "perhaps the shepherd with his dog" is an almost unnoticeable allusion to her physical nearsightedness, which is no longer a symbol of moral nearsightedness. Dorothea has discovered, through personal suffering and moral intelligence, her continuity with involuntary, palpitating nature—a continuity that had been granted effortlessly to Will Ladislaw from the start. What is left unmentioned is that this discovery is not the product of knowledge but of mere error: Dorothea is completely wrong about the episode between Ladislaw and Rosamond that prompted her to her moral revelation. The most profound discovery in the book is an inward discovery about Dorothea's own commitments, the kind of discovery that is no less valid because it was prompted by a mistake about the outer world.

The episode of Dorothea's night and morning is an elaborate restatement of the themes that George Eliot found in the religious writings of Ludwig Feuerbach. Dorothea is brought back to her responsibilities by a feeling for life and humanity in general, not for any one person. She goes to Rosamond determined to help save her from temptation. But the speech Dorothea makes to her is as much about herself as it is about Rosamond. Dorothea had felt a not entirely innocent pleasure in Will Ladislaw's company, when she too was someone else's wife. She had refused her husband's unjust demands, but her refusal had coincided with his decline, and when she speaks to Rosamond of adulterous love as something that "murders our marriage," she is pointing to the way in which her own husband seems to have been killed partly by the strains of his marriage to her. Casaubon had never "loved and trusted" Dorothea except through the distorting lens of his egoism, but Dorothea has learned to be concerned more with the living than the dead, more intent on loving than on being loved. And she has quietly given up her fantasies of an exalted, epic life for the deeper satisfaction of a loving, ordinary one. At the start of the book, Dorothea was out-raged by Celia's remark that Sir James Chettam thinks she is fond of him: "It is offensive to me to say that Sir James could think I was fond of him. Besides, it is not the right word for the feeling I must have towards the man I would accept as a husband." Eighty chap-ters later, when Dorothea confirms that she has accepted Will Ladis-law as her husband, Celia asks, "Is he very fond of you, Dodo?" and Dorothea answers, "I hope so. I am very fond of him."

A few lines later, she quietly affirms that the knowledge that matters most to her is the knowledge gained through sympathy—which literally means *feeling with*. When Celia asks to hear how Dorothea and Will became engaged to each other, Dorothea affec-tionately refuses: "No, dear, you would have to feel with me, else you would never know"—which is to say, you need sympathy in order to know.

The profundity of Dorothea's speech to Rosamond is that she has learned about the awesome "nearness" of all marriages through a marriage that was abysmally unhappy. Here George Eliot throws aside all the grand fantasies of rescue, isolation, and superiority that drive much of Dorothea's story, and acknowledges the quiet realities of forgiveness and need. This moment of reality is brief. George Eliot follows it, a few pages later, with the lightning bolt that unites Dorothea to Will and with the sketchy and unconvinc-ing "Finale" in which Will Ladislaw finds his way to a public career and Dorothea has an "incalculably diffusive" effect on "the grow-ing good of the world" without doing anything in particular.

The myth that George Eliot dismantles in Dorothea's speech is the same myth that she endorses elsewhere in Dorothea's story: the myth that marriage can be a means of escape from unhappiness, that a rescuer like Will Ladislaw can take you away from all this into a permanence of knowledge and love. What marriage brings, Dorothea tells Rosamond, is not escape but *nearness*, an intensity and intimacy in which husband and wife can choose to give each other either misery or happiness, and will probably choose some of both. In the burst of light that recalls Dorothea and Will to their bodies, George Eliot presents in compressed symbolic form the transformation of love into marriage, a change that she does not attempt to portray with all the realism and detail that give shape and texture to the rest of the book. But in the dark sufferings of Dorothea as she confronts her commitment to her egoistic, imperfect husband, George Eliot points tentatively toward a change that is even more profound and more unportrayable: the transfiguration of marriage into love.

5

LOVE: *Mrs. Dalloway*

Mrs. Dalloway is a book about the kind of love that everyone wants but that no grown-up person seriously expects to give or to get. Peter Walsh loves Clarissa Dalloway simply and absolutely for herself. He does not love her for such things as beauty, intelligence, power, warmth, or wit, because all these things, to the degree that she has or doesn't have them, are qualities or attributes which exist in more or less similar combinations in thousands of other people whom he doesn't care about. Peter takes no interest in sets of attributes, and when he is distracted into thinking about Clarissa's attributes, he tends to be annoyed by them. What he loves instead is the unique person he calls "Clarissa herself."

Walking through London, Peter hears church bells sounding the half hour, and thinks of the sound as if it were a person,

> like something alive that wants to confide itself, to disperse itself, to be, with a tremor of delight, at rest—like Clarissa herself, thought Peter Walsh, coming down the stairs on the stroke of the hour in white. It is Clarissa herself, he thought, with a deep emotion . . .

Everyone else sees Clarissa more or less accurately in terms of her attributes: a middle-aged society hostess, welcoming but prudish, enthusiastic but brittle, neither passionate nor capable of inspiring passion. Peter Walsh, whom Clarissa refused to marry thirty years earlier, knows all about her faults and limits, and he never imagines her to be some ideal being who is superior to what she really is. But he also loves her as she really is. In his eyes, she reshapes the world simply by being there. She has, he thinks,

> that extraordinary gift, that woman's gift, of making a world of her own wherever she happened to be. She came into a room; she stood, as he had often seen her, in a doorway with lots of people round her. But it was Clarissa one remembered. Not that she was striking; not beautiful at all; there was nothing picturesque about her; she never said anything especially clever; there she was, however; there she was.

In the final words of the book, his love is rewarded by an ecstatic vision which seizes him that same night, at Clarissa's party, when she comes into the room where he sits waiting for her. Sally Seton, Clarissa's other old friend, having grown tired of waiting for her, has stood up to say a few words to Clarissa's husband before leaving, and Peter is about to follow.

> "I will come," said Peter, but he sat on for a moment. What is this terror? what is this ecstasy? he thought to himself. What is it that fills me with extraordinary excitement?
>
> It is Clarissa, he said.
>
> For there she was.

What Peter Walsh does not know is that, a minute or two earlier, Clarissa had experienced a revelation of her own. She had found herself alone in a "little room" after learning of the suicide of the young shell-shocked veteran Septimus Warren Smith, and had felt an annoyed resentment at the indecorous intrusion of death amidst the pleasures and splendors of her party. Septimus Warren Smith knew he was about to be removed to a sanitarium where his doctors would do his thinking and choosing for him, but he chose to die rather than submit. As Clarissa thinks about him, she perceives that in his suicidal madness he had defended to the death the same personal integrity that she has always betrayed in her own life, not least by giving her parties. Her self-recognition, and her imaginative sympathy with Septimus Warren Smith, transform her inwardly. Restored, even if only for a moment, to the integrity she had so long refused, she returns to her party, where Peter experiences her presence as a visionary glory.

Until almost the end of *Mrs. Dalloway*, Clarissa is scarcely aware that such a person as "Clarissa herself" even exists. She has become a set of attributes, someone whose whole being depends on her husband, on her relation to someone or something else.

> She had the oddest sense of being herself invisible, unseen; unknown; there being no more marrying, no more having of children now, but only this astonishing and rather solemn progress with the rest of them up Bond Street, this being Mrs. Dalloway; not even Clarissa any more; this being Mrs. Richard Dalloway.

Peter feels annoyed when Clarissa introduces her daughter "emotionally, histrionically," as someone who exists in relation to Clarissa, not in her own right: "Here is my Elizabeth." "Why not 'Here's Elizabeth' simply," Peter asks himself afterward. Knowing all about Clarissa's cold contractedness, he persists in loving her for herself. "That was the devilish part of her—this coldness, this woodenness, something very profound in her, which he had felt again this morning talking to her, an impenetrability. Yet Heaven knows he loved her. She had some queer power of fiddling on one's nerves, turning one's nerves to fiddle-strings, yes."

Peter does not know it, but Clarissa feels toward him something of what he feels toward her, although with less intensity, and with more of a sense that her feelings are ghosts of the past rather than intensely alive in the present. She thinks of him as early in the book as the third paragraph: "it was his sayings one remembered; his eyes, his pocket-knife, his smile, his grumpiness and, when millions of things had utterly vanished—how strange it was!—a few sayings like this about cabbages." This is not quite the same as loving Peter himself, but it is far closer to it than the kind of gratitude she feels toward her husband or the possessiveness she feels toward her daughter. She can never entirely recover from Peter's absence: "suddenly it would come over her, If he were with me now what would he say?—some days, some sights bringing him back to her calmly, without the old bitterness."

He is not with her now because she chose to be Mrs. Richard Dalloway, who, when she is not looking back to a past when there was a person named Clarissa, thinks mostly about her party. In her thoughts, she describes her party as "an offering; to combine, to create." She adds, "but to whom?" and tries to justify it:

> An offering for the sake of offering, perhaps. Anyhow, it was her gift. Nothing else had she of the slightest importance; could not think, write, even play the piano. She muddled Armenians and Turks; loved success; hated discomfort; must be liked; talked oceans of nonsense; and to this day, ask her what the Equator was, and she did not know.

She knows that she offers her gift to no one, certainly not to her invited guests. Her feelings about those guests range from mild liking through passive indifference to fearful repulsion. The only two guests whom she urgently wants to be with are Peter Walsh and Sally Seton, to whom she never sent invitations because she did not expect to see them in London, and who appear at her door only because they both chanced to journey to London on the day of the party.

"Must" They Said

The plot of the book, in summary form, is the passage from the opening sentence, "Mrs. Dalloway said she would buy the flowers herself"—in which the woman identified as the wife of Richard Dalloway goes off alone to pay money for something decorative— to the closing sentences in which Mrs. Dalloway has been transformed into Clarissa, even if the only people who notice the transformation are Peter, through the terror and ecstasy of his vision, and Clarissa herself through her revelations in the little room.

Mrs. Dalloway is the deepest and most moving exploration in English fiction, possibly in all fiction, of the love that values another person for the other person's self, the love that values "Clarissa herself" more than anything about her, more than anything she says or does. What gives the book much of its extraordinary depth is its understanding of the inner and outer forces that discourage this kind of love by denying, masking, controlling, or degrading the voluntary, integral self that alone can give love and return it. The force that most opposes love, in *Mrs. Dalloway* as in everything else, is power; and power's most useful ally is passivity. Clarissa Dalloway, for most of the book, insists on remaining passive in the face of love; she spends much of her day reassuring herself that she was right to refuse an entangling marriage to Peter when they both were young; and she admires and wishes she could emulate anyone who is stoical enough to be unmoved by strong emotions. If she could have been someone else, she thinks, she wishes she could have been like "Lady Bexborough who opened a bazaar, they said, with the telegram in her hand, John, her favourite, killed"—killed on the battlefront in the Great War of 1914–18. Yet Clarissa also shrinks instinctively from anyone who wields power, and she is one of the very few characters in the book who has enough moral intelligence to understand both the seductions of power and its cost.

Almost everyone around Clarissa worships in his or her individual way some depersonalizing, elusive, unknowable form of power. The Londoners who stand at attention as an official motorcar with shaded windows threads its way along Bond Street have no idea of who might be inside:

> But nobody knew whose face had been seen. Was it the Prince of Wales's, the Queen's, the Prime Minister's? Whose face was it? Nobody knew.

The crowd outside Buckingham Palace that watches the car approaching the palace gate never sees it enter, because they all turn their attention instead to a newer and even more anonymous kind of power, as they stare up at a skywriting airplane and its invisible anonymous pilot spelling out a trivial advertisement whose letters most of the crowd cannot even decipher.*

The book's most vividly drawn embodiment of power is the medical specialist in nervous disorders, Sir William Bradshaw, who overcomes by social and legal force the autonomy and selfhood of his patients. Only Clarissa Dalloway and Septimus Warren Smith's wife Lucrezia find Sir William repellent—but Clarissa is divided

---

* Sometimes power is worshipped in a less distant and elevated form. In a comic grace note near the end of the book, when Clarissa walks into the little room at her party, the narrator reports that the prime minister and Lady Bruton had left the room a moment earlier, but the chairs "still kept the impress" of them as they sat together, "she turned deferentially, he sitting four-square, authoritatively. They had been talking about India." The book's final image of sexual and imperial power is the imprint of two pairs of buttocks.

into an inner self and an outer hostess, and only her inner self is repulsed by Sir William. The outer hostess is impressed enough by him to invite him to her party, to which he brings the news of Septimus's death. Earlier in the day, when Septimus and Lucrezia visit Sir William in his consulting room, he arranges to have Septimus sent to his private sanitarium, and with unshakable calm urges Septimus to place his whole personality in Sir William's care. "Try to think as little about yourself as possible," he says. "Trust everything to me," he adds, in a casual-sounding phrase that belies the moral and psychological tyranny it imposes. Lucrezia asks if Septimus must be separated from her. "Unfortunately, yes," is the narrator's paraphrase of Sir William's answer: "the people we care for most are not good for us when we are ill." Clarissa Dalloway spends much of her day justifying her willful refusal of all relations that might touch the central core of herself; Septimus Warren Smith spends much of his day anticipating the moment when his relations will be broken and his selfhood suppressed against his will.

Sir William Bradshaw tells Septimus he must rest. Septimus thinks afterward:

> "Must," "must," why "must"? What power had Bradshaw over him? "What right has Bradshaw to say 'must' to me?" he demanded.

The single word "must"—which throughout *Mrs. Dalloway* tends to be emphasized by being repeated two or three times whenever it is thought or spoken—is the complete vocabulary of power. As Lucrezia Warren Smith knows, those who rule over others "saw nothing clear, yet ruled, yet inflicted. 'Must' they said." The force of the word works as much through anonymous social conventions as it does through individual judges and doctors. Clarissa thinks of the word as she withdraws to her attic room with its narrow bed: "Women must put off their rich apparel. At midday they must disrobe." Clarissa's daughter Elizabeth feels its restraints in the same mild form when she ventures out alone into the City: "She must go home. She must dress for dinner."

The same word, however, can also signify an entirely different kind of necessity, an inner necessity, not something imposed from without. Septimus refuses to have children, but Rezia replies, "she must have children . . . she must have a boy. She must have a son like Septimus." But until the end of *Mrs. Dalloway*, all internal voluntary necessity—the kind of inner necessity that says "I can do no other," as Martin Luther reputedly protested when commanded to submit to authority—is overruled by a necessity imposed from outside.

Because She Is Mortal

Mrs. Dalloway, like much of Virginia Woolf's fiction, mingles triumphant satisfaction and elegiac sadness. Clarissa's and Peter's triumphant revelations at the end are shadowed by their knowledge of Clarissa's recent illness and their fears about her death, and above all by the brute fact of Septimus Warren Smith's suicide. The book's triumphant parts and its elegiac parts depend upon each other, because both elegy and triumph, in this book, are ways of valuing the personal uniqueness that is summed up in the idea of "Clarissa herself."

At one point in Peter Walsh's wanderings after his brief unsatisfactory morning meeting with Clarissa, he hears a clock strike, imagines Clarissa entering her drawing room at the stroke of the hour, and asks himself, "why had he been so profoundly happy when the clock was striking." Then his mood darkens:

> as the sound of St. Margaret's languished, he thought, She has
> been ill, and the sound expressed languor and suffering. It was
> her heart, he remembered; and the sudden loudness of the final
> stroke tolled for death that surprised in the midst of life, Clarissa
> falling where she stood, in her drawing room. No! No! he cried.
> She is not dead! I am not old, he cried . . .

Peter values Clarissa as fervently as he does precisely because he
is aware that she must die, and Virginia Woolf portrays in *Mrs.
Dalloway* the emotional truth that you can only value someone
else—Clarissa herself or anyone whose unique self seems infinitely
valuable—if you are also conscious of their mortality. In human
relations, part of the precious value of the loved one is the fact that
she is mortal; if she were not mortal, she could be adored or vener-
ated or perceived as a shining light or a pillar of fire, but never
loved as an equal, never loved with the sense of urgency that comes
with knowing that she cannot receive your love forever.

Virginia Woolf modeled *Mrs. Dalloway* on the *Odyssey*, partly
because she simultaneously modeled it on another book that was
modeled on the *Odyssey*, James Joyce's *Ulysses*. Peter Walsh is a
failed modern Odysseus who returns after five years to a woman
who is married to someone else. He is both like and unlike Homer's
Odysseus who returned after twenty years of war and wandering to
a Penelope who remained heroically faithful. While Odysseus was
away, Penelope wove and unwove a shroud; when Peter bursts in on
Clarissa, she is sewing up a tear in her dress. The earliest statement
in Western literature of the inextricability of mortality and love
occurs in the dialogue between Odysseus and the immortal goddess Calypso when she challenges him to justify his preference for
the mortal Penelope over herself. "Can I be less desirable than
she?" Calypso demands. "Less interesting? Less beautiful? Can
mortals / compare with goddesses in grace and form?" Odysseus

replies with the tact that he always uses when speaking to those he does not love:

> "My lady goddess, here is no cause for anger.
> My quiet Penelope—how well I know—
> would seem a shade before your majesty,
> death and old age being unknown to you,
> while she must die. Yet, it is true, each day
> I long for home, long for the sight of home."

Odysseus, Calypso knows, spends his days weeping by the shore of her island, bored literally to tears by the company of someone who, because she is infinitely less vulnerable than he is, can have no real need for him. (Peter himself is "attractive to women who liked the sense that he was not altogether manly.") Great strength and invulnerability, like great power, tend to be most attractive to those who try to avoid the entanglements of intimacy by seeking partners who don't need them.

Seduced by an Archetype

Every age has its own ways of obscuring or defacing personal integrity while finding great intellectual excitement in doing so. In the early 1920s, when Virginia Woolf was writing *Mrs. Dalloway*, the most exciting of these was the idea of archetypes, Carl Gustav Jung's term for "primordial images," such as the Wanderer or the Great Mother, which, unless revealed by psychologists or artists, are (so Jung and his followers said) present only in the unconscious mind and transmitted across the ages through a collective and impersonal unconscious that shapes all conscious individuality. Before Jung gave it a name, the idea of the archetype had been much in the air of European thought in the late nineteenth century: in the mysterious evocative images of Symbolist art, in the universalizing mythographies of Sir James Frazer's *The Golden Bough,* and in the visionary poetry of W. B. Yeats where the sphinx seen in a visionary moment in "The Second Coming" is "a vast image out of *Spiritus Mundi*"—the mind of the universe. In 1923, when she was also writing *Mrs. Dalloway,* Virginia Woolf and her husband Leonard Woolf, in their roles as publishers of the Hogarth Press, hand-set the type for the first British edition of T. S. Eliot's *The Waste Land,* a poem in which the Grail quest is an archetypal journey taken not by a single individual hero but by multiple figures each of whom is a local embodiment of some aspect of a universal quest-myth. In the same year, 1923, Jung's special use of the word "archetype" became widely known in English when his *Psychological Types* was published in translation.

The idea of the archetype was and remains exciting because it makes vivid a truth that tends to be ignored: your individuality is in fact shaped partly by impersonal models of which you are not consciously aware. The archetype has enough truth in it to make it plausible to believe—as some of the greatest thinkers of the twentieth century were tempted to believe—that archetypes contain the ultimate truth about human beings. Peter Walsh experiences the temptations of the archetype while sitting on a park bench and dreaming the daylight dream that occupies the brief fifth section of *Mrs. Dalloway.* As Peter descends into dream, the nursemaid dressed in gray who is sitting beside him on the bench loses her personal identity and becomes an archetypal figure: "she seemed like the champion of the rights of sleepers, like one of those spectral presences which rise in twilight in woods made of sky and branches." (In English and other languages, archetypes are typically honored with a definite article—"the hero," "the goddess"— while lesser beings get the indefinite one—"a middle-aged man," "a nurse.") Peter himself ceases to be Peter Walsh and becomes instead the archetypal "solitary traveller, haunter of lanes, disturber of ferns," who suddenly sees before him the archetypal goal of his wanderings: "the giant figure at the end of the ride." His transformation exhilarates him: "By conviction an atheist perhaps, he is taken by surprise with moments of extraordinary exaltation." The only things that now seem real to him are primordial images projected outward from his own desires onto the world of dream; ordinary individual human beings seem merely contemptible: "Nothing exists outside us except a state of mind, he thinks; a desire for solace, for relief, for something outside these miserable pigmies, these feeble, these ugly, these craven men and women." Projecting a primordial feminine archetype on the world around him as he advances "down the path with his eye upon sky and branches[,] he rapidly endows them with womanhood."

In writing Peter's dream, Virginia Woolf explores a temptation in order to understand its power, not in order to yield to it. She refuses the desire—to which many modernist writers succumbed— to embrace a vague primordial image as something more real and rewarding than the "miserable pigmies" who are particular persons and things. "Such are the visions," she continues in her account of Peter's dream, "which ceaselessly float up, pace beside, put their faces in front of the actual thing; often overpowering the solitary traveller and taking away from him the sense of the earth, the wish to return, and giving him for substitute a general peace, as if . . . myriads of things merged in one thing; and this figure, made of sky and branches as it is, had risen from the troubled sea . . . to shower down from her magnificent hands compassion, comprehension, absolution."

This is Peter's moment of crisis, the time when he must make his decision at a crossroads. Like any quest hero from Odysseus onward, he is tempted by the sirens' song of comforting but fatal illusion that calls him away from the difficult journey that leads to his real goal. But in Peter's quest, the real goal is not some remote place but something much closer: "the actual thing," the real, ordinary world that can be transfigured by love for a particular person while it remains the actual thing. Peter is tempted to turn instead toward "a general peace," an exalted vagueness. "So, he thinks, may I never go back to the lamplight; to the sitting-room; never finish my book; never knock out my pipe; never ring for Mrs. Turner to clear away; rather let me walk straight on to this great figure [the archetypal female at the end of the journey], who will, with a toss of her head, mount me on her streamers and let me blow to nothingness with the rest."

This vision of "nothingness" is as enticing and as destructive as the sirens' song that tempts Odysseus. As the solitary traveler of Peter's dream emerges from the woods, the great feminine figure shades into an "elderly woman" at the door who is not quite his landlady, because she has become the heroine with a thousand faces. She "seems (so powerful is this infirmity) to seek, over a desert, a lost son; to search for a rider destroyed; to be the figure of the mother whose sons have been killed in the battles of the world." (Virginia Woolf explicitly diagnoses the archetypal imagination as "this infirmity"—a weakness, an inability, a disease.) Finally, "as the solitary traveller advances down the village street," everyone seems still, "as if some august fate, known to them, awaited without fear, were about to sweep them into complete annihilation." The traveler, who is slowly returning toward a waking consciousness of the actual world, goes indoors "among ordinary things." The landlady takes away the marmalade, and asks, "There is nothing more to-night, sir?" And the dream ends with the narrator's question, "But to whom does the solitary traveller make reply?" The "solitary traveller" of the dream and "Mrs. Turner" of the real world live in different universes, and anyone who steps outside Mrs. Turner's universe—such as the "solitary traveller" who is no longer Peter Walsh—loses all knowledge of those flesh-and-blood human beings who remain inside.

When Peter wakes, he says to himself, "The death of the soul." The phrase looks in two directions. It names the kind of annihilation and death that Peter has been dreaming about, in which the personal self dissolves into a collective anonymous archetype, but the phrase also points toward the meaning of Clarissa's persistent and deliberate refusal of her deepest self. As Peter rouses himself awake, "The words [the death of the soul] attached themselves to some scene, to some room, to some past he had been dreaming of. It became clearer; the scene, the room, the past he had been dreaming of." To Peter, looking back on his dream now that he is fully conscious, his dream does not seem at all to have been about preconscious archetypes but instead about an actual moment when he and Clarissa were young, at Clarissa's family home, Bourton, "when he was so passionately in love with Clarissa":

> They were talking about a man who had married his housemaid, one of the neighboring squires . . . Then somebody said—Sally Seton it was—did it make any real difference to one's feelings to know that before they'd married she had had a baby? . . . He could see Clarissa now, turning bright pink; somehow contracting; and saying, "Oh, I shall never be able to speak to her again!" . . .
>
> He hadn't blamed her for minding the fact, since in those days a girl brought up as she was knew nothing, but it was her manner that annoyed him; timid; hard; arrogant; prudish.* "The death of the soul." He had said that instinctively, ticketing the moment as he used to do—the death of her soul.

---

* Thus Virginia Woolf's final revision for the British edition. The earlier state of the text found in the American edition has "timid; hard; something arrogant; unimaginative; prudish." But Clarissa's imagination is not the problem, so

Peter's dream of archetypal vagueness is the opposite of Clarissa's hard arrogant prudery, but both are ways of denying the individuality of real persons, and both require something like "the death of the soul." When Peter remembers Clarissa "somehow contracting," he uses the same metaphor that she herself uses when thinking about her own withdrawal from personal and erotic sympathy; alone in her room at midday, she calls her emotional withdrawal "some contraction of this cold spirit."

The Fertilizing Stain

A few moments after Peter rises from his dream, he is rewarded for having refused its temptations. His reward is a waking experience that counters his distorting dream with an alternative vision of a living person. "A sound interrupted him" at a street corner: "a frail quivering sound, a voice bubbling up without direction, vigour, beginning or end . . . of no age or sex," singing incomprehensible syllables, *"ee um fah um so / foo swee too eem oo."* The voice proves to be that of another woman—"for she wore a skirt"—who is almost but not quite archetypal, an eternal figure of womanhood whose life span is identical with eternity.

> Through all ages—when the pavement was grass, when it was swamp, through the age of tusk and mammoth, through the age of silent sunrise, the battered woman—for she wore a skirt—with

Virginia Woolf removed Peter's reference to it. The last-minute changes that Virginia Woolf made in the British edition published by her and her husband at the Hogarth Press emphasize some of the most important themes of the book in ways that readers of the American edition have never had a chance to see. Other such changes are noted in the following pages.

her right hand exposed, her left clutching at her side, stood singing of love—love which has lasted a million years, she sang, love which prevails, and millions of years ago, her lover, who had been dead these centuries, had walked, she crooned, with her in May . . . and when at last she laid her hoary and immensely aged head on the earth, now become a mere cinder of ice, she implored the Gods to lay by her side a bunch of purple heather, there on her high burial place which the last rays of the last sun caressed; for then the pageant of the universe would be over.

She is both the earth and the body, fertilizing and fertile, combining abstract archetype and coarse reality. Her song issues "from so rude a mouth, a mere hole in the earth, muddy too, matted with root fibres and tangled grass"; it flows "all along the Marylebone Road, and down towards Euston," not through a nameless archetypal landscape; and, in a splendid compressed image, it flows "fertilizing, leaving a damp stain"—because the body's fertility cannot be idealized into something pure, and always leaves a stain. What makes her crucially different from Peter's dream image of the great figure at the end of the ride is that this living woman looks more like a woman and less like an archetype the closer he looks at her: "she wore a skirt."

As Peter comes closer to the singing voice, its nonsense syllables converge into a love song: "give me your hand and let me press it gently . . . and if some one should see, what matter they?" The archetype of Peter's dream had been a delusive form of universality; the voice of the eternal old woman points toward the universality shared by real individual human beings—not a collective unconscious, but the physical body that is love's instrument, medium, and home. Nearby, Lucrezia Warren Smith, who is never deluded into archetypes despite the distractions of her private misery, feels a concerned sympathy for this same old woman. Peter Walsh is enough of a fairy-tale quest hero to give the old woman a shilling as he passes, because only the hero who gives a coin to the old beggar will be rewarded with the princess on the last page—as Peter is rewarded with his ecstatic, terrifying vision of Clarissa herself.

The Pressure of Rapture

Clarissa, meanwhile, has been telling herself that she was right to refuse the kind of intimacy that the old woman sings about. Like everyone at some point in their lives, Clarissa argues to herself that what other people see as her failings are really her merits. She was right, she thinks, to reject Peter for the bland, generous, prudish Richard Dalloway: "For in marriage a little licence, a little independence there must be between people living together day in day out in the same house; which Richard gave her and she him." Peter would have demanded intolerable closeness. "She had to break with him or they would have been destroyed, both of them ruined, she was convinced."

She is so practiced in her self-deceptions that she can make convincing arguments on their behalf. As she walks through the park early in the morning, she remembers throwing a shilling into the pond. "But everyone remembered," she tells herself; "what she loved was this, here, now, in front of her; the fat lady in the cab"— as if her warm feelings to a fat lady glimpsed in a taxi made up for her coldness to everyone close to her. Later, when she thinks of her death, she focuses on the same idea of herself: "no one in the whole world would know how she had loved it all; how, every instant . . ."

She thinks differently when she withdraws to her room at midday. She cannot avoid confronting a chill at the center of herself, "a virginity preserved through childbirth which clung to her like a sheet." The same chill had frozen her intimacy with Richard in the early days of their marriage:

> Lovely in girlhood, suddenly there came a moment—for example on the river beneath the woods at Clieveden—when, through some contraction of this cold spirit, she had failed him. And then at Constantinople, and again and again. She could see what she lacked. It was not beauty; it was not mind. It was something central which permeated; something warm which broke up surfaces and rippled the cold contact of man and woman, or of women together. For *that* she could dimly perceive. She resented it, had a scruple picked up Heaven knows where, or, as she felt, sent by Nature . . .

Suitably enough, the book that Clarissa reads alone in bed at night is Baron de Marbot's memoir of Napoleon's retreat from Moscow after the Russian winter blocked his attempt to breach the city wall.

Clarissa's coldness is not an unchanging, inherent part of her. It can melt, although it does so only at rare intervals and only in chaste moments with women, not with men. The kind of experience in which her coldness melts into passionate warmth is not the experience of a sexual act, but the book describes it in a startlingly detailed sexual metaphor. Clarissa, the narrator reports, partly echoing Clarissa's own thoughts, "could not resist sometimes yielding to the charm of a woman, not a girl, of a woman confessing, as to her they often did, some scrape, some folly." Whatever the cause of her feeling—"whether it was pity, or their beauty, or that she was older," for a brief moment,

> she did undoubtedly then feel what men felt. Only for a moment; but it was enough. It was a sudden revelation, a tinge like a blush which one tried to check and then, as it spread, one yielded to its expansion, and rushed to the farthest verge and there quivered

and felt the world come closer, swollen with some astonishing significance, some pressure of rapture, which split its skin and gushed and poured with an extraordinary alleviation over the cracks and sores! Then, for that moment, she had seen an illumination; a match burning in a crocus; an inner meaning almost expressed. But the close withdrew; the hard softened. It was over—the moment.

"The close withdrew; the hard softened." Clarissa's revelatory emotions are "what men felt," and the masculine sexual metaphors of tumescence and detumescence that describe Clarissa's feelings have much to do with Virginia Woolf's impatience with sexual labels and categories—as in the concluding pages of *A Room of One's Own,* where she speculates that everyone has a mixture of "two sexes in the mind," that no mind is purely male or female. The most thrilling experience that Clarissa remembers is being kissed on the lips by Sally Seton at eighteen; but to ask (as readers often do ask) whether or not Clarissa is a lesbian is to falsify Clarissa and simplify the novel. "Clarissa herself" is unclassifiable into any category. She can experience a rush of emotions in the presence of a woman; she thinks warmly about Peter Walsh as she walks through the park; and she rebuffs equally Peter, Sally, and her husband. Clarissa "could see what she lacked"; she could at moments "see what men felt."

So Peter is wrong about her when he walks through London after waking from his archetypal dream, thinking in a resentful, categorizing way that "women . . . don't know what passion is. They don't know the meaning of it to men"; that is exactly what Clarissa does know. But Peter is bluntly right to complain in his next sentence that "Clarissa was as cold as an icicle." Clarissa fails in her relations with both men and women, fails in her relations with her husband and her daughter—while she insists on praising herself for her success in loving the fat lady in the cab.

Virginia Woolf judges Clarissa's sexuality according to its warmth or coldness, not according to which category of person her sexuality favors. What matters to her in the sexuality of her characters is the depth of their emotions, not the nature of the object of those emotions. In this she takes the opposite approach from one that has governed much of Western sexual morality ever since Plato, in the *Laws,* condemned homosexual acts for being contrary to nature. The trouble with judging human acts according to whether they are natural or unnatural is that moral judgments apply only to voluntary acts and choices, not to involuntary, instinctive behavior, and nature provides no standard for judging one voluntary choice against another. No choices are natural in the way that instinctive behavior is natural. Furthermore, the separate question of whether you were born with your sexuality or whether you chose it is morally irrelevant; probably the only moral question it makes sense to ask about anyone's sexuality is to what extent you use it as a means of treating other people as instruments and objects—something that can occur in a conventional married bedroom as readily as in more unconventional settings—and to what extent your sexual life is one of the means by which you value other persons for themselves. The maternal nature divinity in *Jane Eyre* never thought about different varieties of sexuality, but she too judged Jane's potential relationships by precisely this standard.

He Could Not Feel

The chill at the heart of Clarissa Dalloway has its counterpart in the isolating, ultimately suicidal madness of Septimus Warren

Smith, who discovered, on the day he got engaged to Lucrezia five years earlier, that "he could not feel." In the room in Milan where Lucrezia worked making hats, "the table was all strewn with feathers, spangles, silks, ribbons; scissors were rapping on the table; but something failed him; he could not feel." Clarissa's failure with her husband Richard ("she had failed him") leaves her alone in her bedroom at midday thinking about her party. Septimus's failure leaves him in the uncomprehending, domineering hands of Sir William Bradshaw—although one of the ironies of his death is that he leaps from his window to avoid being carted off to Sir William Bradshaw's private sanitarium when the man ascending the stairs, who in fact has nothing at all to do with Sir William, is the blunt general practitioner Dr. Holmes, who insists that nothing is wrong with Septimus that a mild sedative can't cure.

Virginia Woolf volunteered only two details about the writing of *Mrs. Dalloway,* in the preface she wrote for a cheap reprint in the Modern Library series in 1928, three years after the book first appeared:

> Of *Mrs. Dalloway* then one can only bring to light at the moment a few scraps, of little importance or none perhaps; as that in the first version Septimus, who later is intended to be her double, had no existence; and that Mrs. Dalloway was originally to kill herself, or perhaps merely to die at the end of the party. Such scraps are offered humbly to the reader in the hope that like other odds and ends [which she significantly neglects to provide] they may come in useful.

Septimus was brought into the novel as Clarissa's double, who dies in madness so that Clarissa might live—much as Jane Eyre's double Bertha Mason dies in madness so that Jane may marry. He is unable to feel because he has involuntarily shut down his emotions rather than endure his grief over the battlefield death of Evans, his sergeant and friend. (Septimus's psychological history derives from the account of "the psycho-neuroses of warfare" in W. H. R. Rivers's *Instinct and the Unconscious,* published in 1920 and widely known at the time *Mrs. Dalloway* was being written.) Clarissa's coldness seems to have a similar cause, dating back to her childhood. In a passage that seems extraneous to the story except for its parallel with Septimus, Peter Walsh remembers Clarissa's thoughts about an incident involving her sister and her father, Justin Parry: "To see your own sister killed by a falling tree (all Justin Parry's fault—all his carelessness) before your very eyes, a girl too on the verge of life, the most gifted of them, Clarissa always said, was enough to turn one bitter." Both Clarissa and Septimus suffer the same anxious inability to feel, yet Clarissa's failure is partly her own voluntary failure, partly a failure imposed on her by nature and training, while Septimus's failure is almost entirely forced on him by the engines of war. And while Clarissa can secure herself against despair through the protective powers of wealth, status, and privilege, the same powers make it intolerable for Septimus to live.*

Clarissa is protected and Septimus destroyed by the powers embodied in Sir William Bradshaw, the only person in the book whom the narrator condemns in her own voice rather than through the inner voice of one of the characters. "Proportion, divine proportion, Sir William's goddess," is the thing he worships. "Wor-

---

* Because of their different privileges, the same action, when performed by one or the other, leads to entirely different results. At the start of the book Clarissa remembers how, as a girl at her parents' house, "she had burst open the French windows and plunged at Bourton into the open air," and exults, "What a lark! What a plunge!" Near the end, Septimus too plunges through a window, having "flung himself vigorously, violently down on to Mrs. Filmer's area railings"—to his death.

shipping proportion, Sir William not only prospered himself but made England prosper, secluded her lunatics, forbade childbirth, penalised despair, made it impossible for the unfit to propagate their views until they, too, shared his sense of proportion . . ." Sir William's power to make his patients kneel down before normality corresponds to other kinds of power:

> But Proportion has a sister, less smiling, more formidable, a God-dess even now engaged—in the heat and sands of India, the mud and swamp of Africa, the purlieus of London, wherever in short the climate or the devil tempts men to fall from the true belief which is her own—is even now engaged in dashing down shrines, smashing idols, and setting up in their place her own stern coun-tenance. Conversion is her name and she feasts on the wills of the weakly, loving to impress, to impose, adoring her own features stamped on the face of the populace . . . This lady too (Rezia War-ren Smith divined it) had her dwelling in Sir William's heart, though concealed, as she mostly is, under some plausible disguise; some venerable name; love, duty, self sacrifice.

Conversion is the goddess of the missionary, the propagandist, the organizer, the representatives of authority in British Africa and British India—and of the Harley Street nerve specialist who invokes her to subdue his patients and his wife: "For example, Lady Brad-shaw. Fifteen years ago she had gone under. It was nothing you could put your finger on; there had been no scene, no snap; only the slow sinking, water-logged, of her will into his."

Whenever a novel contrasts oppressors and victims, readers take pleasure in identifying with the victims. Virginia Woolf, as always, undermines her readers' self-flattery. She portrays victims who can be as corrupt as their oppressors, who respond to oppression by finding weaker victims to oppress in turn. Sir William Bradshaw, among his many acts of oppression, "forbade childbirth"; so too does his victim, Septimus Warren Smith, who refuses a child to his wife Lucrezia. Like Sir William, Septimus responds to personal needs with impersonal principles. Lucrezia says that she "must have a son like Septimus"; Septimus thinks in response: "One cannot bring children into a world like this." Clarissa Dalloway is repelled by oppressors, but not enough to refrain from inviting them to her party. Her guests include, in addition to Sir William Bradshaw, representatives of many other varieties of professional and imperial power: the prime minister (who proves to be an absolute nonentity in manner and appearance); the absurd power-worshipper Lady Bruton, incapable of writing a letter to *The Times* without help from men; and Hugh Whitbread, the toady courtier of whom Peter Walsh thinks when he sees him at Clarissa's party: "Villains there must be, and God knows the rascals who get hanged for battering the brains of a girl out in the train do less harm on the whole than Hugh Whitbread and his kindness."

The only oppressor excluded from Clarissa's party is the one at the far end of the pecking order: Doris Kilman, Elizabeth Dalloway's tutor. With her domineering greeds and futile resentments, she is unhesitatingly shut out by everyone else in the human community. "I never go to parties," Miss Kilman tells Elizabeth. "People don't ask me to parties." Dismissed from schoolteaching during the Great War "because she would not pretend that the Germans were all villains," bitter with the humiliations of class, Miss Kilman longs to humiliate Clarissa as she herself has been humiliated. "There rose in her [Miss Kilman] an overmastering desire to overcome her; to unmask her . . . But it was not the body; it was the soul and its mockery that she wished to subdue; make feel her mastery." Having found a comforting delusion of moral superiority in evangelical Christianity, Miss Kilman now wants to convert Elizabeth. Both Miss Kilman and Sir William Bradshaw worship Conversion, but the goddess rewards the doctor and abandons the schoolmistress.

Septimus, having been victimized, frees himself through death. Miss Kilman, having been victimized, stuffs herself with sugared cakes, resents a child for taking a pink cake off a plate, and blunders among the tearoom tables. She almost demands to be rejected; she repels all sympathy—so much so that one editor of *Mrs. Dalloway* calls her "an uncomfortable blot on the book, and quite inessential"—but the book insists that her suffering is no less unjust because she makes it impossible for anyone to care about her. By presenting Miss Kilman as too repellent to be sentimentalized, Virginia Woolf exposes the falsehoods favored by well-meaning propagandists who rouse their audience against injustice by sentimentalizing the victim. The propagandist does not have enough faith in himself or his audience to expect to be believed if he were to insist that oppression is evil in itself, regardless of the worth or lack of worth in the oppressed. Instead he describes a world divided into wicked oppressors and innocent victims, with victims who tend to be so remote in culture and geography that they can be sentimentalized as both primitive and noble. Whether or not the propagandist knows it, this implies that oppression is evil *because* its victims are innocent, and that oppression would be acceptable if committed against victims who are guilty. His argument eventually fails, because his audience sooner or later notices that, in the real world, victims of oppression often become distorted by hatred and resentment, that they were no more noble or primitive than anyone else in the first place, that they have always been as capable of injustice as everyone else is. But because the audience has been convinced that oppression is evil only when the victim is innocent, it now concludes that the victims deserved their oppression after all—and well-meaning liberals are thus transformed into angry reactionaries, and the propagandist, in the end, serves the oppressor whom he hoped to defeat.

The politics of *Mrs. Dalloway,* as of *Three Guineas* a decade later, combine a radical critique of established authority with a skeptical anatomy of national and imperial symbols. Virginia Woolf's political views, here and elsewhere, are effectively those of her socialist husband Leonard Woolf in a more extreme and less pragmatic form. One of the book's most subtly radical moments occurs when Peter Walsh admires the way in which every car pulls aside to let an ambulance pass: he calls this "one of the triumphs of civilization," and contrasts "the efficiency, the organization, the communal spirit of London" with the disorder of "the East." He is right to admire the civilization that defers to the ambulance, but the episode's radical political irony lies in the book's insistence that this same civilization and communal spirit has worked to destroy Septimus Warren Smith, and that the ambulance is bearing Septimus to the hospital where he will be pronounced dead.* Yet Virginia Woolf made politics the servant and instrument of ethics, and never justified falsehood for the sake of political expedience. In her novels, no political cause or party has a monopoly on truth. The only person in *Mrs. Dalloway* who treats Miss Kilman with kindness and respect is Clarissa's husband Richard, a Conservative M.P. with all the conventionalities and limits of his kind, who bores his wife with his concern for Armenian victims of genocide whom no one else in the book even notices, victims whom Clarissa (who muddles them with Turks and Albanians) absurdly tells herself she helps by loving her roses.

---

* This episode is Virginia Woolf's ironic refutation of the unironic paragraph in her friend E. M. Forster's *A Passage to India,* published while *Mrs. Dalloway* was being written, in which the schoolmaster Mr. Fielding, on his return from India, finds in Europe something deeply admirable: "the civilization that has escaped muddle, the spirit in a reasonable form."

Death and the Party

Angrily thinking about Miss Kilman's desperate wish for Elizabeth's love and about Miss Kilman's desperate effort to convert Elizabeth to evangelical religion, Clarissa asks herself—rhetorically, and certain of her own answer—"Had she ever tried to convert anyone herself? Did she not wish everybody merely to be themselves?" She is repelled by the sexless lust of Sir William Bradshaw and the book's other oppressors, but her wish for everybody to be themselves is more of a wish to be left alone by everyone than a wish to have an equal relation, or any other kind of relation, with anyone. Miss Kilman's possessive love for Elizabeth gives Clarissa an excuse to refuse love altogether:

> Love and religion! thought Clarissa . . . tingling all over. How detestable, how detestable they are! . . . The cruelest things in the world, she thought, seeing them clumsy, hot, domineering, hypocritical, eavesdropping, jealous, infinitely cruel and unscrupulous, dressed in a mackintosh coat, on the landing; love and religion.

As she rages, she notices the old lady whom she has often observed looking out the window opposite her own, "quite unconscious that she was being watched." The old lady's autonomy, Clarissa tells herself, plausibly enough, deserves to be preserved against the onslaughts of the world's Kilmans and Bradshaws. "There was something solemn in it—but love and religion would destroy that, whatever it was, the privacy of the soul. The odious Kilman would destroy it."

Phrases such as Peter's "the death of the soul" and Clarissa's "the privacy of the soul" point toward something central in *Mrs.*

Dalloway. Both Clarissa Dalloway and Virginia Woolf try to find a language for talking about the soul and its privacy while rejecting all other religious meanings, especially institutional and doctrinal ones. "Not for a moment did she believe in God," Clarissa says about herself. "One of the most thoroughgoing sceptics," Clarissa has evolved an "atheist's religion of doing good for the sake of goodness" (which was also the essence of Dorothea Brooke's religion). Peter Walsh, "by conviction an atheist," is surprised by moments of exaltation in his archetypal dream. The book endorses their skepticism. Doris Kilman and Sir William Bradshaw exemplify the brutality of Conversion, and when the gray motorcar bears its important personage through the London streets, "the spirit of religion was abroad with her eyes bandaged tight and her lips gaping wide." Septimus Warren Smith points to the falseness of the old religion in his mad fantasies of a new one ("Men must not cut down trees. There is a God"). The "seedy-looking nondescript man" with a leather case full of pamphlets who is glimpsed hesitating on the steps of St. Paul's Cathedral wants to go inside to find balm, company, and welcome, but mostly for simple relief from his own bitter contrariness, "that plaguy spirit of truth seeking which leaves me at present without a situation." Those who seek religion in this novel are looking for an illusion that can protect them from truth.

When Clarissa indicts love as the other great destroyer of the soul's privacy, the book says nothing explicit to dispute her, but her arguments become less plausible as she continues. "Love destroyed too," she tells herself, arguing from the example of Peter Walsh. "Look at the women he loved—vulgar, trivial, commonplace." Peter has come to London for the unpleasant and embarrassing purpose of arranging a divorce for the insignificant younger woman he intends to marry. Clarissa is appalled by what he has been brought down to by his desire for love: "Horrible passion! she thought. Degrading passion! she thought, thinking of Kilman and her Elizabeth . . ." Clarissa cannot let herself understand that Peter Walsh has been wounded by his failures in love, not by love itself. He entangles himself with commonplace women and their undignified troubles because he was refused by Clarissa, the one woman to whom he ever offered love, and he would never have been destroyed had she been able to accept it. The many terrible things done and suffered in the name of love do not discredit love itself, any more than the terrible things done and suffered in the name of justice discredit justice itself as something worth seeking and having and doing.

Only the discourteous intrusion of death into Clarissa's party can make her rethink her conviction that love is the enemy of the self, that love destroys "the privacy of the soul." Shortly after Sir William and Lady Bradshaw arrive late, Lady Bradshaw murmurs an excuse to Clarissa: "A young man (that is what Sir William is telling Mr. Dalloway) had killed himself. He had been in the army." Clarissa's first response is a mild shock at the indecorousness of it: "Oh! . . . in the middle of my party, here's death, she thought." As if nothing seriously bothersome had happened, she continues into a little room where the prime minister had earlier gone with Lady Bruton. There she experiences the deeper shock of sudden and complete isolation: "There was nobody. The party's splendour fell to the floor, so strange it was to come in alone in her finery."

Thus begins one of the most magnificent episodes in modern literature. Clarissa first evades, then embraces, the recognition which the book has been preparing for her all along, and she experiences the transformation that in some obscure way makes possible Peter Walsh's concluding vision of her. She begins by complaining, in the nervous repetitive manner she falls into when angry, that her party's effect had been ruined: "What business had the Bradshaws to talk of death at her party? A young man had killed himself. And they talked of it at her party—the Bradshaws, talked of death."

The book had earlier pointed to Clarissa's "horror of death," and the party is now revealed as her futile attempt to escape death.* The reminder of death that was once commonly engraved on tombstones, *"Et in arcadia ego"* (Death itself saying, "I too am in Arcadia"), is the same reminder that the Bradshaws bring to Clarissa at her party, and she sees in her imagination what Septimus had seen as he died: "He had thrown himself from a window. Up had flashed the ground; through him, blundering, bruising, went the rusty spikes." Lady Bradshaw had in fact told Clarissa nothing beyond the fact that the young man who killed himself had been in the army, yet Clarissa (after wondering, "He had killed himself—but how?") somehow sees what her double had seen. The uncanniness of this detail resembles the uncanniness of Victor Frankenstein's landfall at the spot where his double had earlier deposited the body of Henry Clerval.

The Thing That Mattered

For Clarissa, the uncanny event is a moment of transformation. Until now, she has suffered the chronic loneliness that comes with indifference—the indifference that prompted her to feel anger at having death brought into her party. But her vision of Septimus's death is an act of sympathy that overcomes her indifference, start-

* Surprisingly enough, many critics treat Clarissa's party as a triumphant example of woman's work, something like Lily Briscoe's painting in *To the Lighthouse*. This view seems to overlook Clarissa's power-worshipping invitations to the prime minister and Sir William Bradshaw and her snobbish annoyance at being pressured into inviting her insignificant cousin Ellie Henderson.

ing with her tentative question to herself about Septimus's death: "But why had he done it?" Finding her way to the answer to her own question, she remembers that all day "she had been thinking of Bourton, of Peter, of Sally," of the days when she had not yet closed herself off from intimacy by marrying Richard. All of them would go on living as they had done for the past three decades, but Septimus "had flung it away." Now, by naming to herself what it was that she betrayed—betrayed by isolating herself from Sally and Peter—she understands what it was that Septimus defended by dying:

> A thing there was that mattered; a thing, wreathed about with chatter, defaced, obscured in her own life, let drop every day in corruption, lies, chatter. This he had preserved. Death was defiance. Death was an attempt to communicate; people feeling the impossibility of reaching the centre which, mystically, evaded them; closeness drew apart, rapture faded, one was alone. There was an embrace in death.

Instead of the thing that mattered, Clarissa has chosen to fill her life with something that mocks it by almost rhyming with it, something she names twice in one sentence: "chatter."

The thing that mattered is something she does not name, but it has something to do with integrity, with intimacy, with self-knowledge, and with what Clarissa had earlier thought of as "something central which permeated." It also has something to do with what had been lost when "closeness drew apart, rapture faded." (Clarissa's thoughts here echo her earlier recollection in her attic room of fading erotic intensity: "the close withdrew; the hard softened.") A few sentences later she imagines Septimus in the presence of Sir William Bradshaw, who, she now reminds herself, is "a great doctor yet to her obscurely evil, without sex or lust, extremely polite to women, but capable of some indescribable outrage—forcing your soul, that was it . . ." (Lucrezia Warren Smith had earlier judged him as "not a nice man.") And a few lines later Clarissa again sees the old lady in the window opposite, embodying what she had a few hours ago thought of as "the privacy of the soul." The thing that mattered is the core of what Peter Walsh calls "Clarissa herself," something that induces terror and ecstasy, something that cannot be defeated by death and is deeply connected to love. Virginia Woolf does not want to call it the soul in the paragraph in which Clarissa acknowledges its importance, but Clarissa herself uses the word two paragraphs later when she imagines Sir William Bradshaw inflicting "some indescribable outrage—forcing your soul, that was it."

Clarissa keeps returning to the word "soul" or to a variety of lightly disguised synonyms. Peter remembers that Clarissa had developed "a transcendental theory" about "the unseen part of us" which might survive the death of the visible body and attach itself to other persons. Peter uses the word "soul" as a synonym for "self" when he thinks about his need for the simple companionship of gossip: "For this is the truth about our soul, he thought, our self, who fish-like inhabits deep seas . . . ; suddenly she shoots to the surface . . . has a positive need to brush, scrape, kindle herself, gossiping." The word "soul" occurs more often in *Mrs. Dalloway* than in any of Virginia Woolf's other novels, and about twice as often in *Mrs. Dalloway* as in the book where it occurs next most frequently, the archaizing and parodic *Orlando*.

Septimus had "plunged holding his treasure," but because Clarissa has let her treasure be defaced and obscured, it is now she who feels "the terror, the overwhelming incapacity . . . in the depths of her heart an awful fear," and her party is no defense against it:

Somehow it was her disaster—her disgrace. It was her punishment to see sink and disappear here a man, there a woman, in this profound darkness, and she forced to stand here in her evening dress. She had schemed; she had pilfered. She was never wholly admirable. She had wanted success. Lady Bexborough and the rest of it. And once she had walked on the terrace at Bourton.

When she stepped out this same morning, Clarissa had remembered admiringly how Lady Bexborough had been tough-minded enough to open a fair moments after learning that her son had died in battle. Now, at another festive moment, surrounded by other people, Clarissa learns of another young soldier's death, and is transformed by her sympathy for him. "Lady Bexborough and the rest of it" get and deserve nothing more than a contemptuous sentence fragment.

"And once she had walked on the terrace at Bourton," three decades earlier, when Sally Seton suddenly kissed her on the lips—and "the whole world might have turned upside down" and she experienced "the revelation, the religious feeling!" Her hatred of "love and religion" in all their domineering and institutional forms is consistent with her gratitude for the revelation and the religious feeling prompted by her private relation with Sally Seton—but until now she has forced herself to remember their domineering forms, not their revelatory ones.

The disaster and disgrace that she at last recognizes in herself is her own refusal to give and receive sympathy. The moral crisis that she confronts occurs entirely within herself, and she can resolve it only by transforming herself. Dorothea Brooke's lonely crisis in the final scenes of *Middlemarch* never demands that she confront a disaster and disgrace of her own: Dorothea turns instead to the disaster and disgrace of two other people, Rosamond and Ladislaw, and she performs a noble and generous act that has the unspoken effect of confirming her superiority and demonstrating that she is not required to make any changes in herself beyond learning the price of things in shops (nor are we who admiringly read about her). In the uncompromising psychology of *Mrs. Dalloway,* everyone's moral superiority over Doris Kilman or Sir William Bradshaw exempts no one—certainly not Clarissa—from confronting her own inadequacies.

Having escaped her self-flattering sense of superiority, Clarissa does not yield to the subtler self-flattery that occurs when you are fascinated by your own guilt. She knows perfectly well that she has taken pleasure in her isolation and still takes pleasure in it, and she lets herself be distracted from her thoughts of Septimus. "Odd, incredible; she had never been so happy."* And now she occupies herself in the little room by straightening chairs, aligning a book on a shelf, and reminding herself of her foolish idea that "something of her own" was in the sky above her house. As she does so, she walks to the window, and there—"Oh, but how surprising!—in the room opposite the old lady stared straight at her!" The old lady who embodied for Clarissa "the privacy of the soul" when she saw her earlier in the day suddenly seems to have renounced her privacy by looking at Clarissa face to face. "Could she see her?"—can the old lady looking through the window see Clarissa in the little room—she asks herself, but the answer does not matter: whatever the old lady can see, Clarissa herself has felt the shock of being seen, in the privacy of her soul, by another soul in its own privacy. (This moment is deliberately unspectacular and unmoving, because the kind of moral discovery that Clarissa must make is not the kind that can be induced by a timely flash of lightning.) The

---

* Another last-minute revision: in the earlier text in the American edition this sentence reads "It was due to Richard; she had never been so happy." But it was not due to Richard; she alone chose her isolation.

reason that the privacy of the soul is a treasure worth dying for is that it defends and preserves the closeness, rapture, and embrace, the "attempt to communicate" that Clarissa recognizes in Septimus. "This he had preserved," she thought, a few paragraphs before. Now she remembers his death as a triumph of integrity: "The young man had killed himself; but she did not pity him." The last phrase has multiple meanings: her refusal to pity him has a trace of survivor's heartlessness, but it is also a refusal to feel the kind of loveless pity that elevates itself above the one pitied.

As the light goes out in the old lady's window, Clarissa repeats the lines from the mourning song in Shakespeare's *Cymbeline* that she has remembered at moments throughout the day: "Fear no more the heat of the sun." In Shakespeare, this is a threnody over Imogen, who is not dead after all, and who wakes a dozen lines after the song ends. Clarissa, too, returns from her lonely encounter with death. With her sudden—although perhaps momentary—escape from indifference, she has also escaped from her chronic loneliness:

> The clock was striking. The leaden circles dissolved in the air. But she must go back. She must assemble. She must find Sally and Peter. And she came in from the little room.*

Now the reiterated "must . . . must . . . must" expresses Clarissa's inner imperatives, the obligations that she freely and deliberately chooses—the opposite of what the same repeated words meant when Septimus remembered Sir William Bradshaw's imperatives. Clarissa must "assemble"; and she can only do so by finding indi-

---

* Until Virginia Woolf made her final proof corrections for the British edition, the sentence "The leaden circles dissolved in the air" was followed by "He made her feel the beauty; made her feel the fun" (still present in American editions). The omitted phrases diminished Clarissa's revelation by aestheticizing it into beauty and fun instead of her moral need to "assemble," to "find Sally and Peter."

vidual persons, not by merging into the plural collectiveness of her party, and so her next thought is that she must find Sally and Peter, whose love she no longer mistakes as a domineering intrusion on the soul's privacy. Her decision is explicitly conscious and moral. "She could see what she lacked," as she told herself a few hours earlier in her attic room; she has "a scruple picked up Heaven knows where, or, as she felt, sent by Nature"; she cannot (unlike the young Sally) rely on nature or instinct or inclination to do the work of loving for her. Her knowledge of her lack was her excuse for doing nothing about it; now she has no excuse, and must do her best with what she has.

Virginia Woolf modeled Clarissa Dalloway partly on an elegant society hostess from her parents' circle of friends, Kitty Maxse, who had lost contact with Virginia Woolf and disapproved of Virginia's Bloomsbury circle. Kitty Maxse died in 1922, perhaps by suicide, when she fell over the banister on her staircase. Virginia Woolf had been grateful for Kitty Maxse's kindness, but thought of her as brittle, glittery, and generally unsatisfactory. But when she re-created her as Clarissa Dalloway, she gave her the deepest moral and emotional understanding that she gave to any of her characters in her whole career as a novelist, and in doing so she rescued the fictional woman from the death that the real one seemed to have chosen.

Clarissa Absent and Clarissa Present

After the moment when Clarissa "came in from the little room," she disappears from the book for forty paragraphs. She remains unseen by the narrator, and apparently by everyone else, until, in the final lines, she succeeds in her attempt to communicate, and Peter Walsh experiences what Clarissa calls closeness and rapture, and what Peter calls the extraordinary excitement of terror and ecstasy. Readers seem not to have remarked on Clarissa's disappearance, but her guests notice it. "Where was she, all this time? It was getting late," Peter wonders to himself. "Why did not Clarissa come and talk to them?" Sally asks a few paragraphs later, and then, after some further paragraphs, says, "really she must go, if Clarissa did not come soon."

Where is Clarissa? Why does it take her so long to find Sally and Peter after her revelation in the little room?

Virginia Woolf was careful to write the narrative of her book in strict chronological sequence. Her characters spend much of the day recollecting their pasts, but their acts of recollecting, like all the other events in the book, occur one after the other; the book never suggests that the events in one section occur at the same time as the events in a preceding section. The long interval between Clarissa's exit from the room and Peter's vision may seem unimportant (like any hostess, she has been buttonholed by her guests), but it is essential to the book's emotional depth. Equally essential is the fact that no one but Peter is reported as seeing Clarissa in the final pages of the book—and even Peter is not reported as actually *seeing* her as a visible, physical presence in the room. All that the book says of his experience of her is that he is puzzled by feelings of terror and ecstasy, and shortly afterward tells himself, "It is Clarissa." For there she was, the book concludes. But exactly where was she, and in what way was she there?

The reason Virginia Woolf chooses this indirect way of describing Clarissa's arrival seems to be that the book, in effect, remembers its author's original intention (as described in her 1928 preface) to have Clarissa "kill herself, or perhaps merely to die at the end of the party." In a ghostly invisible form, the original story is hidden within the published version as a parallel or shadow narrative that coincides with the story that takes center stage. In that invisible parallel narrative, Clarissa dies as she steps out of the little room. This shadow version of her death completes an action imagined earlier in the book, when Peter remembers Clarissa's theory of the survival of the unseen part of ourselves. As Peter recalls it, Clarissa's odd sense of affinities between herself and others

> ended in a transcendental theory which, with her horror of death, allowed her to believe, or say that she believed (for all her scepticism), that since our apparitions, the part of us which appears, are so momentary compared with the other, the unseen part of us, which spreads wide, the unseen might survive, be recovered somehow attached to this person or that, or even haunting certain places after death . . . perhaps—perhaps.

At the end of the plausible, realistic, central narrative of *Mrs. Dalloway*, Peter sees Clarissa enter the room. At the end of the parallel shadow narrative, Peter's earlier premonition of the bell that tolled for death—"Clarissa falling where she stood, in her drawing-room"—has been fulfilled, and the "unseen part" of her has been, as she imagined, "recovered somehow attached to this person or that"—attached to the person of Peter Walsh, who more than anyone else loves her for the invisible center of herself.

A triumphant conclusion can be deeply moving only when it is shadowed by the possibility of death and defeat. Shakespeare's comedies always include the threat of death, even when the sources of his plots included nothing of the kind. Virginia Woolf invented for *Mrs. Dalloway* a complex interweaving of triumph and elegy in which Peter Walsh's vision of the living Clarissa conceals the buried traces of a story in which his vision can occur only after Clarissa has died. This double narrative is consistent with the complexity of the book's moral depths. For all its exhilarating excitement, Peter's vision of Clarissa will not produce any change in his life: Virginia Woolf says nothing about the day after the party, but the only possible outcome is that Peter will return to India to marry his insignificant divorcée, Sally will return to her rich husband and six children, and Clarissa will resume her life as Mrs. Richard Dalloway.

If D. H. Lawrence had written the story, Clarissa would perhaps have gone off to live in a rural cottage with Sally and Peter. But Virginia Woolf deliberately made her characters too old and too stable for fantasies of drastic change. Vision is not discredited by its inevitable fading in the moments after the book's closing words, but the emotional force of the concluding vision is immeasurably deepened by a reader's understanding that it is simultaneously sufficient and too late, that Clarissa's visionary love remains detached from any possibility of physical love.

The Bootboy at Claridge's

Like *Ulysses*, *Mrs. Dalloway* follows its characters from morning to night on a single June day as they wander through a city, remembering their past. Virginia Woolf had some tart things to say about Joyce while she was reading *Ulysses*. She thought "the poor young man has only got the dregs of a mind compared even with George Meredith"; some of the early chapters were "merely the scratching of pimples on the body of the bootboy at Claridge's"—the grandest London hotel. When she finished reading it, she told her diary she thought it "a mis-fire." She added:

> Genius it has I think; but of the inferior water. The book is diffuse. It is brackish. It is pretentious. It is underbred, not only in the obvious sense, but in the literary sense. A first rate writer, I

mean, respects writing too much to be tricky; startling; doing stunts.

Virginia Woolf was as dismissive and snobbish in her novels as she was in her diaries and letters, but in her novels, unlike her diaries, she was distrustful of her snobbery and knew what was wrong about it even if she was unwilling or unable to renounce it. She took *Ulysses* seriously enough, despite its pimples and under-breeding, to use it as a model for the single-day narrative of *Mrs. Dalloway* and for her own borrowings from the *Odyssey,* many of them lifted directly from Homer rather than taken secondhand from Joyce. *Mrs. Dalloway,* which in manuscript had been titled *The Hours,* is organized into twelve chapters,* as *Ulysses* is orga-nized into eighteen, each with its own hour of time and style of consciousness. Peter Walsh is as anonymous when he arrives in London as Odysseus is anonymous when he arrives disguised on Ithaca: "And just because nobody yet knew he was in London, except Clarissa, and the earth, after the voyage, still seemed an island to him, the strangeness of standing alone, alive, unknown, at half-past eleven in Trafalgar Square overcame him." In his recol-lection of Clarissa, he unconsciously echoes the final word of *Ulysses:* "She had some queer power of fiddling on one's nerves, turning one's nerves to fiddle-strings, yes."

Critics have argued over the literary merits of Virginia Woolf's dismissals of and borrowings from *Ulysses* ever since Wyndham Lewis accused her in 1934 of plagiarizing Joyce. But the heart of

---

* This is apparent only in the first edition, which was seen through the press by Leonard and Virginia Woolf, and in almost all later British editions. Three of the chapter breaks are absent from American editions, evidently because of miscom-munication between author and printer.

the matter is Virginia Woolf's deeper sense of the relation between aesthetic genius and moral intelligence. Complexity is not the same as depth, and she understood that Joyce's book, with all its surface intention to shock and disturb, was finally soothing and flattering to its readers. Joyce's openness about sexual and excretory matters was to her less revolutionary than adolescent; and she used Peter Walsh's thoughts about the five years since the end of the 1914–18 war to make a subtle joke about *Ulysses*. "People looked different," Peter observes as he walks through London, and he goes on to think about other changes:

> Newspapers seemed different. Now for instance there was a man writing quite openly in one of the respectable weeklies about water-closets. That you couldn't have done ten years ago—written quite openly about water-closets in a respectable weekly.

Joyce's most shocking episodes, that is, were no more shocking than last week's *Spectator* or *New Statesman*.

Joyce's aesthetic method was flattering in a more subtle and elusive way. *Ulysses* was ultimately shaped and governed by the aesthetic theories that Stephen Dedalus expounded in *A Portrait of the Artist as a Young Man*. True art, Stephen said, "arrested" the spectator, as opposed to false art which left the spectator either attracted or repelled. Art that attracted the spectator—made you want to do or have something—was pornographic, Stephen said; art that repelled the spectator—turned you away from something— was didactic; neither was true art. Novels were especially difficult to write in accordance with Stephen Dedalus's specifications, because any extended narrative about human beings must include incidents that attract or repel. Joyce solved the problem in *Ulysses* by balancing both kinds of response with an exactness unparalleled in literature. Aesthetically, Leopold Bloom is ridiculous: misinformed, clumsy, cuckolded, masochistic; he is sexually pitiable, exchanging erotic fantasies by mail with a woman he has never met and masturbating at the distant sight of a young woman on the shore. No one wants the humiliation of appearing to others or oneself as Bloom does. Morally, however, Bloom is perfect, generous to strays and strangers, tolerant of his wife's adultery, and, unlike anyone in the real world, apparently incapable of doing or causing harm to others. The fantasy of a hero who is aesthetically flawed but morally perfect encourages readers to conclude that because they (like all ordinary human beings) have the same sort of aesthetic flaws that the hero has, they may also have the same sort of moral perfection. For this fantasy Virginia Woolf had no patience, and Clarissa Dalloway's revelation in the little room is a moment of self-discovery of moral failings, not aesthetic ones.

The later chapters of *Ulysses* move gradually away from a world of life and death toward a timeless, cyclical, anonymous world of myth and dream—the same world that tempts Peter Walsh in his daylight dream of the solitary traveler. Leopold Bloom settles at last into the passivity of sleep, reflecting on "the lethargy of nescient [unknowing] matter: the apathy of the stars." He has traveled with "Sinbad the Sailor and Tinbad the Tailor and Jinbad the Jailer" and a dozen more alliterative archetypes. Molly Bloom becomes the mythical embodiment of earth, reclining like a doubly archetypal earth goddess "in the attitude of Gea-Tullus," and in her final monologue she remembers everything and accepts everything. A funeral occurs in one of the early chapters, but a birth occurs in a later one, and everything remains in balance. No one in *Ulysses* does any serious harm to anyone in the course of the day; nothing is seriously or irrevocably lost.

Mrs. Dalloway refuses to offer such reassurances. In the world portrayed by Virginia Woolf, time does not move in circles, and the loss that occurs in the course of the action is irrevocable and real. No new birth balances Septimus's death. And Septimus's death is not a natural event but a murder provoked by others and committed by himself. Clarissa's vision, magnificent as it is, occurs too late.

Virginia Woolf gave new depths to the material she lifted from *Ulysses* in the same way that Shakespeare did with his sources. At the end of the phantasmagorical "Circe" chapter in *Ulysses* a "wonderstruck" Leopold Bloom has a vision of his long-dead son Rudy as "a fairy boy of eleven, a changeling, kidnapped, dressed in an Eton suit with glass shoes and little bronze helmet." The moment is one of Joyce's triumphs: at once superbly moving and absurdly sentimental because sentimentality and cliché are part of the real language of strong human emotions. Virginia Woolf seems to have been stimulated by this passage to give Peter his concluding vision of Clarissa, but she chose to give Peter a vision of Clarissa herself, not a projection of his fantasies about her.

Bloom's son Rudy had died eleven years earlier, having lived little more than a week. Bloom's fifteen-year-old daughter Milly is working for a photographer away from Dublin and never appears in *Ulysses*. Virginia Woolf transformed these separations of father and children in *Ulysses* into the emotional distance between mother and daughter in *Mrs. Dalloway*. Clarissa finds Elizabeth opaque, and thinks of her more as a flower than a person: "now at seventeen, why, Clarissa could not in the least understand, she had become very serious; like a hyacinth . . ." Elizabeth keeps her distance from her mother, not only during her Telemachos-like expedition through London, but also in her silences at home, her distaste for all of Clarissa's urban social excitements: "she so much preferred being left alone to do what she liked in the country, but they would compare her to lilies [and, Elizabeth complained earlier, to poplar trees, early dawn, hyacinths, fawns, and running water], and she had to go to parties, and London was so dreary compared with being alone in the country with her father and the dogs." On the last page of the book Elizabeth stands beside her father, who makes her happy by telling her how lovely she is—although the last of her thoughts is not about human beings at all, but her worry that "her poor dog was howling."

Clarissa is baffled by her daughter's wish for the privacy of the soul, the same privacy that Clarissa insists on protecting for herself and that she is grateful to Septimus Warren Smith for preserving. Virginia Woolf portrays Clarissa's vision in the little room, like Peter's vision of Clarissa, as triumphant, even though it can change nothing in Clarissa's future, and even though its sunburst of illumination leaves in shadow Clarissa's marriage and all the possible futures that might emerge from Clarissa's parenthood.

6

PARENTHOOD: *To the Lighthouse*

Mrs. Ramsay nurtures and comforts her eight children. Mr. Ramsay enrages and terrifies them. Every reader of *To the Lighthouse* sympathizes with the six-year-old James Ramsay's fantasy of killing the father who destroys all youthful hope. A year after she finished *To the Lighthouse*, Virginia Woolf noted in her diary that her father, Leslie Stephen, would have been ninety-six years old if he had lived, but that "mercifully" he had not. His life, she wrote, "would have entirely ended mine. What would have happened? No writing, no books;—inconceivable." Leslie Stephen was the model for Mr. Ramsay, but Virginia Woolf was subtler and deeper when writing novels than when keeping her diary, and her novel portrays the nurturing parent as the one who holds back her children in an attempt to preserve and sustain her own past—while the tyrannical parent is the one who points them toward their own future.

To the Lighthouse is, among many other things, a study in the double nature of parenthood, its simultaneous impulses to hold back and push forward a child. For her children, and for her guests, whom she treats like children, Mrs. Ramsay provides a warmth at the heart of life. She gives them a maternal protection that unites them, calms their fears, and wins their worship and gratitude. Yet in order for her children and her guests to grow into themselves, they must venture into the colder, isolating world outside her household. What Mrs. Ramsay offers is not a relation between individual persons with their own personal histories—she finds it "painful to be reminded of the inadequacy of human relationships"—but a recurring cyclical world of ritual and myth in which unique personality dissolves into undifferentiated unity. Under Mrs. Ramsay's care, the family has the steamy intensity of a hothouse, and also has a hothouse's isolation from the changing climate of wind and rain outside. Mrs. Ramsay wants everything to remain stable and wants everyone to remain together in a unity that she provides for them. "My dear, stand still," she tells her youngest son at the start of the book, and, near the end, Lily Briscoe remembers "Mrs. Ramsay bringing them together; Mrs. Ramsay saying, 'Life stand still here.'"

Mr. Ramsay, with his histrionic self-pity, his insatiable demands for sympathy, his infuriating harshness and indifference, his anxiety over the future of his books (not over the future of his children), seems to embody all the worst faults of parenthood. He makes his first misstep on the first page when he denies James, his youngest son, the extraordinary joy of looking forward to a voyage to the lighthouse the next morning. He continues to stamp through his children's lives, in the boots about which he is absurdly vain, until ten years later, when he forces James, and James's sister Cam, to make that same voyage—and James and Cam, in their anger against him, hope the wind will remain calm and force them to remain on shore. But Mr. Ramsay in his impossibly annoying way is forcing his children out of their nest.* In the last pages of the

---

* This is a metaphor that Virginia Woolf liked to use about herself. In her 1928 introduction to *Mrs. Dalloway* she explained the difficulty of writing about her earlier work. The author's mind, she wrote, "is as inhospitable to its offspring as the hen sparrow is to hers. Once the young birds can fly, fly they must; and by the time they have fluttered out of the nest the mother bird has begun to think perhaps of another brood."

book, when their boat arrives at the lighthouse, Mr. Ramsay praises James's steering—"Well done!" he says, triumphantly—and Cam, who knows that James too is triumphant, silently addresses herself to her brother: "You've got it at last. For she knew that this was what James had been wanting, and she knew that now he had got it he was so pleased that he would not look at her or at his father or at anyone." James wins for himself a satisfaction that his mother could never have given him: the satisfaction of having performed a difficult task, and being recognized by an incorruptible impartial judge as having done it.

Virginia Woolf's mature novels superimpose two (sometimes more) measures of time in the same narrative. She does so most plainly and playfully in *Orlando,* where a single human life extends across four centuries, and more subtly but just as pervasively in *Mrs. Dalloway, To the Lighthouse,* and *Between the Acts.* In the stories that provide the basic plots of these three books, Virginia Woolf portrays time on a local, historical scale that extends across at most a few decades of individual lives; in related stories that she conceals in the metaphoric texture and poetic language of these same books, she portrays time on a vast, epochal scale that spans centuries or millennia and encompasses the rise and fall of civilizations. In *To the Lighthouse,* the passage from the first section, "The Window," through the brief connecting sequence "Time Passes," to the concluding section, "The Lighthouse," brings the characters away from their lives in the secure Edwardian twilight, where Mrs. Ramsay provides them with a criterion and focus, through the shattering transitions of the Great War, and on to their new lives without Mrs. Ramsay in the transformed society of the 1920s. But in the hidden story told through the metaphors of the book's poetic prose, the narrative also passes from an archaic, impersonal world of ritual and myth into a modern world of individuality and choice—while, at the same time, its characters pass from childhood into adulthood. *To the Lighthouse* is a novel that half conceals its happy endings, and it is much less a nostalgic celebration of Mrs. Ramsay than many readers have taken it to be.

The Mother-Goddess and Her Children

Mrs. Ramsay's maternal genius is her power to create a changeless world in which individual persons willingly dissolve their separate selves into a shared unity. She understands this quality in herself; what she does not understand is that she embodies the ancient matrilineal principles of communal life that the classicist Jane Harrison—whom Virginia Woolf deeply admired—imagined in her book *Themis: A Study of the Social Origins of Greek Religion* (1912).* The book is in effect a study of archetypes, written a few years before anyone referred to them by that name. Themis is the goddess who presides over the banquets on Olympus and summons the gods to assembly in the meeting place called the *agora;* as Jane Harrison writes, "she is the very spirit of the assembly incarnate. Themis and the actual concrete [i.e., material] agora are barely distinguishable." Themis, Jane Harrison continues, "is the force that brings and binds men together, she is 'herd instinct,' the collective conscience, the social sanction." She is not merely the social imperative, but also the embodiment of the fixed doom or fate that reduces to powerlessness and futility every isolated individual will. Jane Harrison emphasizes that the realm of Themis was matrilineal, not matriarchal: "Woman is the social centre not the dominant force."

* I was prompted to look at *Themis* and to think about its connections with *To the Lighthouse* by reading Vicki Tromanhauser's enlightening, unpublished study "Virginia Woolf's Sacrificial Plots," which, however, reads the novel in very different ways from my own.

As *To the Lighthouse* opens, Mrs. Ramsay is sitting with her youngest son James, the two together serving as a modern illustration of what Jane Harrison calls a "point of supreme importance" among the ancients: "In primitive matrilinear societies woman is the great social force or rather central focus, not as woman, or at least not as sex, but as mother, the mother of tribesmen to be . . . The male child nursed by the mother is potentially a *kouros*, hence her great value and his." (A *kouros* is a young male warrior, and *Themis* is in part a study of the ancient hymn to the young warriors who protected the infant Zeus.) Jane Harrison describes ancient images that illustrate the ancient matrilineal structure: the mother is seated with her sons; "The father, Kronos, is . . . nowhere" (Jane Harrison's ellipsis). When Mr. Ramsay announces that "it won't be fine," in contradiction to Mrs. Ramsay's promise that they will go to the lighthouse "if it's fine tomorrow," James is furious enough to want to gash a hole in his father's patriarchal breast.

A few pages later, the hypercritical young academic Charles Tansley is dazzled by the experience of walking alongside Mrs. Ramsay, who is "the most beautiful person he had ever seen," although "she was fifty at least" and has eight children. He sees "stars in her eyes." The dried-up childless widower William Bankes, who lives otherwise only for his work, experiences "rapture—for by what other name could one call it" in Mrs. Ramsay's presence, and cannot say "why the sight of her reading a fairy tale to her boy had upon him precisely the same effect as the solution of a scientific problem, so that he rested in contemplation of it, and felt . . . that barbarity was tamed, the reign of chaos subdued"—just as, for Jane Harrison, the emergence of Themis created a civilization superior to mere tribal loyalties and the rule of force. William Bankes's image of Mrs. Ramsay derives from Jane Harrison's pages; as he speaks with Mrs. Ramsay over the telephone, "He saw her at the end of the line very clearly Greek, straight, blue-eyed.* How incongruous it seemed to be telephoning to a woman like that. The Graces assembling seemed to have joined hands in meadows of asphodel to compose that face." Lily Briscoe, whom Mrs. Ramsay wants to marry off to William Bankes, thinks the same way about her: "All the time she was saying that the butter was not fresh one would be thinking of Greek temples . . ."

The beauty that overwhelms Charles Tansley and William Bankes is more than Mrs. Ramsay's mere physical presence. Tansley is transformed by her into a child who worships her as a mother; he is awed by her beauty in the way that a child is awed by his mother's beauty. Bankes is enraptured by Mrs. Ramsay's maternal presence as she reads to her son, the future *kouros*. Lily Briscoe, too, worships Mrs. Ramsay as prophetic and quasi-divine. Although Lily suspects herself of yielding to "the deceptiveness of beauty," she prefers to think of Mrs. Ramsay as an ark of sacred meaning: "she imagined how in the chambers of the mind and heart of the woman who was, physically, touching her, were stood, like the treasures in the tombs of kings, tablets bearing sacred inscriptions, which if one could spell them out, would teach one everything."

Lily imagines even more than this: Mrs. Ramsay is to her the sanctuary of something even greater than the knowledge of everything, "for it was not knowledge but unity that she desired, not inscriptions on tablets, nothing that could be written in any language known to men, but intimacy itself . . ." Shortly afterward, Lily sees Mrs. Ramsay as a great sacramental building: "she wore, to Lily's eyes, an august shape; the shape of a dome." The image

---

* Thus the American edition; the British edition, in which Virginia Woolf made slightly different revisions in the final proofs, reads "at the end of the line, Greek, blue-eyed, straight-nosed."

seems uncharacteristically forced, as if Virginia Woolf were more intent on the identification of Mrs. Ramsay with sacred places than on mere plausibility.

The Priestess and Her Altar

Later, as her family and guests gather for dinner, Mrs. Ramsay is the priestess and hierophant of her dining room, tending the flame of her shrine, surrounded by worshippers. Fourteen people are gathered at the table: she and her husband, their children, and four of their six guests, Lily Briscoe, Charles Tansley, William Bankes, and the poet Augustus Carmichael. At first, everything is sullen and tentative, as Charles Tansley makes unpleasant remarks and William Bankes worries that Mrs. Ramsay will "find out this treachery of his; that he did not care a straw for her," and all privately hope that their lack of feeling will be invisible to the others. Then the candles are lit and the separate selves coalesce into a visionary oneness. The surrounding night is excluded by the glass of the windowpanes, "which, far from giving any accurate view of the outside world, rippled it so strangely that here, inside the room, seemed to be order and dry land; there, outside, a reflection in which things wavered and vanished, waterily." Nothing has changed in the real world, but everyone experiences an inner transformation as they begin to engage in the mythical struggle of stasis against fluidity: "Some change at once went through them all, as if this had really happened, and they were all conscious of making a party together in a hollow, on an island; had their common cause against that fluidity out there." Mrs. Ramsay has given them purpose, rapture, and peace.

Just as the first dish is about to be brought in, the two remaining guests, the youthful Paul Rayley and Minta Doyle, arrive together, and Mrs. Ramsay realizes that she has brought about their engagement to marry. As Lily watches, Mrs. Ramsay takes in hand the unity that she has created, presiding like a priestess over "this terrifying thing"; Mrs. Ramsay "exalted that [terrifying thing], worshipped that; held her hands over it to warm them, to protect it, and yet, having brought it all about, somehow laughed, led her victims, Lily felt, to the altar"—a double-edged image when applied to Paul and Minta newly engaged to be married. "There was something frightening about her," Lily tells herself. "She was irresistible . . . She put a spell on them all, by wishing, so simply, so directly . . ."

Like all religious ritual, "this terrifying thing" brings a glimpse of eternity into the secular world of transient time. For Mrs. Ramsay, the celebrant of the ritual, its meaning is more intense, more complete, than it can be to mere worshippers:

> she had reached security; she hovered like a hawk suspended; like a flag floated in an element of joy which filled every nerve of her body fully and sweetly, not noisily, solemnly rather, for it arose, she thought, looking at them all eating there, from husband and children and friends; all of which rising in this profound stillness . . . seemed now for no special reason to stay there like a smoke, like a fume rising upwards, holding them safe together. Nothing need be said; nothing could be said. There it was, all around them. It partook, she felt . . . of eternity . . . there is a coherence in things, a stability; something, she meant, is immune from change, and shines out . . . in the face of the flowing, the fleeting, the spectral, like a ruby . . . Of such moments, she thought, the thing is made that endures.*

Immediately after she thinks this, she assures one of her dinner guests that "there is plenty for everybody." The temptation to dissolve yourself into the comforting unity of an archetype is rela-

---

* In the British edition: "the thing is made that remains for ever after. This would remain."

tively easy to resist when it comes to you in a dream, as it does to Peter Walsh in *Mrs. Dalloway*. It is harder to resist when it comes to you in the person of your hostess at the dinner table.

The ritual atmosphere intensifies as Mrs. Ramsay looks again at "the window in which the candle flames burnt brighter now that the panes were black." At first the voices around the table—men's voices together and Minta's voice speaking alone—"reminded her of men and boys crying out the Latin words of a service in some Roman Catholic cathedral." Then the words seem even more removed from persons, time, and space, "as if no one had said them, but they had come into existence of themselves." The moment is the climax of Mrs. Ramsay's priesthood. Even Augustus Carmichael, having held himself aloof all day, now stands and "bowed to her as if he did her homage."

The moment when one individual pays homage to another is also the moment when a collective unity breaks up. Mrs. Ramsay stands "with her foot on the threshold," on the line between the eternal presence inside and the world of time outside, and "waited a moment longer in a scene which was vanishing even as she looked." She takes Minta's arm so that they may talk in private, and as she leaves the room, "it changed, it shaped itself differently; it had become, she knew, giving one last look at it over her shoulder, already the past." As soon as she leaves, "a sort of disintegration set in."

Away from the dining room, while the party breaks up into the atoms of its separate personalities, Mrs. Ramsay seeks a different stillness: "She felt rather inclined just for a moment to stand still after all that chatter, and pick out one particular thing; the thing that mattered; to detach it; separate it off; clean it of all the emotions and odds and ends of things . . ." As in *Mrs. Dalloway*, "chatter" is contrasted by rhyme with "mattered," but the thing that Mrs. Ramsay discovers is the opposite of what Clarissa discovers.

Clarissa looks out the window at the old lady opposite going to bed, and is moved to action as she goes off to find Sally and Peter. Mrs. Ramsay seeks stasis, stability, and inhuman nature. "So she righted herself after the shock of the event, and quite unconsciously and incongruously, used the branches of the elm trees outside to help her stabilise her position. Her world was changing; they [the branches] were still." She cannot separate the stability she seeks from a flattering sense of her own permanent importance in the lives of those around her. The engagement of Paul and Minta having been accomplished, "it seemed always to have been, only was shown now and so being shown, struck everything into stability. They would, she thought . . . however long they lived, come back to this night; this moon; this wind; this house and to her too. It flattered her, where she was most susceptible of flattery . . ." Everything at the house on the island, she thinks, "would be revived again in the lives of Paul and Minta . . . Paul and Minta would carry it on when she was dead," as if they were her children, and she could expect, through them, to achieve something like immortality. She knows she cannot have her wish that her children would remain always the same ("Oh, but she never wanted James to grow a day older! or Cam either. These two she would have liked to keep for ever just as they were . . ."), so she guards against change by bringing about a marriage that will repeat a unity that cannot in itself be preserved against age or death. As in any religious ritual, the essential thing is preserved by repeating it.

Infidel Ideas of Change

Everyone yields to Mrs. Ramsay's unifying embrace, but no one wants to stay in it forever. Her daughters "sport with infidel ideas which they had brewed for themselves of a life different from hers." Mrs. Ramsay, who like Dorothea Brooke is both physically and psychologically shortsighted, opposes everything that makes her children become themselves: "Strife, division, differences of opinion, prejudices twisted into the very fibre of being, oh, that they should begin so early, Mrs. Ramsay deplored." Lily Briscoe, more realistic and more subtle than her hostess, perceives that unity is always in conflict with individuality. A few paragraphs after she imagines Mrs. Ramsay wearing the shape of a dome, she considers, and fails to resolve, a problem in her painting:

> It was a question, she remembered, how to connect this mass on the right hand with that on the left. She might do it by bringing the line of the branch across so; or break the vacancy in the foreground by an object (James perhaps) so. But the danger was that by doing that the unity of the whole might be broken.

Everyone except Mrs. Ramsay is willing to risk breaking the unity of the whole and returning to their individual selves, which is why the marriages that Mrs. Ramsay demands—Lily Briscoe and William Bankes, Minta and Paul—either fail to occur, or occur but turn into something different from the sort of marriage that she had in mind.

The "charge against" Mrs. Ramsay made by those who know her is—as she perceives—that she wants to impose her will over others: "Wishing to dominate, wishing to interfere, making people do what she wanted." And she half endorses the charge by reading to James the fairy tale of the fisherman's wife, as collected and retold by the Brothers Grimm. An enchanted, magical fish has granted wishes to a poor fisherman; the fisherman's wife keeps sending him back to the fish with a wish that she be given ever-greater powers and an ever-richer house—she works her way up to become emperor and then pope—until she finally asks to become lord of the universe, and is reduced to the poor hovel in which she and her husband began. The smaller version of this ambition that Mrs. Ramsay worries over in herself is the pressure she has put on Minta Doyle to marry Paul Rayley, her insistence "that people must marry; people must have children." But Mrs. Ramsay, unlike the fisherman's wife, wants nothing as crude as a crown or palace; she wants to preside over a state of unity and permanence that she and everyone around her can dissolve into. It never occurs to her that an exhilarating sense of unity may not be what the others need in order to become themselves, because it never occurs to her that becoming oneself is a goal worth seeking. Even the autonomous existence of other selves in distant places is enough to disrupt the unity she wants. When the talk at dinner strays toward the Mannings, a family whom she had last seen twenty years ago, she is unsettled by the thought that they had changed: "For it was extraordinary to think that they had been capable of going on living all these years when she had not thought of them more than once all that time . . . Yet perhaps Carrie Manning had not thought about her either. The thought was strange and distasteful."

Mrs. Ramsay wants a static unity, but like all other would-be tyrants, she does not subject herself to the rule she tries to impose on others. She is far more changeable than she wants anyone else to be. Among the technical triumphs of *To the Lighthouse* is its rendering of the emotions in any marriage that change from hour to hour or minute to minute. Where earlier English novelists portrayed either constant love or constant hatred, or the slow transformation of one into the other, Virginia Woolf portrays the ebb and flow of love over the course of a few minutes or hours. At the start of her dinner party Mrs. Ramsay sees her husband frowning at the far end of the table and "could not understand how she had ever felt any emotion or affection for him." A few pages later, still at the table, she looks again at him and thinks, "if he said a thing, it would make all the difference . . . Then, realising that it was because she admired him so much that she was waiting for him to speak, she felt as if somebody had been praising her husband to her and their marriage, and she glowed all over without realising that it was she herself who had praised him."

Selfless, Without a Self

Other people—Minta Doyle's mother, for example—charge Mrs. Ramsay with a wish to dominate, but Mrs. Ramsay senses that the wish originates in some greater power that holds her in its grip, that "she was driven on"—rather than voluntarily choosing—to insist that everyone marry and have children. And when she insists on marriage for everyone, she does so "too quickly she knew, almost as if it were an escape for her too." No one can live for more than an hour or two—the duration of the Ramsays' dinner party—in the unity that Mrs. Ramsay desires, and she herself knows, in some obscure way, that she desires it *because* she embodies some deep impersonal force that seeks stability and rest. Like the physical and biological forces that operate in nature, the force that Mrs. Ramsay embodies is powerful, indifferent, and, in all senses of the word, selfless. "So boasting of her capacity to surround and protect, there was scarcely a shell of herself left for her to know herself by; all was so lavished and spent." Her private answer to the charge against her, her claim that she is driven to do what she does, sounds like an excuse, but it points to a deeper truth. Her effect on others, as she tells herself accurately, is not the work of her own will; it is the work of a power outside her control. As for her startling, compelling beauty: "How could she help being 'like that' to look at," she asks herself, indignantly.

Marriage and children—her own and others'—provide her

with an escape from an inner darkness which others, blinded by her maternal aura, cannot detect. Only her husband senses "that solitude, that aloofness, that remoteness of hers," the aloneness of the maternal goddess who unifies everyone else. Like Clarissa in *Mrs. Dalloway*, Mrs. Ramsay learns unsettling truths about herself when she finds herself alone, but unlike Clarissa, she exults in isolation and distance: "One shrunk, with a sense of solemnity, to being oneself, a wedge-shaped core of darkness, something invisible to others . . . and this self having shed its attachments was free for the strangest adventures." She becomes a "core of darkness," free from all human entanglements,

> for no one saw it. They could not stop it, she thought, exulting. There was freedom, there was peace, there was, most welcome of all, a summoning together, a resting on a platform of stability.

Mrs. Ramsay treasures her escape into herself for the same reason that she tries to make "life stand still" and urges marriage on Lily and on Minta: she wants an escape from the uncertainty and change inherent in all relations among individuals.

But she is deluded when she exults in her withdrawal. As she recedes into her private darkness, the language of the book records a withdrawal deeper than her mere isolation from others: in an obscure but crucial way, she withdraws from herself. Her phrase "being oneself, a wedge-shaped core of darkness" turns out to mean something different from *having* a self or *becoming* oneself in the sense of having a unique personality. Instead of going deeper into her personality, she escapes from it into a darkness where personality no longer exists. "Not as oneself did one find rest ever, in her experience . . . but as a wedge of darkness. Losing personality, one lost the fret, the hurry, the stir; and there rose to her lips always some exclamation of triumph over life when things came together in this peace, this rest, this eternity." In this mood, she increasingly feels herself attached to a remote object, "to one thing especially of the things one saw"—and she now loses herself in the beam of the lighthouse.

And while looking out at the lighthouse, as she annihilates herself and "became the thing she looked at," she repeats phrases in her mind—"when suddenly she added, We are in the hands of the Lord." The conventional piety of the phrase startles her:

> But instantly she was annoyed with herself for saying that. Who had said it? Not she; she had been trapped into saying something she did not mean . . . What brought her to say that: "We are in the hands of the Lord?" she wondered. The insincerity slipping in among the truths roused her, annoyed her.

This is one of Virginia Woolf's most splendid and unsettling moments, written with exact moral and psychological insight. Mrs. Ramsay delights in slipping away from personality, then is startled and annoyed to discover that when personality is lost, what takes its place is not the detached, bodiless wedge of darkness that she imagines, but a cliché. And although Mrs. Ramsay brushes away the insight and returns to her knitting, the novel has made its point that when personality is renounced or denied, the void it leaves in the self is filled by impersonal speech, automatic sentiments, empty slogans, trivial formulas, party lines, fashionable chatter. When Mrs. Ramsay tries to escape from personality, she does not escape it at all: she merely does to it what Clarissa Dalloway accused herself of having done to it, leaving it "wreathed about with chatter, defaced, obscured . . . let drop every day in corruption, lies, chatter."

The language of this moment in the novel derives from a

famous sentence in T. S. Eliot's essay "Tradition and the Individual Talent" (published in book form in Eliot's *The Sacred Wood,* which Leonard Woolf had reviewed in 1920): "But, of course, only those who have personality and emotions know what it means to want to escape from those things." Mrs. Ramsay's experience as a wedge of darkness suggests that Virginia Woolf perceived that the very wish to escape from personality and emotions, to evade everything that mattered, was itself the unhappiness that afflicted T. S. Eliot. The passage away from personality was not, as Eliot hoped in his essay, the entryway to a great cohesive tradition in which all of European literature is simultaneously present and into which all individual writers are subsumed; instead it leads to the inane wilderness that Mrs. Ramsay finds when she withdraws into darkness and that Eliot himself portrayed a few years later in "The Hollow Men."

Among the clichés of postmodern aesthetics in the late twentieth century was the discovery that the self is not a stable and coherent whole but a shifting and provisional gathering of bits and pieces derived from external culture, what Virginia Woolf in *Between the Acts* (in a phrase adapted from Shakespeare's *Troilus and Cressida*) called "scraps, orts and fragments." As Mrs. Ramsay's experience implied, long before postmodernism was thought of, this insight is accurate, but only to the extent that the personality in question is detached from all others. As soon as it commits itself to something or someone, the fragments converge; they become purposive and whole; you become yourself. The postmodern theory of personality, like Eliot's theory, tells more about the theoretician than about the theory's ostensible subject—about the failures of selfhood in those who refuse to be anyone in particular, not about any inherent limits of selfhood.

Fathers and Children

Virginia Woolf rebuked the patriarchal social order in her two political books, *A Room of One's Own* and *Three Guineas,* and throughout her essays, diaries, and letters. *To the Lighthouse,* however, is not a political or social tract, but a historical and psychological novel—or, as she speculated in her diary, something other than a novel for which she could only guess at a name. Perhaps it could be, she wrote, "A new —— by Virginia Woolf. But what? Elegy?" After mourning the past, elegies always look toward the future: as in the last line of John Milton's "Lycidas," "Tomorrow to fresh woods, and pastures new." *To the Lighthouse* is a family history in which the timeless maternal past is supplanted by a patriarchal world of change—and a time approaches somewhat like the one imagined at the end of *A Room of One's Own,* when sexual differences will no longer matter, when neither matriarch nor patriarch can rule the future.

The matrilineal past imagined by Jane Harrison brought civilization into being, but everyone who lived in that past lived under the assumption that fate or doom is more powerful than freedom. For better or, mostly, for worse, history is made by Themis's patriarchal successors, blundering toward a future; not by Themis herself, trying to preserve things as they were. Mrs. Ramsay has convinced herself that Paul and Minta will carry on her kind of life when she is dead, that the present will be revived in the next generation; but the middle section of the book, "Time Passes," contradicts her even in its title. In the section's opening sentence William Bankes says, "Well, we must wait for the future to show." And Andrew Ramsay says, not quite as a reply, "It's almost too dark to see." What the dark future shows, in the next few pages, are the disasters and dissolutions brought about by the Great War—in Virginia Woolf's view, the disastrous work of the patriarchy—as the Ramsays' house on the island is abandoned to the elements, as Mrs. Ramsay dies "rather suddenly," as Mrs. Ramsay's plans for her children are destroyed when Prue dies from "some illness connected with childbirth" and Andrew is killed on the battlefield.

Then, in the final section of the book, "The Lighthouse," the surviving Ramsays and Lily Briscoe gather again at the house on the island; Mr. Ramsay impels a reluctant James and Cam to brave the voyage to the lighthouse; and Lily Briscoe completes the painting that she had left unfinished on her previous visit ten years before. Mrs. Ramsay is mourned by everyone, but the section titled "The Lighthouse" is Virginia Woolf's variation on George Eliot's theme in the section of *Middlemarch* titled "The Dead Hand." In *To the Lighthouse* as in *Middlemarch,* the living must triumph over the will of the dead. But *Middlemarch* treats their struggle as a morally simple matter of thwarting the will of the dead tyrants Mr. Casaubon and Peter Featherstone, while *To the Lighthouse* portrays a more complex and plausible struggle against the will of the loving and maternal Mrs. Ramsay.

The triumph of the living requires the defeat of someone loving and maternal, and is no less satisfying because of it. Paul and Minta recover from the failure of their marriage by making a relationship unlike anything Mrs. Ramsay could have approved. Minta, "tinted, garish," has had affairs; after their marital crisis, Paul has taken up with a serious woman who shares his views. "Far from breaking up the marriage, that alliance had righted it," Lily observes; Paul and Minta now "were excellent friends." (On Minta's first visit to the island, perhaps anticipating the new kind of life she would later find for herself, she had "left the third volume of *Middlemarch* in the train and she never knew what happened in the end.") Lily fantasizes about gloating over Mrs. Ramsay's failure to make the future behave like the past. "She would feel a little triumphant, telling Mrs. Ramsay that the marriage had not been a success"— which seems closer to Lily's real view of the matter than her earlier thought that it had been "righted" by its failure.

Throughout the first part of the book, ten years earlier, Mrs. Ramsay had tried to shape the future of her children and of anyone else who was younger than she was. Mr. Ramsay meanwhile had been equally anxious about his reputation among the young, about changes in literary fashion that denigrated his beloved Sir Walter Scott, about the probability that his books will be forgotten, about his frustrated ambition to move beyond the letter Q in his quest to extend human thought toward its culmination at Z. But Mr. Ramsay never imagines he can control the future by controlling other people, and in the last chapter of the first section he finds satisfaction merely in reading Sir Walter Scott, and that satisfaction is enough to let him dismiss his anxieties and ambitions: "now, he felt, it didn't matter a damn who reached Z . . . Somebody would reach it—if not he, then another." Mrs. Ramsay never gives up her ambition, and at the end of the same chapter, when she lets her husband know that she loves him while refusing him the words of love that he wants from her, or that she thinks he wants from her, "she had triumphed again." (Her triumph may, however, occur only in her imagination: Virginia Woolf is careful never to report directly that Mr. Ramsay wants words of love from her at this point, only that Mrs. Ramsay is convinced that he wants them.)

Mr. Ramsay gives up his ambition, which is why, no matter how overbearing and absurd he remains, no matter how insistently he coerces his reluctant children, he never blocks them from becoming adults, while Mrs. Ramsay has grown so accustomed to maternal success, so unwilling to accept anything less than victory, that only death can defeat her. And the whole process of life and growth in *To the Lighthouse* requires that she be defeated.

This is a very different way of thinking about masculinity and femininity from those that permeate Virginia Woolf's political writings and her notes in her diaries about her family background. She was the only one of the great modernists of the 1920s who refused in her imaginative writings—her novels—the enticing equation, favored by James Joyce, T. S. Eliot, and D. H. Lawrence, in which family politics are understood to be a microcosm of world politics, so that if you understand family relations you understand such large-scale things as the relations of Ireland and England or the moral crises of Europe. (She made this exact equation in *Three Guineas,* but not in her fiction.) In *Mrs. Dalloway* actions and emotions that have murderous results when they occur on the public scale of international relations may have very different effects within the intimate scale of personal relations. What is murderous between nations may be liberating among individual men and women. The patriarchal horrors of the Great War are parodied, not duplicated, by the patriarchal poses of Mr. Ramsay as he recites "The Charge of the Light Brigade" or rushes across the lawn in search of a woman who will pity him, or at least admire (as Lily obligingly does) his boots.

At the Lighthouse

When Lily Briscoe, in the third part of the book, begins to paint the picture she had left unfinished on her last visit, she remembers Mrs. Ramsay as the organizing principle of the place, the one who had gathered everything together as if she too had been organizing a work of art. The scene on the beach ten years earlier "seemed to depend somehow upon Mrs. Ramsay sitting under the rock, with a pad on her knee, writing letters." The permanence that Mrs. Ramsay had hoped to leave behind her comes into being—for the moment—in Lily's memory of her: "That woman sitting there writing under the rock resolved everything into simplicity; made these angers, irritations fall off like old rags; she brought together this and that and then this, and so made of that miserable silliness and spite . . . something—this scene on the beach for example, this moment of friendship and liking—which survived, after all these years complete . . . and there it stayed in the mind affecting one almost like a work of art."

Lily repeats to herself the phrase "Like a work of art" and then proceeds through a long paragraph of admiration and understanding in which she imagines Mrs. Ramsay "making of the moment something permanent." Lily's painting, too, she thinks, is an attempt to make something permanent, and she thinks of Mrs. Ramsay as an artist who succeeded where Lily has not yet been able to succeed:

> In the midst of chaos there was shape; this eternal passing and flowing . . . was struck into stability. Life stand still here, Mrs. Ramsay said. "Mrs. Ramsay! Mrs. Ramsay!" she repeated. She owed it all to her.

Ten years before, on the night of the party, when Paul Rayley told Mrs. Ramsay he was engaged to Minta Doyle, he too had said, "I owe it all to you."[*]

A vision may be captured and made permanent in a work of art, but in life it rarely persists longer than a moment. For a painter or writer working at a canvas or a page, the command "Life stand still here" is the command that brings into being a work of art. When that command is imposed on other human beings, as it is by Mrs.

---

[*] The echo of Paul Rayley and Lily Briscoe both owing "it all" to Mrs. Ramsay occurs only in the American edition; in the British edition Lily ends her thought with "She owed this revelation to her."

Ramsay, it requires them to submerge themselves into a unity that deprives them of their personalities and their future. The vision Mrs. Ramsay makes possible to others is an image of wholeness that acts like any moment of passionate satisfaction that unites parents and children in a state of intensity and security, a state which seems infinitely valuable and desirable. But that sense of unity becomes constraining and tyrannical when it is used as a model or guide for everyday life—rather than as something inaccessible and profound which perhaps gives ultimate meaning to everyday life, but cannot govern its details.

Mrs. Ramsay never understands this. Lily Briscoe, almost despite herself, does. At the end of *To the Lighthouse,* both James, at sixteen, and Lily, at forty-four, escape in different ways from Mrs. Ramsay's maternal hearth and become autonomous adults. Both achieve something that had long been delayed, something that needed years to pass before they could find it. Having spent the day annoyed with Mr. Ramsay and longing for Mrs. Ramsay, Lily feels for the last time the "old horror" of her unsatisfied longing for the unity that Mrs. Ramsay promised—"to want and want and not to have," as Lily says of her old feelings. "Could she inflict that still?" she wonders about Mrs. Ramsay.

Then, suddenly, she realizes that Mrs. Ramsay can no longer inflict that. Lily's unsatisfied longing which had once been the "old horror" is now quietly transformed into "part of ordinary experience, was on a level with the chair, with the table." Freed from the past, Lily wonders about the present and future—and she no longer wants Mrs. Ramsay. "Where was that boat now?" she asks herself. "And Mr. Ramsay? She wanted him."

Then, after James has steered the boat to the lighthouse, and Mr. Ramsay has congratulated him and "sprung" off the boat "lightly like a young man," Lily thinks aloud, "He must have reached it," and feels "suddenly completely tired out." This moment is entirely unlike the triumphant unity of Mrs. Ramsay's dinner party with its glow of permanence and endurance. Lily senses without knowing that James's life has arrived at a moment of great change. Thanks to his father's insistence, he has had his own autonomous success. When his father says "triumphantly: 'Well done!,' " the triumph that Mr. Ramsay celebrates is not his own but his son's. There is nothing shared or unifying about this moment; Mr. Ramsay seems entirely unaware of what his son is feeling.

Lily feels tired after James's and Mr. Ramsay's success because, in the same way that Clarissa understood Septimus, Lily understands what James and Mr. Ramsay feel, and is exhausted because some great effort has been completed. Tired as she is, the experience rouses her to her own triumph. When she looks at her canvas, she has none of Mrs. Ramsay's fantasies of permanence and endurance, no hope that anyone will care about her painting after she is dead. "It would be hung in the attics, she thought; it would be destroyed." She has told herself this repeatedly all day; now, after James's achievement, she thinks differently about it. "But what did that matter? she asked herself, taking up her brush again." And with the realization that what she makes on her canvas need not be permanent after all, she frees herself to find her own way. The steps of the house are empty; her canvas is blurred; but she brings everything into focus with a single stroke, and creates in art the kind of order that Mrs. Ramsay could not create in life. "With a sudden intensity, as if she saw it clear for a second, she drew a line there, in the centre. It was done; it was finished." Just before she closes the book with the words "I have had my vision," she lays down her brush "in extreme fatigue." It is the fatigue of someone who, having completed something, can turn to things that matter to her future.

7

Everything comes to an end in *Between the Acts*, and then, as the book itself comes to an end, something unknowable begins. The events of the book take place in and around an English country house, Poyntz Hall, during the twenty-four hours from one evening to the next in the last June before the Second World War. In the afternoon, the villagers perform an ironic fragmentary pageant, written for them by an outsider, Miss La Trobe, and composed of imaginary episodes from a thousand years of English history. The official purpose of the pageant is to raise funds to illuminate the village church, Bolney Minster, with electric lights. But the villagers, the church, and the surrounding landscape all share what one character calls "The doom of sudden death hanging over us."

Ten years earlier, in the closing words of *The Waves*, the novel by Virginia Woolf that is composed almost entirely of the thoughts of six characters, one of the characters, Bernard, confronts death like a hero who is part chivalric knight, part Don Quixote:

Death is the enemy. It is death against whom I ride with my spear couched and my hair flying back like a young man's, like Percival's, when he galloped in India. I strike spurs into my horse. Against you I will fling myself, unvanquished and unyielding, O Death!

This melodramatic fantasy of what it feels like to face imminent death has the manner of someone who does not quite believe that death is real. In *Between the Acts* the characters and the narrator face death more plausibly and less dramatically. Some face it with resignation, some with anger, some with blind denial or mere indifference. *Between the Acts* takes an old person's view of death: the disappearance of any individual seems less momentous than it might in youth or middle age. "For us," an old man in the book tells his sister when she reminisces about a children's game, "the game's over."

The characters in *Between the Acts* divide into those who see the disaster approaching even if they know they can do nothing about it and those who by inclination or willfulness try not to see it at all. The only future that most of the characters think about is one that has been foretold of the next few hours, the forecast by the "weather expert" in the morning newspaper whose prophecy is limited to: "variable winds; fair average temperature; rain at times." Even this simple formula seems to have been forgotten by the afternoon when a sudden shower falls: "No one had seen the cloud coming." Giles Oliver, the middle-aged heir to Poyntz Hall, listens in fury as his aunt, Mrs. Swithin, says of the view from the garden: "It'll be there when we're not." (This is the same conviction of permanence that Mrs. Ramsay feels about Paul and Minta and the house on the island.) Giles says nothing, but rages against "old fogies who sat and looked at views when the whole of Europe—over there— was . . . bristling with guns, poised with planes. At any moment guns would rake that land into furrows; planes splinter Bolney Minster into smithereens and blast the Folly." (Hogben's Folly— the word means a costly and usually decorative or extravagant structure—is the other notable building in the vicinity.)

In the eyes of her nephew, Mrs. Swithin seems complacently unaware of disaster and change. But her imagination encompasses epochal changes that Giles never thinks about. The kind of change that Mrs. Swithin thinks about, however, takes place over such vast periods that it does not threaten the peace and quiet of anyone in particular. Near the start of the book she reads in her favorite *Outline of History* (it is by H. G. Wells, though the book never says so) about a time far more distant than the merely historical past that is recalled in the village pageant, a time before words were thought or spoken, before men and women emerged from their caves, when the British Isles did not even exist, "when the entire continent, not then, she understood, divided by a channel, was all one; populated, she understood, by elephant-bodied, seal-necked, heaving, surging, slowly writhing, and, she supposed, barking monsters; the iguanodon, the mammoth, and the mastodon; from whom presumably, she thought . . . we descend." Changes that occurred in more recent centuries seem less important to her, more easily assimilated. She says of the earnest Victorians portrayed in the pageant, "I don't believe that there ever were such people. Only you and me . . . dressed differently." Mrs. Swithin's family bought Poyntz Hall a little more than a hundred years earlier. Showing a visitor a picture on the wall, she says it is "not an ancestress. But we claim her because we've known her—O, ever so many years."

The Scene Changes

Seen from the terrace at Poyntz Hall, the world seems changeless. The place still corresponds to its description in a nineteenth-century guidebook: "1833 was true in 1939. No house had been built; no town had sprung up." The Oliver family looks out over the view from the house "to see if what they knew might be different today. Most days it was the same."

Most days—but not this day. A few hours earlier, Mrs. Swithin had told her brother Bartholomew Oliver (Giles Oliver's father) that she had nailed up a placard about the pageant; her words had been overheard by Giles's wife Isa:

> Every summer, for seven summers now, Isa had heard the same words; about the hammer and the nails; the pageant and the weather. Every year they said, would it be wet or fine; and every year it was—one or the other. The same chime followed the same chime, only this year beneath the chime she heard: "The girl screamed and hit him about the face with a hammer."

The sentence that Isa hears for the first time comes from a newspaper report of a trial at which guardsmen at Whitehall were convicted of the rape of a young girl; this was an actual event, not Virginia Woolf's invention. "That was real," Isa thinks as she reads about it in the newspaper, while Mrs. Swithin comes into the room carrying a hammer of her own into a world that seems—but only seems—domestic, innocent, and unchanging.

The pageant that Miss La Trobe has written for the village is a skeptic's history of England, in which change is almost always for the worse. Miss La Trobe is rumored to have failed at keeping a tea shop, to have failed when she went on the stage, to have failed in an erotic relationship with an actress. In the modernistically disconnected scenes of her script, England first emerges as an innocent child who then becomes a hopeful girl in the age of Elizabeth, and then, after a long episode of Restoration cynicism, transforms itself into an evangelizing imperial bully, whose truncheon-armed policemen rule over minds and morals at home and abroad. Behind Miss La Trobe's educated dismay over the brutalities of history lies a romantic fantasy about nature, which she imagines as having the stability that human beings lack: *"The earth is always the same,"* says a chorus of villagers in the pageant. But Mrs. Swithin, having read her *Outline of History,* knows that the earth is never the same, that it too is a place of struggle and extinction.

The history told in the pageant ends at the same moment when the performance is over. "The hands of the clock had stopped at the present moment. It was now. Ourselves." Everything stops; change ends. The performers hold mirrors up to the audience so that they can see themselves as they are and be changed by what they see. "The mirror bearers squatted; malicious; observant; expectant; expository." Like all admonitory art, the pageant inspires no one to change. No one is willing to be taught by an author's malicious attempt to "show us up, as we are, here and now." Miss La Trobe's attempt to shame and enlighten her audience says more about Miss La Trobe's artistic vanity than about the audience, and Virginia Woolf more than half sympathizes with them when they all turn away—all except the "vulgar . . . over-sexed" visitor Mrs. Manresa, who looks directly into one of the proffered mirrors, powders her nose, and rearranges a curl in her hair.

Elusive Harmonies

In her earlier books, Virginia Woolf had half ironically and half seriously evoked the visionary, liberating, and unifying powers of the artist. Vision in *Mrs. Dalloway* and art in *To the Lighthouse* revived lost meanings and joined together things that had been divided. In her final novel Virginia Woolf takes a more jaundiced view of vision and art, as if she were preparing herself, without regrets, to abandon both.

William Dodge, who arrived in the village with Mrs. Manresa, looks at one of the pictures in Poyntz Hall, but "The picture looked at nobody. The picture drew them down the paths of silence." Miss La Trobe's accusing mirrors also reveal nothing; in the midst of the pageant she thinks to herself, "A vision imparted was relief from agony"—that is, by giving a vision to others, she can relieve her own agony—but even while she thinks this, she knows she has given and imparted nothing:

> She hadn't made them see. It was a failure, another damned failure! As usual. Her vision escaped her.

It escapes because she tries to force it on others. She strides about, "often with a whip in her hand," and ends the play with a hectoring moralizing complaint spoken by the dehumanized voice of a loudspeaker connected to a gramophone—the kind of voice familiar in the later 1930s from broadcasts by European leaders. "Whose voice it was no one knew. It came from the bushes—a megaphonic, anonymous, loud-speaking affirmation." The voice rebukes the audience for their snobbery and selfishness, then complains that they cannot see the reality of love and integrity because they do not yet see the unity they really share: *all you can see of yourselves is scraps, orts and fragments.* Then it proceeds to lecture them about what they do not know: *Well then listen to the gramophone affirming . . .* But at this moment the records get jumbled, and the pageant seems to end inconclusively, halfway through a sentence. The vicar stands up to improvise a puzzled speech about the meaning of what they all have seen, and he too is interrupted by a dozen airplanes that chance to fly overhead in military formation, asserting a lethal technological reality that the pageant, despite all its historical and political skepticism, has entirely ignored.

The vicar cannot find words to acknowledge the airplanes' existence. They appear as he speaks the first syllable of a word (the word is "opportunity," something that, in his world, is soon to be in short supply), and after the airplanes pass overhead, he speaks the remaining syllables of the word as if nothing had happened. The national anthem is sung, making the patriotic statement that some in the audience had hoped would be part of the pageant itself. Then the gramophone finally continues its interrupted affirmation: "*Dispersed are we; who have come together. But,* the gramophone asserted, *let us retain whatever made that harmony.*" The gramophone's speech had been recorded in advance to look back on a harmony that the pageant never manages to achieve.

Nor does anything else achieve it. At one point Mrs. Swithin and Miss La Trobe gaze at each other: "Their eyes met in a common effort to bring a common meaning to birth. They failed." Until the final paragraphs, all sexual desires in the book issue in frustration or anger; no meaning at all is brought to birth. Isa Oliver suffers from an unspoken passion for the gentleman farmer Rupert Haines and wishes that he, not Giles Oliver, could have been the father of her children; Rupert Haines scarcely notices her existence. Giles Oliver is drawn magnetically to the indifferent Mrs. Manresa, who is traveling with the homosexual William Dodge, who is transfixed by Giles, who despises him. The aesthetic world of the pageant—the world of art in which Lily Briscoe triumphed— offers nothing better. The young lovers in Miss La Trobe's pastiche of seventeenth-century comedy are no less selfish and calculating than the old roué and harridan who try to thwart them, and offer no promise of a youthful future better than the aging past. The earnest young Victorian couple in the pageant's final scene choose mates who can help them in converting the heathen (as if St. John Rivers had found a kindred spirit), not for any more immediate satisfactions.

Older and younger generations are always isolated from each other in Virginia Woolf's world, but in *Between the Acts* they cannot find even the ambivalent, incomplete relations that they achieve in her earlier books. Isa Oliver is furious with her father-in-law Bartholomew for terrifying her son by springing out on him with a newspaper folded in front of his face to look like a monstrous beak; Bartholomew dismisses his grandson as a crybaby and a coward. Ancient relations give no comfort; new ones bring no hope. Isa and William Dodge can speak freely, she says, "perhaps because we've never met before, and never shall again." Miss La Trobe and William Dodge, having met for the first time in the morning, part in the evening: "Putting one thing with another, it was unlikely that they would ever meet again." Every meeting, every moment of contact, brings with it the prospect of a future without shape or meaning: "The future shadowed their present, like the sun coming through the many-veined transparent vine leaf; a criss-cross of lines making no pattern."

Playful Amidst the Catastrophe

In 1938 Virginia Woolf finished her ferocious tract *Three Guineas*, in which she placed the blame for injustice, inequality, and war more or less entirely on the patriarchal vanities of men. In 1940 she echoed this argument in *Between the Acts*, where she alludes to the guardsmen's rape of a young girl, to Bartholomew Oliver's colonial career in the Indian Civil Service, to a colonel at the pageant asking, "Why leave out the British Army? What's history without the army, eh?" But now, in her novel, she is less intent than she was in her tract on placing the blame for the disaster, and *Between the Acts* has no convenient focus of social and political villainy who can satisfyingly be hissed like Sir William Bradshaw in *Mrs. Dalloway*. Giles Oliver, "hirsute, handsome, virile," seems as if he might personify the warlike patriarchs of *Three Guineas;* and as a stockbroker he is implicated in the financial maneuverings that his father reads about in the morning paper. But among all the characters, only Giles foresees the coming war and has the moral intelligence to be furious about it. When someone at the pageant says to him, "Surely, Mr. Oliver, we're more civilized" (alluding to the defunct tradition of the village idiot), Giles can only answer, *"We?"*

Between the Acts is narrated by a calm ironic voice that knows all about the coming disaster but refuses to be agitated by it into heroics or despair. Instead, in a way that does not pretend to be anything more than chilly and appalling, the book is resolutely playful in the midst of catastrophe—with a gallows humor that it shares with none of its characters, and perhaps with none of its readers. It treats words as toys, inventing rhyming games that extend across a half dozen paragraphs, indulging in word-making games in which syllables taken from separate words combine and recombine into other words as the syllables recur from one sentence to the next. A sequence of rhyming words can weave from one page to another, while the characters alter their thoughts to chime with the unheard rhyming words that other characters think to themselves. Sometimes their rhymes take their cue from the pageant. After one of the many instances when the gramophone says *"Dispersed are we,"* Mrs. Manresa rhymes, "Follow, follow, follow me . . . I'm for tea." Isa Oliver adds a second set of rhymes while extending the first: "The wave has broken. Left us stranded, high and dry . . . Broken is the three-fold ply . . . Now I follow . . . to have tea." Someone else adds more rhymes: "Shall I go or stay? Slip out some other way? Or follow, follow, follow the dispersing company?" And the rhymes continue in the thoughts of others: "the monkey puzzle tree . . . the play we acted in the nursery."

The narrator's rhyming games are echoed in apparently random moments in Miss La Trobe's script for the pageant. In the middle of its final speech, the gramophone's voice briefly forgets that it is anonymous and megaphonic, and calls uncomfortable attention to the authorial personality of Miss La Trobe: *"Take myself now,"* the voice says, explaining that she knows she shares the faults she finds in others: *"Do I escape my own reprobation, simulating indignation, in the bush, among the leaves? There's a rhyme, to suggest, in spite of protestation and the desire for immolation, I too have had some, what's called, education."*

Virginia Woolf had exulted in the virtuosity and depth of her verbal artistry during thirty years of her literary vocation. Now, with cool deliberation and something close to self-contempt, she reduces that artistry to Miss La Trobe's nervously self-conscious verbal games and the narrator's irrelevant and indifferent ones. In *Orlando* the playfulness of the book's historical pastiche was closely woven into the playfulness of its biographical content. In *Between the Acts* the playfulness of the words is emphatically at odds with the misery and foreboding of the characters, who need no poetic or literary words to express it, and sometimes no words at all:

> He [Giles] said (without words) "I'm damnably unhappy."
> "So am I," Dodge echoed.
> "And I too," Isa thought.

Now that death is imminent, art is less important, less serious than it seemed in *The Waves*, ten years earlier, when the unhappily artistic Rhoda entered a concert hall and experienced an apotheosis of art. Through art, Rhoda said, one could see beyond mere appearances and analogies to "the thing that lies beneath the semblance of the thing." Art was simultaneously a victory over death and a compensation for it:

Percival [the young man mourned by everyone in *The Waves*], by his death, has made me this gift, let me see the thing. There is a square; there is an oblong. The players take the square and place it upon the oblong. They place it very accurately; they make a perfect dwelling-place. Very little is left outside. The structure is now visible; what is inchoate is here stated; we are not so various or so mean; we have made oblongs and stood them upon squares. This is our triumph; this is our consolation.

In the same way, the personal integrity that mattered to Clarissa Dalloway no longer carries much weight. Nor does the shaping and decisive stroke of Lily Briscoe's paintbrush. Instead, Miss La Trobe indulges resentful fantasies of being either "an outcast" or "the slave of my audience," and her one experience that resembles a vision occurs in a distinctly unvisionary way, blurred by an alcoholic haze as she sets down her glass in the village pub, trying to forget the failure of her pageant: "There was the high ground at midnight; there the rock; and two scarcely perceptible figures . . . She heard the first words." Such is Miss La Trobe's vision. But the book omits to report what the words say.

Words can amuse themselves in *Between the Acts* because they have their own autonomous existence, indifferent or antagonistic to human beings. Early in the book, when Giles first arrives at Poyntz Hall, "Words . . . ceased to lie flat in the sentence. They rose, became menacing and shook their fists at you." Not long afterward, as old Mrs. Swithin shows a guest the nursery in Poyntz Hall, "Words raised themselves and became symbolical." Near the end, as Miss La Trobe drowses and nods over her drink, words grow from the soil like flowers: "The mud became fertile. Words rose above the intolerably laden dumb oxen plodding through the mud. Words without meaning—wonderful words."

Seen from the detached, almost indifferent perspective of *Between the Acts,* all of life, in its individual and collective forms, flows and ebbs without much human intervention. The work of making a future is no longer aesthetic, visionary, or moral, no longer dignified or intense. To the extent that the future is made by anything at all, it is made by primal and archaic impulses; this does not mean (as it would have meant to Mary Shelley or Emily Brontë) that it is therefore made well. Virginia Woolf, unlike Miss La Trobe, is untempted by romantic nostalgia for an unconscious nature that has been ruined by human beings. Nature often gets the most crucial things wrong. When Giles Oliver walks angrily away from his aunt and father, kicking a "barbaric . . . pre-historic" stone, he encounters a "monstrous inversion," "birth the wrong way round":

> There, couched in the grass, curled in an olive green ring, was a snake. Dead? No, choked with a toad in its mouth. The snake was unable to swallow, the toad was unable to die. A spasm made the ribs contract; blood oozed. It was birth the wrong way round—a monstrous inversion.

Four weeks after finishing *Between the Acts,* Virginia Woolf, despairing over a future of private and public madness, drowned herself in the river Ouse. Her book portrays a world of futility and despair that she did not expect her readers to enter—none of her earlier books withdraw into a remote emotional distance in the way this one does—and in the final paragraphs she points toward an unknowable future different from anything she was then able to imagine.

After the old people, Mrs. Swithin and Bartholomew Oliver, have gone up to bed, Giles and Isa find themselves alone with each other for the first time all day:

Alone, enmity was bared; also love. Before they slept, they must fight; after they had fought, they would embrace. From that embrace another life might be born. But first they must fight, as the dog fox fights with the vixen, in the heart of darkness, in the fields of night.

The war, which everyone but Giles has tried to ignore, will soon begin. As the world of the book prepares for its private and public battles, it sheds all traces of civilization and regresses to the distant past.

The window was all sky without colour. The house had lost its shelter. It was night before roads were made, or houses. It was the night that dwellers in caves had watched from some high places among rocks.

Then the curtain rose. They spoke.

The book closes here, without reporting the words they spoke—in the same way, a few pages earlier, Miss La Trobe in her vision in the pub "heard the first words" that no one else hears. The entr'acte has ended; the next act has begun. The words spoken by Isa and Giles will issue in antagonism and battle; they "must fight, as the dog fox fights with the vixen," because their fight is forced upon them by instincts that precede words, impersonal instincts that overrule all private individual choices. Yet, in the world of this book, as in life, the thing that must happen is not—thanks to chance and choice—the only thing that will happen.

Giles and Isa's first spoken words, like all other words, are instruments of choice that instinct cannot entirely control. After their quarrelsome words, "they would embrace"; from their embrace "another life might be born"—through the workings of instinctual powers that choice cannot entirely control. And that new life, partly through its own choices, partly through instinctive necessity, will be both like and unlike the lives that conceive it. Choice and instinct will fight each other and embrace each other. Giles and Isa's words and bodies, which now threaten them with struggle and death, may issue, despite themselves, in change and renewal, and bring a new meaning to birth.

AFTERWORD *to the Anchor Books Edition*

As I sent the final proofs of this book to the publisher, I saw in my mind's eye the familiar image of a man sealing a letter in a bottle and throwing it hopelessly out to sea. As it turned out, the number of responses I received after publication and the depth of feeling that went into many of them were as gratifying as they were unexpected.

This book is about personal feelings and personal commitments as they are portrayed in seven novels, and many readers wrote that they were grateful to find novels that they love being discussed in these terms without sentimentality. Each reader seemed to find the center of the book in a different chapter. Each wrote to me in the same first-person spirit that the book was written in, almost always disagreeing on one or more points of interpretation, often, I think, because each of us placed more emphasis on one or the other side of the same question. More than one reader complained that in writing about *Mrs. Dalloway* I had given too much credit to Peter Walsh. Yes, they said, Peter Walsh loves Clarissa, but he gets her wrong and he himself is mostly futile and absurd. This is of course true, but if a person's love deserves to be discredited because it misunderstands its object, or because the lover has made a mess of his own life, then few people's love would be worth anything at all.

In the same way, a few readers insisted that Virginia Woolf, because she had committed suicide, should not be praised as a moral and psychological genius. But great writers tend to see more clearly when they are writing than when they are doing anything else. Virginia Woolf said of herself, "nothing makes a whole unless I am writing." This book does not set up any of its five novelists as a mentor or role model or guide or any other of those fantasy leader-figures to whom people turn when they have abandoned hope of finding their own way. Instead they are examples of writers who saw some things clearly and got some things right, although each of them entirely failed to see other things and at times got things woefully wrong.

I realized after I finished the book that this approach to the five novelists—as examples who were partial and imperfect, not as teachers or guides—was an essential part of the way in which the book approaches the idea of individuality. In setting out to write a book about individuality, I wanted to avoid writing a general account that would be vague enough to apply to anyone, because most things that are interesting about any individual are unique, and a general account would be false precisely because it generalized. I also wanted to avoid presenting any one person as a model of individual life, because this would imply that the model on offer was the best or true model that other people should follow. But of course no one, certainly none of these novelists, can provide a model for anyone else's life, and no one can become a unique individual by imitating someone else's individuality. My solution was to tell a life story that extended from birth to death, like everyone's life story, but which was divided among five individual lives, five contradictory facets of the same problem, none of which embodied the full meaning of the story as a whole.

In choosing this solution, I had in the back of my mind the method that T. S. Eliot used in *The Waste Land*. Eliot's poem tells the story of a legendary quest to restore fertility to a sterile kingdom, not with a traditional quest hero at its center, but through a shifting population of partial and imperfect figures from ancient myths and modern society who each carry a fragment of the whole story. Virginia Woolf used similar methods throughout her work, especially in *Jacob's Room* and *The Waves*, where multiple figures combine to tell a story that would be distorted and falsified by telling it through any single character.

One recurrent question in the letters I received was why I had chosen these particular novels and authors in preference to others. Why not Jane Austen, or Charles Dickens, or Elizabeth Gaskell, or Thomas Hardy? All I could answer was that I had considered writing about each of these authors, and that I could easily imagine a similar book to this one made up of entirely different examples. Some of the books I thought about including were Jane Austen's *Mansfield Park,* Charles Dickens' *Great Expectations* or *Bleak House,* Elizabeth Gaskell's *Cranford,* and Thomas Hardy's *Tess of the D'Urbervilles.* One that was on my list until the table of contents took final shape was Anthony Trollope's *Barchester Towers,* a novel in which the irresistible power of sex disrupts the decorous society of an English cathedral town and reveals the unique ways in which every individual responds to a universal instinct.

A day or two after I sent off the final proofs, I realized that one thing that I ought to have included was a sentence about the differences between the legal meaning of marriage and its moral and emotional meaning. Morally and emotionally, marriage is a sexual relation governed by mutual vows of fidelity; these vows are the moral parallel of a legality, the joint ownership of property that is also essential to marriage. In many of these seven novels, especially *Wuthering Heights*, *Jane Eyre*, and *Middlemarch*, one of the many dilemmas of marriage is the failure of the legal and moral meanings to coincide. This failure is only one example of a larger contradiction between legal rules and moral commitments in a world where everyone lives both a public life shaped largely by legal and economic systems and a private life shaped largely by moral and emotional choices.

I wrote this book because I was deeply moved by all seven novels, but I found it difficult to say just how I was moved by them, in that every attempt I made seemed to harden into pomposity or falsehood. The next few sentences are a brief attempt to get it more or less right.

What moves me most deeply in books are the moments when the characters or the images or the ideas or the rhythms enter into a new relation with each other, or when they discover for the first time the relation that they had been in all along—as when Jane Eyre and Mr. Rochester first wend their way homeward, or when Clarissa Dalloway can at last tell herself, "A thing there was that mattered." At such moments, a world—or a small part of a fictional world—that until then had been disordered, unjust, and unloving transforms itself into a world with at least some traces of coherence, justice, and love. The effect of this, for me and I think for others, is a mixture of two contradictory emotions that otherwise never occur at the same time. The transformation that occurs in the book induces happiness at the vision of a just and loving world—and grief at the recognition that it only exists in a book, that no one can ever live there. Other emotions may be deeper or more intense, but this one is unlike any other: a vision of a world you can never enter, which is still worth trying for, and a triumph you can never share, which is still worth exulting in.

NOTES ON THE NOVELISTS

Mary Shelley

Born Mary Wollstonecraft Godwin, 1797, in London, daughter of the philosopher William Godwin and the writer Mary Wollstonecraft; died 1851 in London. Eloped with Percy Bysshe Shelley in 1814; married him in 1816 after his first wife's death. Their first three children died in infancy or childhood; her last child, Percy, survived her. Her fiction—published anonymously, although her authorship seems to have been widely known almost from the start—includes *Frankenstein* (1818; revised version, 1831), *Valperga* (1823), *The Last Man* (1826), *Perkin Warbeck* (1830), *Lodore* (1835), and *Falkner* (1837).

Emily Brontë

Born Emily Jane Brontë, 1818, in Thornton, Yorkshire; daughter of Patrick Brontë, an Anglican minister, and Maria Branwell; died 1848 in Haworth, Yorkshire. Her works were published under the name Ellis Bell, and her authorship became known only after her death. Her poems, together with poems by Charlotte and Anne Brontë, appeared in *Poems, by Currer, Ellis, and Acton Bell* (1846). Her only novel was *Wuthering Heights* (1847).

Charlotte Brontë

Born 1816 in Thornton, Yorkshire, daughter of Patrick Brontë and Maria Branwell; died 1855 in Haworth, Yorkshire. She married A. B. Nichols (her father's curate) in 1854, and was pregnant when she died. She published her books under the name Currer Bell, although her authorship was widely known after the early 1850s. Her poems appeared in *Poems, by Currer, Ellis, and Acton Bell* (1846). Her first novel, *The Professor,* was published posthumously (1857). During her lifetime she published *Jane Eyre: An Autobiography* (1847, "edited by Currer Bell"; second edition, 1848), *Shirley* (1849), and *Villette* (1853).

George Eliot

Born Mary Anne Evans, 1819, in Nuneaton, Warwickshire; daughter of Robert Evans, an estate agent, and Christina Evans; died 1880 in London. (She was baptized Mary Anne, but used the spelling Mary Ann until 1851, when she began using Marian.) She lived with G. H. Lewes from 1854 until his death in 1878; she married John Cross in 1880, a few months before her death. She translated David Friedrich Strauss's *The Life of Jesus, Critically Examined* (1846, anonymously) and Ludwig Feuerbach's *The Essence of Christianity* (1854, as Marian Evans). Her novels, stories, and poems were published under the name George Eliot, although after 1859 her authorship was widely known. Her fiction includes *Scenes of Clerical Life* (1858), *Adam Bede* (1859), *The Mill on the Floss* (1860), *Silas Marner* (1861), *Romola* (1863), *Felix Holt the Radical* (1866), *Middlemarch* (published in eight parts, 1871–72), and *Daniel Deronda* (published in eight parts, 1876).

Virginia Woolf

Born Adeline Virginia Stephen, 1882, in London; daughter of Leslie Stephen, writer and editor of the *Dictionary of National Biography,* and Julia Duckworth; died 1941 in Rodmell, Sussex. Married Leonard Woolf, writer and social reformer, in 1912. Her novels include *The Voyage Out* (1915), *Night and Day* (1919), *Jacob's Room* (1922), *Mrs. Dalloway* (1925), *To the Lighthouse* (1927), *Orlando* (1928), *The Waves* (1931), *The Years* (1937), and *Between the Acts* (published posthumously, 1941). Her extensive criticism and journalism includes *The Common Reader* (first series, 1925; second series, 1932), *A Room of One's Own* (1929), and *Three Guineas* (1938).

FURTHER READING

Whole libraries have been written about the seven novels and five authors that are the subjects of this book. This note lists a few of the books from which I learned the most, and which I most enjoyed reading, while working on this one. For each author, I have listed one or more biographies, some collections of letters and journals, and a highly selective list of critical studies. Some of the best brief critical works on these novels are the introductions to paperback editions published by Oxford and Penguin; in the case of Virginia Woolf, these editions are available, for copyright reasons, only from the United Kingdom. Brief, entertaining problem-solving essays by John Sutherland on the first five novels in this book may be found in his three collections, *Is Heathcliff a Murderer?* (1996), *Can Jane Eyre Be Happy?* (1997), and *Who Betrays Elizabeth Bennet?* (1999); the three books were reprinted in a single volume as *The Literary Detective* (2000).

Frankenstein

Miranda Seymour's *Mary Shelley* (2000) is a thorough and readable biography. The fullest collections of documents are *The Journals of Mary Shelley, 1814–1844*, edited by Paula R. Feldman and Diana Scott-Kilvert (1987), and *The Letters of Mary Wollstonecraft Shelley*, edited by Betty T. Bennett (three volumes, 1980–88). Anne K. Mellor, *Mary Shelley: Her Life, Her Fiction, Her Monsters* (1988), is a lively general study. *The Endurance of Frankenstein: Essays on Mary Shelley's Novel*, edited by George Levine and U. C. Knoepflmacher (1979), includes studies of the novel's intellectual background, literary technique, and cultural effects. Maurice Hindle's *Mary Shelley, Frankenstein* (Penguin Critical Studies series, 1994) is brief, accessible, and wide-ranging. The same author's introduction and notes to his Penguin Classics edition of Mary Shelley's revised version of the novel (1992) are equally fascinating, as are Marilyn Butler's introduction and notes to her Oxford World's Classics edition of the first version (1993).

Wuthering Heights

The little that is known about Emily Brontë's life may be found in Winifred Gérin's *Emily Brontë: A Biography* (1971) and Edward Chitham's *A Life of Emily Brontë* (1987). A fanciful but intriguing reconstruction of Emily Brontë's Gondal myth, written in the form of a prose narrative that frames some of her poems, is *Gondal's Queen: A Novel in Verse,* arranged by Fannie E. Ratchford (1955). A more straightforward edition is *The Complete Poems,* edited by Janet Gezari (1992). Charlotte Brontë and Emily Brontë, *The Belgian Essays,* edited and translated by Sue Lonoff (1996), prints all the *devoirs* that the two sisters wrote while studying French in Brussels. *The Brontës: The Critical Heritage,* edited by Miriam Allott (1974), collects early reviews and appreciations. Edward Chitham reconstructs the process of writing *Wuthering Heights* in his *The Birth of Wuthering Heights: Emily Brontë at Work* (1998). Modern critical studies began with Charles Percy Sanger's still-fascinating and widely reprinted *The Structure of Wuthering Heights* (first published with the author's initials only, C.P.S., 1926). Ian Jack's introduction to his Oxford World's Classics edition of the novel (1981) is especially illuminating.

Jane Eyre

Elizabeth Gaskell's *The Life of Charlotte Brontë* (1857; widely available in modern reprints) has the excitement of a good novel because it is the work of a major nineteenth-century novelist, but as a biography it is somewhat airbrushed and protective of its subject. Winifred Gérin's *Charlotte Brontë: The Evolution of Genius* (1967) is more thorough, and Lyndall Gordon's *Charlotte Brontë: A Passionate Life* (1994) convincingly justifies the adjective in its subtitle. *The Letters of Charlotte Brontë,* edited by Margaret Smith (three volumes, 1995–2004), include fascinating notes on Charlotte Brontë's family and friends. See also the suggested reading for

Wuthering Heights, above, for books on Emily, Charlotte, and Anne Brontë. The long chapter on *Jane Eyre* in Kathleen Tillotson's *Novels of the Eighteen-Forties* (1954) remains a valuable starting point for thinking about the book. *The Madwoman in the Attic*, by Sandra M. Gilbert and Susan Gubar (1979), revealed depths that had been waiting more than a century to be found. Michael Mason's introduction to his Penguin Classics edition (1996) takes an illuminating approach to the religion and psychology of the novel. Adrienne Rich's essay, "Jane Eyre: The Temptations of a Motherless Woman," is reprinted in her *On Lies, Secrets, and Silence* (1979).

Middlemarch

Rosemary Ashton's *George Eliot: A Life* (1996) is both readable and scholarly. Nine volumes of *The George Eliot Letters*, edited by Gordon S. Haight (1954–78), will be too much for most readers, but the same editor's single-volume *Selections from George Eliot's Letters* (1985) is consistently interesting. A Penguin Classics volume, *Selected Essays, Poems and Other Writings*, edited by A. S. Byatt and Nicholas Warren (1990), conveys the depth and range of George Eliot's interests, as does the Oxford World's Classics volume, *Selected Critical Writings*, edited by Rosemary Ashton (1992). *George Eliot*, by Gillian Beer (1986), is a sharply intelligent study of her entire career. *The Real Life of Mary Ann Evans: George Eliot, Her Letters, and Fiction*, by Rosemarie Bodenheimer (1994), weaves a subtle psychological portrait from her letters and novels. Also worth reading are Rosemary Ashton's brief study *George Eliot* (1983); Jennifer Uglow's *George Eliot* (1987), which focuses on George Eliot's feminism; and *George Eliot: The Critical Heritage*, edited by David Carroll (1971), which collects early reviews.

 Middlemarch: Critical Approaches to the Novel, edited by Barbara Hardy (1967), is a collection of rewarding essays. *Middlemarch from Notebook to Novel*, by Jerome Beaty (1960), describes the genesis of the book. Two helpful introductions are Rosemary Ashton's in her Penguin Classics edition of *Middlemarch* (1994) and David Carroll's in his Oxford World's Classics edition (1988). Gillian Beer's *Darwin's Plots: Evolutionary Narrative in Darwin, George Eliot and Nineteenth-Century Fiction* (1983; second edition, 2000) casts light on a wider field of knowledge and emotion than the subtitle suggests.

Mrs. Dalloway

Among many biographies of Virginia Woolf, the most illuminating include Quentin Bell, *Virginia Woolf: A Biography* (1972); Phyllis Rose, *Woman of Letters* (1978); Lyndall Gordon, *Virginia Woolf: A Writer's Life* (1984); Hermione Lee, *Virginia Woolf* (1996); and Julia Briggs, *Virginia Woolf: An Inner Life* (2005). The essential documents are *The Diary of Virginia Woolf,* edited by Anne Olivier Bell (five volumes, 1977–84), *The Letters of Virginia Woolf,* edited by Nigel Nicholson (six volumes, 1975–80), and *The Essays of Virginia Woof,* edited by Andrew McNeillie (four volumes, 1986–94). Some short stories related to *Mrs. Dalloway* (but not quite the "sequence" suggested in the subtitle) are collected in *Mrs. Dalloway's Party: A Short Story Sequence,* edited by Stella McNichol (1973). A concise and illuminating critical study is Hermione Lee's *The Novels of Virginia Woolf* (1977). Alex Zwerdling's *Virginia Woolf and the Real World* (1986) is a refreshing study of the social vision of the novels. Also worth reading are Elizabeth Abel, *Virginia Woolf and the Fictions of Psychoanalysis* (1989); Maria DiBattista, *Virginia Woolf's Major Novels* (1980); Mitchell Leaska, *The Novels of Virginia Woolf* (1977); and Harvena Richter, *Virginia Woolf: The Inward Voyage* (1970). Contemporary reviews of the novels are collected in *Virginia Woolf: The Critical Heritage,* edited by Robin Majumdar and Allen McLaurin (1975).

Three worthwhile introductions to *Mrs. Dalloway* are Claire Tomalin's in her Oxford World's Classics edition (1992), David Bradshaw's in a later Oxford World's Classics edition (2000), and Elaine Showalter's in her Penguin Modern Classics edition (1992); the last of these is reprinted in *Virginia Woolf: Introductions to the Major Works,* edited by Julia Briggs (1994). The only edition of the novel available in the United States that uses Virginia Woolf's final revision of the text is the Everyman's Library edition (1993). An incomplete early draft of the novel may be found in *Virginia Woolf, "The Hours": The British Museum Manuscript of Mrs. Dalloway,* transcribed and edited by Helen M. Wussow (1996). Virginia Woolf's introduction to the 1928 Modern Library reprint can be found in *The Essays of Virginia Woolf,* volume 4 (see above), in a scholarly edition of

Mrs. Dalloway edited by Morris Beja (1996), in *The Mrs. Dalloway Reader,* edited by Francine Prose (2003), and in the many used copies of the Modern Library edition in American used-book shops.

To the Lighthouse

Almost every critical and biographical study of Virginia Woolf has something useful to say about *To the Lighthouse;* see the list of books about *Mrs. Dalloway* in the preceding section. For another perspective on the originals of Mr. and Mrs. Ramsay, see Virginia Woolf's essay "A Sketch of the Past," in *Moments of Being: Unpublished Autobiographical Writings,* edited by Jeanne Schulkind (1976; second edition, 1985). In addition to the books listed above, two especially rewarding introductions to the novel are Margaret Drabble's introduction to her Oxford World's Classics edition (1992), and Hermione Lee's in her Penguin Modern Classics edition (1992), the latter reprinted in *Virginia Woolf: Introductions to the Major Works,* edited by Julia Briggs (1994). *To the Lighthouse: The Original Holograph Draft,* transcribed and edited by Susan Dick (1982), shows how the novel took its final form.

Between the Acts

This novel tends to leave critics and biographers somewhat baffled or uneasy. See the list of books about *Mrs. Dalloway* for a selection of studies of Virginia Woolf's novels. By far the most illuminating readings of *Between the Acts* are Frank Kermode's in the introduction to his Oxford World's Classics edition (1992) and Gillian Beer's in the introduction to her Penguin Modern Classics edition (1992), the latter reprinted in her *Virginia Woolf: The Common Ground* (1996) and in *Virginia Woolf: Introductions to the Major Works,* edited by Julia Briggs (1994). *Pointz Hall: The Earlier and Later Typescripts of "Between the Acts,"* edited by Mitchell A. Leaska (1983), shows the novel taking shape.

ACKNOWLEDGMENTS

Many friends helped me to improve this book. Jenny Davidson, Maria DiBattista, Barbara J. Fields, and Jesse Rosenthal gave advice on the entire manuscript. Rebecca Mead, So Young Park, and Vicki Tromanhauser commented on one or more chapters. In writing about specific details and themes I have relied on Julie Crawford, Nicholas Dames, Stephen Marcus, Ben Parker, Wayne Proudfoot, Michael A. Seidel, Gauri Viswanathan, and Daniel Ziff. Alice van Straalen is the most sympathetic and bracing of editors. Cheryl Mendelson kept an attentive eye on every word of the book at each stage of its composition. On a page which exists as a place for giving thanks, the last words should be for her and for James.

INDEX

Footnotes are indicated by a page number followed by an italic *n*.